California Sober

W. E. Simmons

SVDC INDUSTRIES

California Sober

The Science of Recovery

By W. E. Simmons

Published by
SVDC InDUSTries
An imprint of California Sober™
P.O. Box 181
Venice, California 90294
TheSVDC.com

DEDICATION

First and foremost, this book is dedicated to the memory of the casualties of the War on Drugs, those dear to me being too many to list here, and to the prisoners of that War who were unjustly incarcerated for choices, mistake or otherwise, that every human has the right to make for themselves. May we one day live in a world where education replaces the whipping post and personal freedom reigns supreme.

Next, to those still struggling, I hope these words help you find a path that works for you. For far too long, those who we turn to for help have pointed to an Exit sign on a door that is locked for most, keeping the hallway dark enough that we couldn't see another way out. With the lights on, it becomes obvious that the exits are everywhere, as long as we can open our eyes to the possibilities.

And finally, to the Spyder that leads the way and the Moon that lights the path, you reminded me where I was heading before I lost my way, may my course stay true. To the one who brought them to me, I am forever in your debt.

Contents

Chapter 1 - What is California Sober?

Walking along Venice Beach, contemplating the addiction that had me on my knees for more than a decade, I was reintroduced to a long-forgotten concept that I was too young and naïve to understand when it was first offered to me. It wasn't that I couldn't grasp the idea, just that I didn't fully understand a truth I had no real need for. I wasn't yet addicted to anything when I was first shown the way. My emotional struggles seemed *normal* for someone in my situation. Life had yet to take a bite out of me that I couldn't recover from. By the time those facts changed, I had forgotten the wisdom that had been passed on to me all those years ago. As fate would have it, on the night of one of my biggest struggles I was reunited with a concept that would transform my relationships, my life, and my entire way of thinking: The California Sober method of recovery.

You may have heard the phrase *California Sober* while reading the tabloids or an article about celebrity lifestyles. If you live in or travel to California, or maybe you know someone that does, you may have even heard someone say that they or someone they know are California Sober. Popular songs have even been written about the practice. Lately, the term has even been used in the addiction and recovery community with varying connotations - both positive and negative. With all of its newfound fame, there is a lack of awareness regarding the concept of California Sober, and even those who believe they have some knowledge about it are quite often mistaken.

California Sober is a method of recovery from addiction to *drugs* and alcohol that far exceeds any other method of recovery to date. Its success rate is unprecedented in the field of recovery and is backed by a lifetime of scientific research. The only reason that California Sober hasn't been the standard model of addiction recovery for the past half-century is due to the perpetuation of false ideas by other recovery methods, the government administration of the late 1960s, and the media of that era due to a collective fear of the unknown and the misconception that components of the treatment were impeding the Vietnam War effort.

The California Sober method of recovery has been scientifically proven to be the best treatment for a multitude of conditions of the body and mind. Its benefits include higher recovery rates for alcoholism and *drug* addiction as well as behavioral addiction, but addiction is only one of many conditions California Sober can alleviate. Treatment-resistant depression, existential depression, grief, anxiety, PTSD, and OCD are all shown to be reduced by its techniques. As if that weren't enough, California Sober methods also lower the risk of heart disease, diabetes, and more. While there is no true *cure* for most of these conditions, the California Sober method of recovery is as close as anyone has ever gotten. California Sober methods can be used to *reset* the brain in the same way that rebooting your phone or computer works as a *fix* when those devices get *stuck.*

The best part of California Sober is that it is as easy as changing your mind. California Sober methods rewire your brain by creating new neural pathways. These techniques, when performed along with the California Sober path, can change the way you think about addiction while simultaneously relieving the above-mentioned conditions of the mind. In addition, classic psychedelics stimulate neurogenesis, reduce neuroinflammation, and provoke neuroplastic changes. They literally rewire the brain. For these reasons, classic psychedelics are also being looked at as a treatment for Alzheimer's Disease, Dementia, Parkinson's disease, and Multiple Sclerosis. As new as it sounds, the California Sober method of treating these conditions (and each individual component) has been praised by the psychiatric community for almost a century.

Psychiatric interest in the California Sober methods that were halted in the late 1960s (against the recommendation of the psychiatric community) have been reawakened as of late. New studies are simply confirming what the scientific community has long known. The California Sober method of recovery significantly outperforms other systems of recovery and works as well as other psychiatric medications to treat a host of disorders without the need for Big Pharma and its *drugs.* But what *is* California Sober? The term has been around for some time, but what does it really mean? Before we get into the specifics of what makes it tick, let's explore what it is not.

Through the Myths and the Madness
Trying to get the Message to You

One of the most common misconceptions is that California Sober is a new fad. In reality, California Sober has been around under various names and incarnations since at least the late 1800s, although the majority of studies proving its effectiveness have been done between 1950 and the present. California Sober methods of recovery have been scientifically examined, tested, and proven to be effective in scores of studies over the last 60-plus years. While the term California Sober has only been around for a few decades, the treatment is one that countless patients have used in their recovery for more than a century. The long list of those who have maintained their freedom from addiction using the California Sober method even includes that of the most famous name in recovery, Bill W., the founder of Alcoholics Anonymous.

Another common misconception is that California Sober is simply exchanging one addiction for another. This could not be further from the truth. Substituting one addiction for another is not, by definition, recovery from addiction. California Sober treatments are done with the express intention of relieving the user of all addictions, not just the ones that are holding them back today. This is accomplished by guiding the addict to a new way of thinking while promoting better habits that take the place of bad ones. If someone truly wants to break their addiction, California Sober methods are proven to have the highest success rate among all recovery systems.

While you may have heard the falsehood that California Sober means that you simply smoke marijuana instead of drinking, this is not at all the case. If it were that simple, if weed was the true cure-all for addiction, everyone would simply switch their substance of choice to Cannabis and the world would be a better and addiction-free place. Unfortunately, it's not that simple. While cannabis can aid in the treatment of addiction, California Sober is not just trading in your favorite high for a new one. In addition, a small percentage of the population can become addicted to marijuana. Consequently, a method of recovery with only Cannabis at its center would never work for those individuals. Any form of recovery should work for every type of addiction, as California Sober has been proven to do.

Another misinterpretation is that California Sober is just for alcoholics and drug addicts. Studies show that California Sober Treatments work for a host of other conditions. Anxiety and depression are shown to be significantly reduced by the methods contained herein. Employment fatigue, also known as burnout, can subside, giving way to productivity and an increase in creativity. If you've found yourself in a rut caused by the routine of everyday life, California Sober can help. Before we get into how and why California Sober works, let's explore other methods of recovery and why they fall short in their attempts to do the same.

Kick it

Most people who struggle with addiction, whether it be to alcohol, prescription drugs, or street drugs (like Fentanyl, Crack, or Crystal Meth), have limited choices when it comes to turning their life around and breaking the cycle that has led them down this dark and dreary path. A rare few simply decide that they have had enough. They sink so low that they can no longer bear the heartache that their addiction has caused. Realizing that enough damage has been done to their lives, they walk away from their addiction, never looking back and never again ingesting the substance that nearly ruined their lives. While this would be a wonderful and empowering way to beat addiction if it worked, this is the exception, not the rule.

Far more often than not, this method of kicking the habit results in repeated relapse. In other words, most of the people who try to quit on their own go back to whatever substance was controlling them in a vicious cycle of complete abstinence from all substances, followed by failed attempts at controlled use, and ending in the same pattern of destruction that brought them to their knees in the first place. Going it alone and without a plan is the hardest possible way to beat addiction. This is due to the fact that the craving addicts are fighting lives in the mind. Who better to outsmart you in your efforts to remain sober than yourself?

When you are addicted to a substance that causes your life and well-being harm, you instinctively want to stop. You're coming down, possibly hungover, and generally feel like shit when you finally decide that enough is enough. You're going to sleep it off and, as soon as you feel better, you will change your life around. Sometimes the feeling lasts but a few short hours. Other times it lasts for days, maybe even weeks. As soon as the problems your last binge caused begin to fade from memory and your brain realizes that it isn't going to get that boost that it so desires, the enhancement that it has become accustomed to leaning on, it begins the process of plotting against you, calculating the best way to get what it wants whether you like it or not.

While the conscious mind lives in the illusion that it has control over the actions of the body, choice is truly limited. You may decide what style to wear, which people you like versus who you don't, what career path to follow, or what you prefer to do for fun. You may even decide what to eat for dinner (although even that simple choice is up for debate). Inconsequential choices are yours to make all day, but when it comes to what the body needs (or thinks it needs) you don't have the only say in the matter.

You can physically stop yourself from breathing by simply not taking another breath. Through sheer will, the diaphragm stops moving. Air no longer enters or exits the nostrils. You've made a choice. You are no longer going to draw breath. Unlike your beating heart, this is something you can consciously control - that is, until you've hit the point where your body has decided it's had enough. Your cells scream for oxygen until suddenly, and without your permission, the diaphragm begins to contract. You refuse to let the air into your lungs, but the body persists. In addition, thoughts that you should take a breath consume your mind. Eventually, your will means nothing. The lungs will have air whether you like it or not. You gasp and lose the battle. You are no longer in control.

Perhaps a more fitting example is the sailor lost at sea. As the days go by, he runs out of drinkable fresh water. The sailor knows that he cannot drink from the sea. He understands that doing so will hasten his demise because seawater contains salt. The human body can only make urine that is less salty than seawater. To get rid of the salt, the body needs to eliminate more water than it takes in from the sea. This speeds the process of dehydration. Every sailor knows this to be true. Still, after a couple of days of thirst, even the smartest of seamen will begin to quench that thirst with a swig of the ocean, knowing full well that it will likely be the last thing that they will ever drink.

When the body decides that it needs a substance in order to function, it will do whatever it takes to convince the rational mind that ingesting that substance, whatever it may be, is better than the alternative, no matter the consequences. Like air and water, the brain considers regularly used substances to be necessary to its survival. This is the battle one faces when they try to overcome addiction on their own, without the benefits of a scientific approach to the problem. Quitting an addictive substance without help usually leads the addict back to their Substance of Choice, eventually. This is known as relapse.

How long one stays sober often directly correlates to how bad things have gotten. The bottom (the user's lowest point in a cycle of addiction) is different for different people and is as individual as your situation and your addiction. For some it's an eviction notice from the landlord or getting fired from a job for being late too often or for multiple absences. For others it's losing their children to *the system* (commonly known as child services). For many, it can be pressure from a partner or family member telling the addicted individual to either change their ways or be removed from that loved one's life forever. What motivates some may not motivate others. Still, once one realizes that their addiction is destroying some part of their world that they hold dear, many try to simply say no to their Substance of Choice and get on with their lives.

At some point the mind begins the process of lying to you. It can start as soon as you sober up, telling you that everything is fine or that getting drunk or high once more won't change anything. Your brain begins to dismiss and push aside the part of you that knows this just isn't the case. You were so sure that all of your problems were caused by your substance of choice not long ago. Now you feel like one thing has nothing to do with the other, or that one more time can't make things any worse. The brain fools you so it can get the drug it wants even if you didn't think you wanted to use in the recent past, that past being several months ago or mere hours.

Sometimes the motivation only lasts until the issue your addiction has caused resolves itself. The landlord dropped the eviction when you promised to have the money by weeks end, or your boss had a change of heart and agreed to give you one more chance. Everything is looking up for you. Everything worked out after all. What better time to celebrate? Once your guard is down, the organ that benefits the most from your addiction begins its mission to get more. This is why addiction is often referred to as a demon. It possesses the user and makes them do illogical things in order to get what it wants. More.

When the addict finally realizes they cannot do it on their own, that's when they start to look for help. The problem here is that traditional treatment is hard for most people to accept, and for good reason. Traditional addiction recovery treatments are based on a quasi-religious, cult-like system of rules and steps that must be precisely followed in order to (possibly) find relief from addiction. There is no science to the *steps* they make one follow, resulting in little to no chances of success. In addition, they require total abstinence from any and all substances, which may not be the best course of treatment for the individual. This is one of the many reasons that traditional addiction recovery methods have been proven to be less successful than the California Sober treatment.

Conscious control over addiction can be obtained, but it takes more than will itself. The addict needs to rewire and reboot the brain. A new way of thinking must be achieved, and the sooner the better. While seeking help and knowing that you have a problem are the best first steps on a journey to freedom from addiction, the addict needs to see another way to live their same life. They need to be shown that they can still be their favorite version of themselves without the substance they crave. The California Sober method of recovery can help the user do just that.

The Cult of Anonymity

Most of those seeking traditional recovery turn to Anonymous groups like Alcoholics Anonymous, Narcotics Anonymous,

Cocaine Anonymous, and so on, with minimal success. While they may fare better than the first group, their success is dependent on joining what is essentially a religious cult (by design) in which there is a direct correlation between the addict's rate of victory over the substance that is destroying them and their level of indoctrination into the Anonymous cult of their choosing. The more the addict *drinks the Kool-Aid*, the higher their limited chances of success are. When they don't immediately succeed (as most do not) they are told that it's because they're not truly conforming to the program, when in fact it's more likely that their failure is due to their disbelief in one or more aspects of the 12 steps and their resistance to proselytization.

In the *how it works* section of the Anonymous group's bible, this blame on the individual for failure to successfully abstain is clearly stated. "Rarely have we seen a person fail who has thoroughly followed our path" it begins, although studies show that less than 10% of those who attempt to abstain using their method of recovery actually succeed. They expect you to believe that the other 90% who try their steps fail because they are not honestly following the procedure. The truth is most people fail in 12 step recovery because it doesn't work for everyone. It's that simple.

To further add insult to injury, the *how it works* portion of the Big Book goes on to say that "those who do not recover are people who cannot or will not completely give themselves to this simple program, usually men and women who are constitutionally incapable of being honest with themselves...They are not at fault; they seem to have been born that way. They are naturally incapable of grasping and developing a manner of living which demands rigorous honesty. Their chances are less than average." In short, the Big Book blames the addict's failure on their ability to grasp A.A.'s simple concept and to be honest with themselves. If the 12 steps do not work for you, you must either not be smart enough or you're lying to yourself. This couldn't be further from the truth and is just an excuse for the failure of the 12 step programs themselves.

The California Sober method of recovery never blames failure on the individual. Addiction is not easily overcome. If it were, it would be a non-issue. What California Sober can claim, however, is that our system has a success rate that is 500-800% higher than that of any 12-step program, partially due to the fact that we do not fault the individual for their failure to achieve. Saying that an addict has fallen short of recovery because they didn't try hard enough is the leading cause for them rejecting a program. They know they are trying their best. Telling them otherwise is a slap in the face. California Sober recognizes that relapse is a part of the initial process and that it may take a few tries before one finds their true path. With a higher success rate, California Sober makes it easier to do just that.

Finally, *how it works* (or, more accurately, why it doesn't work) goes on to claim that "there are those, too, who suffer from grave emotional and mental disorders, but many of them do recover if they have the capacity to be honest." The truth is that said *mental disorders* make recovery harder. To say that someone suffering from a diagnosed mental illness need only *have the capacity to be honest* in order to successfully stay off of their substance of choice is not only insulting to those individuals, it's simply untrue. We aren't all built the same. Each individual has their own unique struggle and some of us have a harder time than others. California Sober recognizes that everyone's recovery path is different and allows the individual to find their own path without judgement and labels. We are all human and no person is incapable of recovering through the California Sober method of recovery.

In traditional recovery, addicts are given a set of twelve steps that they must complete in numerical order, beginning anew with every failure. The first of these tasks is to remind themselves that they are powerless over their addiction and that their lives have become unmanageable. California Sober recognizes that asking an addict to reinforce, in their hearts and minds, that they are powerless over addiction on a daily basis, while at the same time asking them to muster the power to abstain, is counterproductive and hypocritical. If one were truly powerless, they could never recover. The mind is the most amazing and powerful part of the human body. Worlds can be created or destroyed through sheer will. People overcome unfathomable obstacles, sometimes even death itself, pushing past their struggles until their goals are achieved. This is the power of positive thinking.

The brain processes input and makes decisions on how best to approach a task at hand. If we tell ourselves we can do something, we can often accomplish seemingly unachievable goals. When we set the bar too low for ourselves, we often cease trying altogether. Why then would we tell an addict that they are powerless over their addiction? We have already admitted that we have a problem simply by seeking some sort of help. If our lives hadn't become unmanageable, we wouldn't have embarked on a quest to become a better version of ourselves. If we omit the falsehood that we are powerless, the first step has been completed the moment we seek help.

Once someone has decided that it is time for a change in how they're living, California Sober gives the user tools to stay away from their substance of choice, simultaneously teaching techniques in which one can change their way of thinking about their individual life and addiction. This leads them to the discovery of a new way of living that is best for them. No one is powerless. Some of us are just having a hard time ridding ourselves of behaviors that we have incorporated into our lives for far too long. When you're stuck in a rut, you're not powerless, you just need to see your world through new eyes. That's what California Sober delivers.

As much damage as the first step can do, it's the second step that has the most power to turn people away from recovery. The second of the 12 steps is coming to the belief that only a higher power, essentially a God, can restore our sanity. This step forces the addict to believe in multiple very specific ideas. First, they have to believe in a higher power, which can be hard for a large percentage of individuals. Second, they have to believe that this higher power is the only thing that can restore their sanity. In addition, the consequence of disbelief is to be sentenced to a life of addiction. What purpose does that serve?

During the California Sober process, many individuals find their way to a belief in a higher power in their first session. That said, there is no requirement that that happen in order for the individual to have success. One's own belief in a higher power has nothing to do with their ability to recover. It's a personal choice that may or may not help someone on their journey to recovery, and not something that the California Sober method of recovery forces upon them. Religion, or lack thereof, is not a factor in any scientific approach to any type of sobriety. Some may find it essential while others find it useless. A recovery method should not rely on, or be interested in, someone's religious beliefs. All that serves to do is exclude individuals that desperately need our assistance.

The 12 steps go on to include surrendering your will and life to God, having God remove your defects, asking God to remove your shortcomings, and praying for the knowledge of God's will. That's a lot of religion being forced upon vulnerable individuals. In addition, simply having faith that you will get better will not get you better. If you have a compound fracture, you cannot pray for your bone to straighten and reattach itself. Not with any success, that is. It's the 21st century. It's time to admit that, while the power of prayer is similar to the power of positive thinking, prayer alone will not heal disease.

While prayer can help many through hard times, and the power of meditation and prayer are strong in those who truly believe that they work, telling an addict that they will be delivered from addiction through these steps alone is detrimental to their recovery. If nearly every step in one's recovery is asking God for help, it seems the addict is being asked to put all of their eggs in one divine basket, rather than creating a multiple approach method like California Sober. Then, like any good cult, the final step is for those with the highest level of indoctrination to spread the message of success, thus increasing the group's numbers and legitimacy.

The 12 steps have tried to do damage control, when faced with the facts I have presented, by stating that a higher power can be anything from a God to the Universe, to the program itself. Their smoke and mirrors are revealed again in *how it works,* which clearly states that "there is One who has all power – that One is God. May you find Him now! Half measures availed us nothing. We stood at the turning point. We asked His protection and care with complete abandon."

While we have no qualms with anyone's belief system, as we all have our own, California Sober knows that one's religious beliefs, or lack thereof, are inconsequential to their recovery and, quite frankly, none of our business. If you believe in prayer, it may help you on your journey to California Sobriety. If you believe in the power of meditation, that can help as well (and has been scientifically proven to). If you believe in neither, the California Sober method of recovery will still work.

The Anonymous groups also swear that the key to success is taking their battle with addiction *one day at a time*, sometimes moment by moment, yet they constantly torture themselves (and each other), measuring their triumph by counting the exact number of days it has been since the last time they used their substance of choice, rewarding themselves with tokens or *chips* that come in 30-day increments of abstinence. As long as they spend every waking moment *working the steps*, going to (often multiple) daily *meetings* where they recount the worst days of their addiction and its awful consequences, and concentrating on the menial tasks of daily life, with any luck they won't have time to use the substance(s) that once ruled their days.

Each of these *Anonymous* groups require full abstinence from any and all mind-altering substances, hypocritically allowing for drugs like caffeine (which can be a trigger drug and lead to relapse in those who are addicted to amphetamines and other *up* substances), nicotine (the addiction that killed the founder of A.A.), prescription pharmaceuticals, and other substances not considered by them to be recreational drugs. The problem with putting all mind-altering substances into one category is that they are not all equal in the world of addiction. Demanding abstinence from all but the ones the program approves of is actually detrimental to the addict. Studies have shown that using certain substances to aid in the abstinence from harmful and addictive *drugs* is far more successful than complete abstinence from any and all mind-altering substances. Recovery without the need for asceticism is what California Sober provides.

While twelve-step programs claim a success rate of 70% for those that are truly and fully indoctrinated, studies show that the true success rate for all that attempt to follow their program is only five to ten percent. The reasons are many, from not believing in a higher power to the fact that the program only works if you dedicate your life to it, but the truly indoctrinated will tell you that if you fail it's because you did something wrong. They blame the addict for not honestly following the steps, declaring that *it works IF you work it*, rather than the truth which is twelve step programs are not what most people need.

The sole benefit of these groups is the comradery, the support of those who have been through similar ordeals reassuring each other, that makes some people successful in their struggle to break the cycle of addiction, not the steps they make their members religiously follow. California Sober also incorporates group therapy and regular meetings of like-minded individuals, but without the requirement of unnecessary steps that have little to no proven value. We know what truly works due to the extensive research and scientific studies that prove the California Sober methods to have the highest success rate of all forms of recovery.

Medication for the Soul

When you have a headache, you take ibuprofen or acetaminophen. If the pain is worse, like that of a broken limb, you take stronger pain medication. When you have a cold, you take cold medicine. Diseases are treated with drugs designed to alleviate symptoms and/or in an attempt to destroy the disease. Why then would they recommend treatment for a disease such as addiction to alcohol or other substances be treated by abstinence from all useful medication, especially when there are medications that are proven to alleviate the symptoms of, and even cure, the disease?

The reason other attempts at recovery fail are the reason that California Sober works. The fact that 5-10% of people recover from their addiction by following a 12-step program is remarkable. On the other hand, the truth that 90% or more that try these types of recovery systems fail lies in the falsehood that the 12 steps are the only true way to beat addiction, and that abstinence from any and all substances is the only way to stop the individual from going back to the substance(s) that ruined their lives. California Sober provides the addict with the tools and knowledge of what is proven to work so that they may decide what works best for them.

The majority of addicts have some sort of early trauma, a chemical imbalance, an early exposure to the substance that they are addicted to, or a combination of these and other issues that need to be dealt with in a way that treats the underlying cause of their addiction. Simply denying them any relief from their condition will rarely result in any long-term solution. The California Sober method of recovery teaches the addict how to circumvent the use of their substance of choice in multiple ways, including rewiring their brain to reinforce the desire for abstinence from that substance, as well as through the use of natural and harmless substances to provide relief when they find themselves in a moment of weakness.

There are substances, most of which are naturally occurring, that are not only proven to help addicts recover almost instantaneously, but that combat a variety of conditions from depression to OCD and even lower the risk of heart disease and diabetes.[1] If any one of these medications has that much power, why then would we exclude it from helping the recovering addict in their journey towards freedom from

---

[1] Simonsson, O., Osika, W., Carhart-Harris, R. et al. Associations between lifetime classic psychedelic use and cardiometabolic diseases. Sci Rep 11, 14427 (2021). https://doi.org/10.1038/s41598-021-93787-4

addiction? The studies speak for themselves. Abstinence from any and all mind-altering substances has been proven a detriment to the recovery process. It's time to focus on what works. California Sober methods are proven to do just that.

Another major problem with traditional recovery is that it is much easier to make the changes in our behavior that lead to addiction than it is to make the changes needed to lead us out of it. That's because drugs reward the brain for these bad behaviors, while quitting is exponentially harder because the lack of those same substances denies the brain that chemical reward. The better we do, the worse we feel, at least at first. All of our efforts seem counterproductive to our happiness and therefore we want to use our Substance of Choice again to make the pain and misery subside. Simply put, getting high feels awesome while coming down makes you feel like shit.

The California Sober method of recovery is to combat the need for harmful highly addictive substances by administering harmless, non-addictive mind-altering substances that help the addict to realize the path to recovery, and others that alleviate the *hunger pangs* of addiction in a moment of weakness. The remedies in the California Sober method of recovery reward the pleasure receptors in the brain much as the chemicals that are being abused do, but with a few major differences.

The classic psychedelics used by our method are non-addictive. Classic psychedelics have little, if any, potential for abuse due to their intensity, their instantaneous tolerance (you cannot simply use the same amount to get the same effect the next day), and their lack of symptoms of withdrawal. Classic psychedelics are a one-and-done euphoric experience whose benefits last for several months. They may alter your perception for several hours while providing relief from addiction and depression for several months, yet one doesn't feel the need to do more. Not in the course of the day, as with other substances, or in the short-term future. There is no longing or craving for them as there is with all addictive substances.

In addition, classic psychedelics have the ability to change the user's mind, quite literally. New neural connections are created during the *trip* and neurogenesis is achieved. These substances literally rewire the brain and, with the help of the user's intention toward better behavior, rewire it in a way that reinforces the user's objective, whether that objective is to quit their previously desired substance or to in some other way alter their behavior. In a nutshell, classic psychedelics, used with the intent to better oneself, reinforce the will to succeed by structurally altering the mind to comply with those intentions. They literally help you to change your mind about the behaviors that have led you to seek their help.

Classic psychedelics and Cannabis also have the ability to stop the addict from using in an emergency situation. Cannabis has been shown to lessen the use of the addict's substance of choice on days when it is ingested prior to said substance. In the case of psychedelics, when taken prior to one's substance of choice they not only reduce cravings, but also stop many substances from producing their desired effects. For instance, after taking a standard dose (the dose needed to feel the full effects) of LSD, mushrooms, peyote, or mescaline, alcohol's effects are no longer felt in the same way by the user. The same is true for many other harmful and addictive substances, making their ingestion feel like a waste of time.

The psychedelics used in the California Sober method of recovery are medication for the soul. They cause neurogenesis (the creation of brain cells and neural pathways) and help to rewire the brain towards a new way of thinking about life, a way of thinking that leads one down the path to recovery and to the best version of themself. At the same time, those that choose to use Cannabis or classic psychedelics for remediation benefit from the immediate cessation of cravings. California Sober provides every CS with the tools they need to end their addiction while giving them useful tools for living a better life in general.

Addiction Demystified
The Root Causes of Addiction

People become addicted to substances for a variety of reasons. For some, a seemingly harmless experimental phase leads them down the road to addiction, while others succumb to peer pressure to try things that they otherwise would have never partaken of on their own. For many, early exposure to a lifestyle that they were born into may be the path that led them astray, never knowing that such behavior was not something that *everyone does*. Sometimes that same experimental phase seems to remedy a chemical imbalance that the user was suffering from before they ever ingested any substances at all. Other times experimentation brings to the surface an underlying psychiatric problem that lie dormant.

The reasons people become addicted to substances are as unique as the individuals themselves. Before we get into how to treat substance abuse, we should first take a look at the general causes. Although an addict may fit into one or more of the following scenarios, sometimes addiction stems from something as simple as enjoying the boost that harmful substances give to the pleasure centers of the brain. Still, studies show that there are 3 main causes of addiction. Early exposure to substance abuse, childhood trauma, and a chemical imbalance in the brain, all of which can be worked through with the California Sober method of recovery.

Early Exposure

Studies show that 25% of people who use certain mind-altering substances in the form of recreational drugs, misused prescription drugs, and/or alcohol before their 18th birthday will become addicted. In other words, one out of every four kids that experiment with alcohol or other harmful substances will become addicted to them. The easiest way to ensure that one doesn't become addicted to harmful substances is to never try them. For this reason, drug education should be taught starting in elementary school, especially considering that junior high is where exposure and experimentation usually begins.

In addition, distracting kids from harmful behaviors by challenging them academically and artistically leaves them with less time to be idle and become bored. Music and art lessons, athletic activities like sports and dance, camping and other outdoor activities with family, as well as other methods of distraction, can keep the young mind healthy and engaged while keeping them away from less productive and harmful activities. These positive activities have the added benefit of causing the brain to create new neural pathways, helping it to grow and mature. The more the child experiences, the more completely their brain develops.

The plasticity of the teenage brain ensures that adolescents will become adept in whatever they choose to learn at this time in their lives, be it academic, athletic, artistic, or otherwise. They will master whatever it is they set their mind to. That's awesome if it's a musical instrument, a sport, or academia, but this also means that if a teen is exposed to a life in the streets, they will become masters of that as well.

Everyone becomes good at something. Better that they learn something productive rather than getting a master class in becoming a derelict.

I chose the latter until a dark turn of events led me back to the path I'm currently on. My peers who chose more wisely in those early years benefitted from a major head start in the rat race, some even finishing their careers before I ever started. Many of the ones that chose the path that I took are no longer with us. Keeping a teen busy with positive extracurricular activities lessens their chances of experimentation with substances and raises their chances of having a life of success and happiness. If we can keep the youth busy with positive activities, the odds of a *normal* life are all but certain.

Still, teens can be exposed to drugs and alcohol from other teens in their social groups and, without education and guidance, will often fall victim to addiction. In addition, many teens are exposed to alcohol and other drugs from family members, such as siblings, cousins, aunts, uncles, and even parents. Little can be done to prevent a child from early exposure in these cases until drug education is reformed and taught as early as possible. I, myself, was exposed to alcohol in utero and was sipping Budweiser before I was five years old. I tried pot at age eleven. When my best friend brought alcohol to school in 7th grade, it had already been normalized. When he offered me pills, I thought *why not*, even though I didn't even know what they were.

While the immature mind is evolving into what it is to one day become, its chemistry is constantly changing. Interrupting this process by introducing substances that alter that chemistry results in the brain wanting, even needing, these substances to perform the basic task of mood stabilization. The moody adolescent becomes irate, appearing at times to be insane, even without the addition of substances that alter that brain chemistry. Adding *drugs* to the equation can send them over the edge and into a destructive pattern of behaviors that feed off the continued relief they find from their chosen substance. Thus, the cycle begins.

Mind-altering substances make us feel good when we otherwise do not, a task our brains have to learn how to accomplish in order to regulate the new chemicals puberty has introduced. The brain stops working towards this goal when substances take over this function. During adolescence, we evolve from children, who have a much less complicated brain chemistry, into adults. The transition is hard enough on its own. When we alleviate the discomfort of this transition with mind-altering substances, we throw off the natural regulation of these hormones that comes with maturity, causing the brain to depend on these exogenous chemicals. That dependence is known as addiction.

The human brain does not finish developing and maturing until the mid to late twenties. The prefrontal cortex, the area responsible for skills like planning, prioritizing, and controlling impulses, is one of the last brain regions to fully mature. The underdeveloped prefrontal cortex makes teens more confident when they are pressured to try things that pose a risk to their health and safety. This is why teens seem to think they are somewhat immortal and take risks, such as experimenting with stronger and more dangerous substances.

In addition, mental conditions begin to reveal themselves in adolescence. The use of mind-altering substances can have several negative effects associated with mental health. Intoxication and withdrawal from alcohol and other substances can present as a form of mental illness causing the teen to be misdiagnosed with, and often medicated for, a condition they do not have. As if that's not bad enough, the use of addictive mind-altering substances can also bring out underlying mental health disorders that may not have surfaced otherwise. As I said, the only true cure for addiction is to have never taken a drink or drug in the first place. Unfortunately, that line cannot be uncrossed, only new lines drawn for new beginnings.

The second-best way to avoid addiction is for teens to postpone experimentation with alcohol and other substances until the brain has fully developed. The later into their 20s the better, with an optimal experimental age in their 30s (although adults are not immune to the draws of addiction). Unfortunately, teens think they know more than adults (and occasionally do). Convincing them to wait or remain abstinent is about as easy as convincing them not to have sex. That is why education in a classroom setting, perhaps Science class, is so important. Telling kids that if they must they can experiment in their 30s would likely be more convincing than telling them to *just say no*.

Those who experiment later in life have but a 4% chance of becoming addicted. That means that while 1 in 4 kids who try mind-altering substances become addicted, only 1 in 25 adults who experiment with alcohol and other drugs suffer that fate. Simply waiting decreases the risk of addiction 6-fold. Since early exposure to drugs and alcohol is the number one cause of addiction, it may be convincing enough to empower teens to wait to experiment until they are older, which may in turn lead most to outgrow the impulse and never experiment at all.

The truth is many addicts will simply grow out of it if they survive. The average cocaine addiction lasts about 4 years, although mine was closer to 13 from start to finish. The average Marijuana addiction usually runs its course in six years, while most users never fall into the addiction category. Alcohol and opiates usually take hold for about 15 years. Of all of the addicts that recover, only about a quarter of them seek any treatment at all, and as we know from earlier, only a small percentage of those benefit from the programs they try. A very small percentage of those that recover simply mature and stop using on their own. For those that do not, California Sober has a solution that far exceeds any 12-step program's result.

Childhood Trauma

Another issue that is linked to addictive behavior is childhood trauma. While some childhood trauma may not be preventable, keeping a close eye on your kids and the adults they are left in the care of is an excellent start. Be careful who you trust them with as most childhood trauma is perpetrated by family members. When the trauma is caused by a parent or guardian it's almost impossible to avoid but can be stopped as soon as it is discovered. Watch out for warning signs and pay attention to your child's daily mood. Drastic changes are a key giveaway for abuse.

In addition to guardianship, children need a lot of love in order to grow into healthy adults. Be nice to your children and give them plenty of love and they will be less likely to become addicted in the first place. Children that don't feel parental love, or those that come from dysfunctional families, have a much higher chance of becoming addicts. This is also one of the reasons for the limited success of the 12-step programs. These programs offer comradery and friendship that can fill the hole left by an unloving or abusive parent.

It's for this same reason that some kids will join gangs, criminal organizations, and other clubs that act as a pseudo-family. If a child is consistently abused in any way, odds are they will seek other less healthy ways to feel loved. Addiction can stem from substituting drugs for the love they need and/or from forming social bonds with other addicts, at the very least doubling the addictive properties of alcohol and drugs by associating them with the family they have created outside of the home.

Alcoholic parents and family members, whether they are abusive or not, combined with the early exposure mentioned above, can create a world where these substances become synonymous with love and happiness. The children of alcoholics and addicts are much more likely to become addicts than those from homes of non-addicted parents. This is compounded by the fact that addicted parents are less likely to give a child what he or she needs emotionally, and the fact that addicts are statistically more abusive than non-addicts. Whether or not there is a genetic predisposition to addiction is a possible additional factor but, even if genetics play no part, addicts produce more addicted children than adults that don't use substances do.

Chemical Imbalance (either born with, caused by use, or caused by pharmaceuticals given prior to brain maturity)

Another reason that some people become addicted to mind-altering substances, such as alcohol and other addictive drugs, is that their brain doesn't supply the chemicals it needs to be *normal*. There are so many reasons that this can occur that there is an entire medical field dedicated to it. The number of conditions is astounding, and their explanation is covered by countless textbooks and scientific journals worldwide, and they all contribute to addiction. The causes of chemical imbalances are many but, while they are often genetic, many are the result of some sort of abuse prior to adulthood.

Psychological conditions can be genetic. Those that are not can be caused by, as we mentioned earlier, using alcohol or other substances before the brain has fully matured. They can also be caused, and prolonged, by introducing unnecessary medications at a young age. In the 1990s, and continuing today on a slightly lesser scale, many children were misdiagnosed with psychological conditions such as ADD, ADHD, depression, bipolar disorder, and other mental health issues when in fact these kids were just transitioning from childhood to adulthood.

Adolescence can be trying for some parents that lack the skills needed to raise teenagers. It's easy to dismiss normal teenage behavior as a disorder. Teenagers go through depression, bouts of mania, and some may present as hyperactive. If the parents can't get a handle on the problem, they often seek the help of a psychiatrist. While therapy is awesome for anyone, the prescribing of pharmaceuticals to counter the effects of the normal hormones that teenagers deal with is all too common. SSRIs used to treat depression and other mood disorders have been shown to increase the risk of suicide in people under the age of 25. Also, as a result of supplementing the brain's chemistry, young minds that are medicated don't naturally produce the same proportion of chemicals that they normally would, resulting in the symptoms recurring any time the child is taken off the medication.

The symptoms of adolescence are the symptoms of many mental health disorders, but any trained professional should know the difference between normal teenage behavior and a psychological disorder. The brain's chemistry should never, aside from extreme circumstances, be altered while the brain is still in development. The result of the administration of unnecessary prescription medications during puberty is an increase in the likelihood of addiction in those that experiment with recreational substances.

What is California Sober?

California Sober is a lifestyle change that doesn't require a change in who you are, that is, unless you are looking for that change to occur. It's a reformation of the truest you. Instead of attempting to make you into someone you are not, California Sober is designed to help you to discover your true potential while allowing you to be yourself. It's a way to shed the baggage of addiction that has been holding you down, simultaneously guiding you to the self you once knew and loved. Inside all of us is the person we know we can be, the way we see ourselves without the judgement of others getting in the way. California Sober will help you see the way to that pure version of yourself.

Have you ever felt as if no one knows who you really are because all they see is the actions brought on by your addiction? You say to yourself *I know I messed up, but that's just not who I really am.* I know I have. I spent many years trying to show others the good inside of me, but all they could see were my past mistakes. No matter how many loving gestures I put forth to sway their opinions, all were seen as attempts to make amends rather than what they really were, my true self shining through. I wanted my friends, my loved ones, even people I had only known for a minute, to see me for who I truly intended to be. Still, for all my trying, they could only see the addict who lied, cheated, and sometimes stole to feed the *demon* that was possessing me.

The California Sober way is not designed to change you, per se. The California Sober way is to open your mind to the possibilities of life without suffering the controlling nature of your addiction, and without replacing it with the controlling aspects of traditional treatment. You or someone you know wants help. That's a given. That's why you're reading this.

Rather than tell you how to live your life, California Sober will give you the tools to live your life by your own rules, without the anchor of addiction weighing you down.

None of us are born with an instruction manual. What we do have is our sense of self, a set of values that are important to us and make us who we are. Some of us are religious, others embrace spirituality, and still others believe in a more tangible, scientific view of the world. In any case, the California Sober way is to embrace who we are and, more importantly, who we would like to be. Our faults are but an obstacle to overcome, not a flaw. None of us are truly broken, no matter what we have been forced to believe by society's norms and how we compare to them. Each of us is as individual as our worlds have made us, and each of us lives in a different world from the next. Those born into wealth are barely on the same planet as the street survivors, yet we cannot deny that those lifestyles have brought us to the same place.

While we may not all share an upbringing, and some of our struggles seem completely beyond compare, we still have one thing in common, addiction or some other condition of the mind has held us from (or destroyed) the life we are trying to live. The California Sober Way will not only show us how to live our best lives, but it can also bridge the gap of our struggles. They say that the truth shall set you free, but then they tell you what that truth should be. California Sober simply opens our eyes to what our truths really are, allowing us to use that knowledge for a higher enlightenment and guiding us to what we already know, even if it is deep inside of us.

What separates California Sober from other methods of addiction recovery is that the California Sober Way is not a set of rules you must abide by in order to shed the baggage of addiction. It is not a set of steps to be followed on a path to someone else's view of normalcy. California Sober is a guide to what you, as an individual, see as your true path. What is *normal* is in the eye of the beholder. What we offer you is your own version of a normal life, the you that you may have been had you not fallen into a trap, the you that you wish you were. California Sober is the path to your best self.

You may not even know what you are looking to accomplish. I know I didn't, although I was sure at the time that I did. Sure, you want to abstain from the poison that has taken over your life, but then what? The California Sober way is to help you find your favorite version of yourself and guide you on a path of your own construction. It is a guided journey that will take you to the place you've been looking for since before you lost your way. The California Sober journey ends where you say it does, and only after you have found the enlightenment you've been seeking all along.

On the California Sober journey, you decide how much or how little you want your life (or yourself) to change. There is no right or wrong, other than abstaining from the substance(s) that have taken control of an otherwise awesome you. The California Sober Way allows you to confront and banish the parts of you that are causing you harm without destroying the pieces that you hold dear. Through an intense self-reflection, you will clearly see what it is that you need to do in order to achieve the version of yourself that best represents the person you want to be.

For those of us with a bad self-image, this journey will reveal a version of you that you may not recognize, one that magnifies your best qualities and forgives the things that have brought you to this point. While there is no cure-all for some of the issues that life hands us, California Sober can help us to accept the cards that we have been dealt and make the most of our hand, thus achieving peace with what we have and allowing us to get the most out of the lives we already live. You will realize your true potential and find resolutions to the struggles that have brought you to this moment.

Some of us are born into the struggle, others have had tragedy rip away a part of us that we once knew. The California Sober Way can guide us to a path of true enlightenment that will lead us back to the person we were born to be. Your greatest self is on the horizon. Only you can make the changes necessary to be that perfect version of yourself, but California Sober can give you the tools you need to find, or remember, who that person is. The California Sober journey begins with who you are and ends with who you want to be. While you may not know the difference yet, you will soon enough.

Bill's Story - A Personal History

I, myself, am California Sober. After several decades of alcoholism, almost half a century, I can abstain from alcohol while in the company of those who are drinking. I can have alcohol in my house and never pour a drink. I haven't had a hangover or drank in excess in years. One might say I am cured of my alcoholism, but I don't see it that way. If I were to allow myself to, I could easily fall back into old habits and return to the destructive behavior that consumed my life before I found the California Sober method of recovery.

In addition to being an alcoholic I am, by my very nature, an addict. Specifically, I was addicted to Crack cocaine for more than a decade. Still, I can be around people using cocaine and other substances, never feeling the desire to use again. I was also what some might call a junk head. There was never a substance presented to me that I didn't try, and use to excess. I would consume anything and everything that would produce a mind-altering experience. There aren't many drugs that I didn't try in my career in addiction, and never did I turn one down. Today, there could be a table full of substances of abuse and I wouldn't feel the need to partake in any of them. I was a hard case, one of the hardest, and I owe my new life to the California Sober method of recovery.

I know true addiction and I know it well, perhaps better than many. I've gotten drunk and high with people from all walks of life, from the rich and powerful who could afford to lose more wealth than I have amassed in my half-century on this planet, to those who struggled to scrape together enough for a meal on the dollar menu. All of them had one thing in common. They had lost control of their lives and disregarded whatever they held dear in order to use their Substance of Choice. No matter what they tried, they failed at one thing, controlling their addiction to the substance that had once given them what they thought they needed to cope. I may not have been the worst-case scenario, but I was right up there with them.

You see, I was under the influence in utero. I didn't stand a chance. I was ingesting alcohol and nicotine from the moment of conception and throughout the gestation period. The only day of my mother's pregnancy that she didn't drink alcohol and smoke cigarettes might have been the day I was born, but I doubt she stayed sober the whole day. I'm only assuming she was sober the morning I was born because it was early on a Wednesday, about 8 am. She probably drank the night before and continued by 5pm on the day she got home from the hospital. I don't fault her for it. It was the way things were in her culture, early 1970s poverty-stricken New York.

I was born at least a month premature, 4 pounds and a couple ounces, with a healthy buzz and, likely, a hangover. Had I been breastfed I might have at least benefitted from the relief of the hair of the dog that bit me, but formula was what was on the menu giving me a few months to sober up. I'm sure the cravings of a screaming baby didn't make it easy for my parents to sleep it off and, considering my brother was only 11 months old when I was born, it couldn't have been easy to handle 2 infants while living the lifestyle they had.

It wasn't long until my embryonic cravings were reinforced. For teething, as I was told by my mother herself, mom dipped our pacifiers in whiskey, additionally rubbing the same spirits on our gums to soothe the pain. She reminded us of this not with guilt or embarrassment, but with a smile of pride because, again, it was what was done in her time and social class. It's what her mother did, and her mother before her, Irish Catholics from the ghettos of New York City.

I began experimenting with mind-altering substances on my own at a rather young age, my parents both being semi-functional alcoholics with my father smoking pot on a daily basis and using *drugs* from time to time. The first time I drank a beer all to myself I was about five years old. My parents, my brother, and I were at a barbeque on the back deck of my aunt's house. My mother was too engulfed in conversation to notice that I walked away with the beer she handed me in order to shut me up as I begged for a sip, something that I did since before I can remember. I don't think she, or anyone for that matter, even realized what had happened. In fact, when I finished that Budweiser and went back for another sip, my request was again granted.

By the time I was eleven, I began drinking beer with my brother and his friends. In my little world, it was a bonding experience and a rite of passage. It made my brother's friends think that I was *cool*, plus they knew that I wouldn't rat them out for anything from that moment on, as doing so would expose me as well. From there, they took me to hang out with the older kids, some in their twenties, without the worry that I might be a spying eye for the authority figures in our lives. By the time I was fifteen years old, drinking any form of alcohol we could get our hands on had become a weekend ritual that followed me into my adult life.

I was also eleven when I smoked weed for the first time. Not much later, my brother showed me the weekly stash that was in the top drawer of my father's dresser. While weed seemed like a fun experience for my young mind, my hypocritically strict parents and flawed religious programming, in addition to a child's mind, made me feel as if I was doing something I would be punished for in this life or the next. Some days I would smoke it and have a good time, while on other days I became paranoid and self-conscious. No matter how often or little I smoked, I never formed a regular habit. At the very least, it never became an everyday practice. Cocaine at fifteen years old had a very different result.

What started as a quick pick me up on long nights out with my best friend Mark soon became weekly, and eventually nightly, trips to the Washington Heights area of New York City. The first time I went with Mark to *cop some blow*, my adrenaline was more of a high than the coke ever produced. After climbing three sets of stairs in a shady-looking building, we were let into an apartment where a man sat at a folding table in nothing but his underwear. In his lap sat a 9mm pistol, a triple beam scale and a kilo of cocaine adorning the table in front of him. I didn't know whether to run or shit my pants. When he offered me a bump of cocaine off of a business card, I politely declined. As his other hand patted the pistol, I realized his request wasn't optional.

You might think that that would be the last time that I climbed those stairs. If so, you'd be mistaken. Mark and I became regulars at that apartment. The face of the man who sat in the chair changed from time to time, I never asked where they went or why, but the ritual was always the same. The man would ask *powder or rock* and we would say powder. The man would give us each a bump, or a line when he felt generous, and business would proceed as usual. After the first time, the gun felt more like a prop than a threat. It wasn't that I was unaware that I was in danger, just that that danger was worth the price of admission for the high I was about to receive.

After I blew through the savings from my job as a gas station attendant, I quit cocaine without a problem, or that's how I felt at the time. Cocaine is an expensive habit for a young kid making five dollars an hour and, truth be told, I couldn't afford it. If someone had some to offer, I'd never say no, but I couldn't maintain a supply long enough to become truly and undeniably addicted. Besides, I was finding new drugs that had less of a speedy turnaround. Drugs that would last longer and that could be obtained at a cheaper price.

That same year I tried LSD, mescaline, mushrooms, and PCP, all without anything I would consider an addiction. LSD, mesc, and shrooms all showed me a love of life I never knew being raised in a house of anger, but they were a one-and-done experience that I never sought frequently. I did fall in love with Angel Dust, however, and for ten bucks Mark and I could enjoy an entire Friday night. Shit, the first time we tried it the Bag o' Vapors was so potent that one ten-dollar bag lasted us a couple of days. My girlfriend at the time wasn't a fan, but that just meant more for me and my boy. She wasn't opposed to my new drug, and my friends all went right along, so there was no one to tell me that it might be a bad idea.

For reasons that were unrelated to my drug use, and more

about my parents' problems (I say this because my parents were oblivious to my extracurricular activities), I was thrown out of my house at the age of 16. I moved into the home of my high school friend, Dan, whose single mother was fine with us having a few beers, as long as we kept it on the second floor of the house. The party went full throttle from there. Left to my own devices and with no one to tell me what to do, beer became more common than water, and other drugs were what made the weekends different. Feeling bad that my brother (who had been kicked out of the house at the same time as me) had no place to stay, my parents took me back in. They never once asked me to come home before they accepted my brother back. Had he been able to make it as I had, I may not have heard from them again.

A year on my own, drinking every night and doing whatever else a 16-year-old kid could find to get himself in trouble, had me doing whatever it took to feel good in the moment. Drinking at home was not something that I was willing to give up now that I had a taste of freedom from hypocrisy. At first, my parents had fun with it, drinking with me and telling street stories from 5 pm until we collectively felt the need to pass out. When my drinking was no longer fun for them, I was on my own for good. My independence started with sleeping on couches, in my van, and anywhere else that would have me.

Still, life never gave me a problem I didn't feel I could handle until I tried Crack, the smokable version of cocaine (also known as freebase). I had been smoking it for years on top of PCP, a mixture that we called Space Base, which hid the addiction potential due to the fact that the Angel Dust overpowered the crack's fiendish side effects.[2] I had never

---

[2] This is a possible testament to PCP and Ketamine causing instantaneous, while short lived, addiction relief. At the very least, PCP had the ability to make crack non-addictive when the two were combined.

smoked Crack on its own until another friend of mine convinced me that it would be just as *harmless* as it was when it was on top of dust. From that moment on, I was hopelessly addicted to the rock.

Not having parents to deal with allowed my life to be free from any and all rules. This lawless lifestyle led me to believe that I didn't have to follow any of the rules of society either. Breaking the law is something you have to do in order to do drugs. From there I found myself on a slippery slope. Disregarding drug laws made me question any and all laws, for if one law is bullshit, the rest must be as well. Stealing food to survive led to stealing other things in the supermarket that could be sold in order to get money for *drugs*. One thing led to another and before I knew it, I was in jail.

Now, one might think it would be hard to get drugs in county jail. That person would be wrong. The first morning that I had breakfast with other inmates I found out how easy it actually was. After a brief introduction, a slightly overweight man with a broken leg presented me with a deal I couldn't refuse. If I were willing to give him half of my breakfast he would reward me with a Percocet, a strong opiate pain medication. For my whole breakfast, he would give me two. Needless to say, I was quickly down to two meals a day and nodding out until lunch.

I was only 20 when I first took a hit of strait crack, and the addiction followed me on and off (mostly on) for over a decade. What started as something to do on a Friday night quickly became a habit that caused me to lose jobs, something I had never experienced in the past, and to sell anything of value that I owned. When I did work, I refinished wood floors and worked as a finish carpenter. Every house I entered I scoped out for drugs. You might be surprised to learn that at least 70% of the medicine cabinets I raided in the

1990s had some form of opiate painkiller, and I wouldn't take just one, I'd steal the bottle.

By the time I realized that I had to stop using these substances, I didn't have the power to do so. There was no playbook for this, no instruction manual to follow. My parents were in no way equipped to give me advice on the matter, *just stop doing it* was the best they could come up with, and my understanding of addiction was limited to what I had learned in Rehab and jail, which was nothing but 12 steps that seemed to make less sense than they had before I needed them. After ten years of selling my soul for any form of cocaine I could find, I had to leave my home in New York, and all of my friends and family, in order to escape.

Like most addicts that are forced to, or voluntarily attempt to quit, I had tried rehab and the 12-step programs starting when I was just seventeen. It never took. I had no problem admitting that I had an addiction that had grown beyond my control. I was sure that I was nearly powerless. I did, however, have a strong disdain for the 12 steps. The idea that turning my will over to some magical force, some higher power that would help me out of my situation, never felt real. I had prayed for things as a kid that never came to fruition, like escaping my abusive home life. How could praying for relief from addiction work? Even if God were real, he obviously didn't grant my silly requests. My problem was real, and I couldn't see the logic in believing that surrendering my will would help me out of a situation that was caused by surrendering my will. It seemed counterproductive, and it was.

Something miraculous DID happen

After a decade of addiction, while facing an eviction for six months of back rent (and no job prospects), I spent my evenings hopelessly addicted and my nights begging the Universe for a way out. The problem with that was that I wasn't actively looking for that way out, just pleading for it with whatever power might grant these wishes. I wasn't looking for a job, a place to live, or a way out. I was simply hoping these things would find me. I spent my days recovering from the previous night's drug use, and that didn't leave any time for figuring out my shit. Still somehow, as if a gift from the Universe itself, an old friend invited me to stay with her in Venice, California, if only until I could land on my feet again. This was what I was looking for, an escape plan, and in the one place that I'd wanted to visit since reading *No One Here Gets Out Alive*[3] a decade prior. This *must* be the Universe finally having my back, I figured.

When I left New York for California in 2002, shortly after my 30th birthday, I found myself in the same situation. I didn't actively look for Crack, yet somehow it found me in the bathroom of a Venice bar the day after I had landed. Still, without a large circle of friends that had the same problem as I did, I found it easier to do it less often until, eventually, my use was rare enough that I didn't consider it a problem that I couldn't handle. I still found myself in a pattern of wasted nights and lost paychecks, but the rent was paid, I was eating at least a couple of meals most days, and I could once again hold a job.

Instead of PCP, I drank way too much alcohol. The least I ever drank was when a friend bet me that I couldn't go a week without a beer. I cheated daily, having a 40-ounce beer whenever no one was around, but I drank far less that week than I had in years. When the week was over, I rode back into drinking full throttle without missing a beat. Like my parents

---

[3] No One Here Gets Out Alive - Jerry Hopkins and Danny Sugerman - 1980 Plexus Publishing paperback: ISBN 0-85965-038-3

before me, and theirs before them, I had become a functional alcoholic. I could hold a job and pay my bills, but I never felt like I could (or even wanted to) stop drinking, which in turn lowered my will and occasionally lead me back to smoking crack. My escape plan wasn't 100% foolproof, I quickly discovered.

Baby Steps and the first Revelation - Bill's story

So, there I was alone, still broke, and living in a motel. I had cut all of my past lifelines, ensuring that no one but myself could contribute to my undoing while simultaneously leaving myself with no way to reach out for help in my struggle to survive, eat, and find shelter from the elements. I had run nearly 3,000 miles to escape a life of addiction with very limited results. I was better than before, I figured, yet I was stuck in a similar cycle that, no matter how sincere my intentions at the start of each day, repeated itself regularly. The only difference now was that the daily crack use had lessened itself to a weekly problem.

Being able to hold a job, eat food on a regular basis, and spend most days without some form of cocaine running through my veins left me complacent. I was content to exist in a sleazy motel with a crack dealer neighbor, crack-addicted sex workers and meth heads for acquaintances, and barely two coins to rub together in an emergency, as long as I could be in the land of eternal sunshine, just a mile from the ocean's edge, with several days to enjoy between bouts of addiction that usually only lasted a few hours (rather than the days or even weeks long binges of my New York life). Baby steps. Still, I drank every night, although I thought that was normal adult behavior and didn't consider it a problem as long as it didn't end with me hitting the rock.

To escape the longing to get high on weekend nights before it had a chance to set in, I would often walk to the beach as soon as my post-work shower was under my belt. At a shady bar in Venice, I would fill the void that existed where my life used to be with the conversation of strangers and as many pints of cheap American beer as I could fit. Afterward, I would stroll the Ocean Front Walk, with a tall can of Budweiser wrapped in a brown paper bag, before braving the lonely walk up Brooks Street to my motel, past the crack dealers on Sixth Avenue that would end up with any cash that I had forgotten to leave at home.

On one such Ocean Front stroll, I decided to venture further than usual, to another bar called Hinano at the land's edge of the Venice Pier. Hinano stayed open until 2 am, unlike the beachfront bars that closed shortly after sunset, and I wasn't ready to end the night alone. Hinano was also where I found my first California crackhead and, after several pints at the Bistro, I had a bug in my brain that was nagging me to find my substance of choice. It had become easy to be sober when I was sober but after a few beers that notion seemed stupid. *I can just do a little*, I thought. *Just a 20 and a few beers to chill.*

As I walked hurriedly down the path to my destination, looking forward to the adventure, I was distracted by what looked like a group of gypsies having a gathering on the sand between myself and the ocean, twirling various objects that were set ablaze and lighting up the beach. The waves crashed to a soothing rhythm to which they all seemed to dance. Fire roared from the end of large chains and hoops, wielded by men and women in loose-flowing outfits of purples, yellows, and black. One man blew a flame 10 feet into the air above him while another lit a cigarette off of a burning log that he had pulled from the fire pit in the center of their little world. I couldn't help but wander over to get a closer look. They reminded me of what my friends and I used to be before our addictions took control.

As I neared the group's outer circle, a young blonde woman met me with a smile and a teacup, two fingers pinching the handle as the other hand gently cradled its delicate body as if shielding a candle's flame from the wind. As she extended her arms, she asked but one word. *Tea?* I graciously accepted my new hostesses offering, sipping the hot beverage until it was gone and taking my place among them to watch their celebration of life, an improvised dance of spinning fire and gyrating bodies known as poi.

As the minutes multiplied, the dance became more intense, the fire creating trails in the darkness that grew longer and longer until the flames seemed to be chasing each other through the night air, the crashing waves delivering a symphony that seemed timed to the rhythm of the performers themselves. Everyone, all of nature, and the night felt as if they were involved in a synchronized event put on by the universe itself for my personal entertainment. Before I knew it, some time had passed without me thinking about getting another beer. What was more striking to me was that I was no longer thinking about the mission at hand. I was no longer yearning to hear the sizzle of crack in my pipe. I didn't care to leave and get high.

Enjoying your tea? the blonde woman asked, even though I had given her back her teacup twenty minutes prior. It was at that moment that I realized what was happening. Still, I felt the need to ask.

What was in that?

Mushrooms, silly, she responded. *I thought you knew. You look like...*

I didn't, I interrupted with a smile I couldn't peel from my face *but thank you. Thank you so very much.*

I was grateful for the fire show, I was grateful for the company of these nomads that had accepted me into their night, but most of all I was thankful that I had no desire to drink alcohol or smoke cocaine. I was more than content watching these misfits harness the energy of the universe than I could have ever been peeking out of the blinds of a dingy motel, listening to pimps scold their girls, sirens wailing down the boulevard and the sounds of madness that were brought on by crack induced auditory hallucinations and the inner voice of paranoia screaming in my brain. It all became so obvious so quickly. This was where I was meant to be at this moment. This was the way to freedom.

After another hour or so of entertainment, and a kindness and love from my hosts that I hadn't felt since I left my chosen family in New York, I decided that I wanted to spend some time alone. It wasn't that this moment of life wasn't exactly what I needed, and it wasn't like I felt in any way out of place among my new friends, but I was overcome with the feeling that I needed to be alone with my thoughts. I needed to contemplate what had just happened to me. Without a word, I wandered off the beach and into the dark streets of Venice. In that moment, my mind and the warm night air of my new hometown were the only comforting friends that I needed. I was finally home.

As I stepped out of the bright streetlights and into the darkness of the sleazy motel that I had so happily called home, my new eyes saw the lie that I had been telling myself for more than a year. The *once were white* cracked plaster walls revealed themselves in a way that I hadn't previously acknowledged and, as I lay on the mattress where God knows what atrocities had taken place, staring at the water-stained ceiling, I grew frighteningly depressed by my situation. While I was definitely doing better than I was when I was dying from my addiction, I could finally see that I hadn't come as far as I had previously imagined.

Sure, I was holding a job and I wasn't smoking Angel Dust and Crack on a daily basis, but I was still drinking every second that I wasn't working or sleeping, and I was occasionally breaking my own rules, getting high on crack in moments of weakness, loneliness, and boredom. As more sirens roared down Lincoln Boulevard, as the crack dealer next door screamed at his wife and best moneymaker, as the sex workers fought with their pimps in the parking lot, the mushroom tea didn't let me tune these things out as I normally had. The feeling of dread overwhelmed me, and I jumped up and hurriedly made my way back towards the beach.

I had been broken for so long that I really thought, until that moment, that I had recovered as much as I was going to. I thought that I would have to forever live a life of controlled alcohol addiction with bouts of crack fiending. I had accepted my fate as an alcoholic and now part-time drug addict and that I had come as far as I could. The truth was that I had come as far as I could without another change of mind. Almost dying in New York forced me to accept a change. Mushroom tea with the gypsies made me *want* to change. I was no longer driven by mere survival; I was shown that I could go back to who I was before my addictions took hold. I now knew that I could be the me I was before this whole mess got out of hand.

By the time I got back to the beach, the gypsies were gone. The only trace of them were the ashes left in the pit of fire. Had it not been for that, I would have thought that I was on the wrong beach, or that it had all been a dream. It was then that I realized that it wasn't the gypsies I was running back to find. It was the sand, the ocean, the sound of the waves crashing on the beach. It was home that I was looking for.

The place where I was when I saw the whole picture unfold with clarity. The mushrooms had reminded me of who I was, and why I had left my home and everything that I loved. They also reminded me of where I was supposed to be headed. Towards freedom from substance use disorder.

More Baby Steps

While the psychedelics had opened my eyes, I wasn't quite ready to see. We have all had this experience. We see the path clearly but close our eyes because we are not ready to change direction just yet. I stopped smoking crack that night, for the most part, but kept drinking after work every night, and my weekends started with mimosa breakfasts at the Sidewalk Cafe' on Venice Beach. Being a functional alcoholic was a major step up from being a strung-out junkie who couldn't hold a job. It was as *normal* as I had ever been and two steps ahead of my parents, which made it feel like success.

Years later, when my first daughter was conceived, her mother being my drinking buddy and the only person I knew with a worse alcohol problem than me, I had to slow down a bit. I was filled with love for that little girl, and she didn't deserve to grow up in the same environment that I was tortured with. I attempted to limit my drinking so that I was relatively sober, at least until her bedtime, but that just didn't feel like enough. Waking up without the memory of going to bed, panicking until I saw her chest rise and take a breath, was driving me crazy. By the time work was done, I had forgotten about the morning's worries, and I'd crack a beer. I knew that I had to do something, I just didn't remember how.

By the time she was old enough to start school, her mother and I had forced ourselves, through sheer will and a little

Cannabis, to limit our drinking to mostly non-school nights. Still, when Thursday night rolled around, we drank until we ran out of whiskey and slept Saturday and Sunday away while our child learned to feed herself breakfast. When we finally emerged, we probably weren't the most pleasant people to be around.

We joined a gym and worked out every night after work. We were striving to be the best versions of ourselves. Still, after the gym we would go to the CVS next door and buy a handful of 22oz. Budweisers and a pack of smokes. We knew that we were being counterproductive by partying after the gym, but old habits are hard to change. That's when we decided it was time for another change. While we were using some of the California Sober methods, we had no intent when we did and, therefore, didn't see the full results.

Neither I nor my baby's mom had the desire to be 100% sober, but we knew that we had to provide a better life for our young daughter. We struggled every day to be better than the day before, to little avail. We set rules on Monday that we would simply break by Thursday's end. Our problem was the problem of many addicts, we were trying to abstain from any and all substances, while our problems were limited to alcohol (by that point at least). Other substances, like weed and mushrooms, were things that we could do once in a while without feeling any need to do them again anytime soon. Still, the programming that came from our combined histories with the 12-step programs, and from anyone we knew who had temporarily overcome addiction by these methods, reinforced that the only way to stop drinking and using other harmful substances was abstinence from any and all mind-altering substances.

On more than one occasion, we decided to take acid or mushrooms as a change of pace. We would spend the night talking about how far we had come since we had quit freebasing cocaine and what we needed to do to get our lives together. For several days after, drinking was less of a priority, our new life as parents becoming our main focus. Still, Thursday would roll around again and we would, mostly out of habit, stop at the store and grab a case of beer and a pack of cigarettes. Had we only known why we hadn't had a craving for a drink all week, or why we were grabbing beer without even craving it, things might have been different sooner than later.

Years of struggling to control our alcoholism finally came to a head when my wife decided to get pregnant with our second daughter. She never drank during either of her pregnancies, a self-control that I can only attribute to her love of the unborn child growing inside of her, a self-control that I never helped with or practiced as I drank away the weekends while she watched in simultaneous envy and disgust. Her astounding discipline went out the window as soon as drinking would no longer physically endanger our children. Shortly after our second child was born, my soon-to-be wife started getting migraines. The headaches were unrelenting, and she returned to marijuana to relieve them.

She found that if she smoked Cannabis prior to drinking, the urge to drink was virtually nonexistent. That, coupled with the fact that alcohol made the headaches worse, caused her to stop drinking altogether. Still, every Thursday through Saturday, I continued my alcohol consumption with no reasonable end in sight. Not having my drinking buddy added to the looserish feeling of guilt that came with my morning hangovers. I wanted to join my fiancé in her newfound California Sobriety, but cannabis was something that I still found unpredictable, and often torturous (likely due to my unresolved issues). A few years later I began taking Opium for back pain and my life changed.

It seemed ridiculous that a long-forgotten substance with a high potential for addiction could be the remedy for my alcoholism. Still, when I took Opium, I could let a beer sit beside me until it was warm and flat before wanting to take a sip. I knew that the morphine and codeine that Opium contained were the most physically addictive naturally occurring substances on the planet. I also knew the dope dealer's philosophy, as was told to me by my late friend Jeff Balk. *The first day, I'm your friend, the second day I'm your best friend, by the third day, I am your dealer.* With that in mind, I only took the Opium on days that I would normally drink. I also took only enough to lessen my back pain and subdue my cravings.

Marijuana made my baby's mother avoid alcohol and Opium took my craving for it away. Neither of us had an addiction to the substances we were using to relieve our alcohol fiend. Neither of us had any negative problems associated with our newfound friends. We were happy, healthy, and better people as a result. We weren't *sober* in the classical sense, but we were free from our addictions. The longer we went without alcohol (we hadn't smoked cocaine since our first child was born), the less we thought about it and the less we relied on our newfound alternative medications to help us stop drinking. Admittedly, though, I was worried that I had traded one addiction for another. Even if it wasn't causing me any problems, I still *needed* Opium in lieu of alcohol.

To be clear, I don't advocate the taking of Opium as a remedy for addiction. Opium is the root form of the most highly addictive substances on the planet and, as such, should be respected and not taken on a regular basis. My mission in this writing is to speak honestly about the California Sober method of recovery, and I cannot be honest while hiding this truth. I am a rare case of someone who, for a very short period of time, was able to self-prescribe a dosage and regimen that allowed me to find temporary relief from using a dangerous and addictive substance by using a slightly less dangerous and addictive substance. That is not the California Sober way, and it could lead anyone down a path to another addiction. When I began to feel a need for Opium, a need I could no longer deny, that's when I truly realized the California Sober method of addiction recovery.

Some envy of my wife's less addictive supplement made me experiment with low-THC Marijuana gummies, an edible form of marijuana in gelatin. I took the 5mg candies nightly at bedtime to build a slight tolerance and allow my mind to get used to it again. When I started taking them on Friday nights, I realized that the paranoia that weed had traditionally caused me only came with certain strains. For me, Indicas were torture and Sativas were the relief I needed. I started taking Sativa based gummies on nights that I would usually drink. That's when I stumbled upon the first aspect of the California Sober method that is scientifically proven, one that I still use today.

With my alcoholism at bay and my Opium use discontinued, I decided it was a good time to enter the psychedelic realm once more. LSD and psilocybe mushrooms were something that I had done dozens of times, using alcohol *to take the edge off*. For the first time in my life, I was about to take mushrooms without anything else to enhance them (like marijuana) or to soften the sharpness (as alcohol can do). The other main difference between that day and all the other times I had tripped, I was taking these mushrooms with the sole intent to finally stop *needing* something to get through the weekend. At 45 years old I hadn't had a truly sober weekend, other than 28 days in rehab or 90 days in jail, since I was about 14 years old. I wanted the freedom that normal people took for granted, I wanted to be able to get to the end of the week without feeling the need to use harmful and addictive substances.

The Real Bill W. – How A.A. was Almost California Sober since 1956

Let's face facts. Some rules are there for a reason. Take for instance diet and exercise. It is proven that moderate exercise prolongs life, keeps you in shape and healthy, and boosts the manufacture of pleasure-inducing chemicals in the brain. It is also a fact that eating a healthy diet does each of those things as well. These facts, presented in such a way by the media as to insinuate that we must all follow a strict set of rules, lead people to a constant roller coaster of fad diets and exercise routines that they feel they have to be vigilant at in order to succeed, ultimately leading to failure and self-loathing.

People who are overweight are often told that they need to cut out all sugar and go on diets that have them eating things that they don't like in order to lose the weight they have accumulated. While it works for a time, they cannot sustain a diet that is torturous to their palate and so they ultimately fail. In truth, the same individuals may have succeeded with simple goals like portion control and substituting a couple of their more processed meals for healthier options. They could still eat the occasional sugary snack, just not as often, and not in the portions in which they used to consume them. A person of average weight doesn't eat salad three meals a day and completely abstain from sugar, nor should the overweight person have to in order to accomplish a more average weight. Moderation is the key to success.

The health media tells us that we have to go to the gym nearly every day, or perhaps run seven miles per day, in order to live to a ripe old age. People who read this go from sitting on the couch every evening, after working in an office cubicle all day, to attempting to be a triathlete overnight. As a result, there is a spike in gym memberships right around the time of New Year's resolutions that sharply drop off as soon as February comes around. That's because people are trying to dramatically change who they are at a moment's notice, quickly leading them to a feeling of being overwhelmed and, eventually, giving up completely. That is because no one can change who they are overnight. It's a process. Baby steps.

Science tells us that a moderate diet consisting of portion control and limited added sugar is what is necessary to maintain a healthy weight. The average Joe eats what he or she likes, but in a way that doesn't become harmful to his or her health or weight. Science also tells us that moderate exercise is what propels us into healthy longevity, not the extreme athletics that can lead to injury or that are unsustainable for the average person's daily routine. Again, moderation is the key.

Just because the overweight person might be addicted to food (or worse, sugar) and the overly sedentary person might have habits that need to be broken in order for them to find a healthy norm, neither should be told that the only way to their life-changing success is by a change so unthinkable that it will surely cause them to fail. Food addicts cannot abstain from food. They have to learn to control their intake and look for better options for what they are putting in their bodies. Healthier options and controlled portions are the keys. Those who don't move as often as they should cannot will themselves into becoming Mr. or Mrs. Universe in a day. However, they can go for a walk around the block at the end of the day, and that may be all that they need. Improving a little each day is more productive than trying to transform in an instant.

Therein lies one of the problems with pure abstinence. Trying to get addicts to follow a set of rules that force them to abstain from any substance in order to achieve sobriety is not only difficult for them, but also scientifically proven to be a detriment. While a select few may need this regimen, the 5-10% that the 12 steps truly help, most people fall short of this strait edge philosophy. You wouldn't tell a person who struggles with their weight to never eat again. You can't force a person who lives a sedentary life to become a triathlete. Why, then, would you tell someone who self-medicates to cut out any and all external substances?

The fear of never feeling exogenous pleasures granted them through self-medication turns off the average addict from even attempting recovery, and the ones who do take that plunge usually fail, mostly due to this extremist idea. The hardest thing for some people who legitimately want to break their addiction is reckoning with the fact that they will never experience an elevated perception again. Since we now know that classic psychedelics are harmless, reduce addiction, and are even proven to be beneficial to our physical and mental health, why would we demand that someone seeking a path to *sobriety* abstain from them?

In addition to abstinence from any and all mind-altering substances, the 12-step programs tell you that you can't have new relationships, making love and sex additionally frowned upon addictions. Now they're lonely, horny, and unable to do anything that makes the pleasure sensors of the brain fire. On top of that, the brain hasn't yet begun replacing the endorphins that it used to get from getting drunk, high, or having sex, so one tends to feel like a depressed lonely loser who is not allowed to do anything to relieve the agony, other than attend meetings. One day at a time doesn't even feel possible, let alone a lifetime vow of misery. Asceticism is not the way to recovery. California Sober is.

The need for abstinence from any and all substances is a fallacy that was never a part of the original 12-step system of recovery to begin with. Caffeine and nicotine are more than welcome in 12-step meetings, in addition to anything prescribed by a physician (which is more often than not the problem their members really need help with). It may interest you to know that the founder of the 12-step program never advocated abstinence from any substance, other than alcohol. Not only that, but he also wanted to incorporate the California Sober lifestyle into his 12-step system of recovery, famously known as Alcoholics Anonymous.

The True First Step was the Twelfth Step - A.A.

What you probably haven't read in any literature provided by a twelve-step program is that its inventor William Griffith Wilson, better known to all members of any of the Anonymous programs as Bill W., was California sober. That's right. The founder of Alcoholics Anonymous was not a believer in abstinence from all substances. A.A. acknowledges this fact, and even has publications that are honest about it (including the Big Book), but you'll likely never hear it in a meeting. Many A.A.s come to me with the same sad story. *I was practicing the steps and following the program, I was staying sober, but I told my sponsor that I smoke cannabis to relieve my anxiety and they told me that they could no longer be my sponsor. Then they told me that I should go to rehab.* If they would only read their Big Book, they would realize their hypocrisy, but too many of them are programmed that a straight edge life of pure abstinence is the only way.

The truth is, Alcoholics Anonymous doesn't say anything about abstaining from other substances. William Wilson didn't concern himself with the problems of any substance other than alcohol. He never preached abstinence from mind altering substances. As long as you weren't drinking, in Bill's mind you were sober. While he remained abstinent from alcohol from December 11th, 1934, until his death from an addiction to tobacco on January 24th, 1971, Bill W. found relief in California Sober substances and held the belief that any substance use, other than alcohol, was between the user and their higher power.

The reason 12 step programs are associated with abstinence from all mind-altering substances actually has nothing to do with old Bill. As a matter of fact, his well-documented stance that drug addiction is not something A.A. should be involved in disregards other substances altogether. The truth is, Bill would only allow a *drug addict* into Alcoholics Anonymous meetings if they were also alcoholic. Alcoholics Anonymous was, and is, about abstinence from alcohol, and not mind-altering substances, something its members (and even its highly regarded sponsors) often do not know.

Bill's concern was with personally refraining from drinking and helping others to do the same, nothing more. Due to this exclusion, those wishing to use the limited success of Alcoholics Anonymous had to find another way. With no other reliable programs to follow, later Anonymous groups (those focused on substances other than spirits) plagiarized what Bill had come up with, rewriting his steps to include abstinence from any and all mind-altering substances, except those that they deemed to be acceptable vices, such as caffeine and nicotine.

Those other Anonymous groups, most notably Narcotics Anonymous, borrowed so heavily from Bill W.'s work that groups and treatment centers mistakenly attributed their philosophies to him. These groups went so far as to incorporate A.A.'s Big Book into their programs, adding to the falsehood that Bill W. supported their beliefs. The truth is the

Alcoholics Anonymous founder was never opposed to psychedelic therapy. The A.A. group's official frequently asked questions go so far as to spell out exactly that. As a matter of fact, W.'s first *spiritual awakening* was the result of using hallucinogens.

Bill Wilson was on his fourth stay at Town's Hospital for Drug and Alcohol Addictions in New York City, where he was being treated for alcoholism. He was administered what was known as the *Belladonna treatment*, a cutting-edge treatment in 1900 that was so successful that it became the most widely used method for treatment of alcoholism by the 1920s. The treatment was derived from the alkaloids of the belladonna and henbane plants in the deadly nightshade family, which have been used for thousands of years as both a poison and a hallucinogen. Patients were given the treatment every hour for fifty hours.

To read Bill Wilson's account speaks volumes. Bill wrote in his Big Book, *my brother-in-law is a physician, and through his kindness and that of my mother I was placed in a nationally known hospital for the mental and physical rehabilitation of alcoholics. Under the so-called belladonna treatment my brain cleared.* The treatment didn't fully take the first time and he was readmitted to the hospital. After a spiritual conversation with an old friend (one who had refused a drink that Wilson had offered), and the notion that alcohol would kill him or leave him in an asylum, Bill was administered the treatment once more.

Suddenly the room lit up with a great white light, Bill W. recalled, *I was caught up into an extacy which there are no words to describe. It seemed to me, in my minds eye, that I was on a mountain and that a wind not of air but of spirit was blowing. And then it burst upon me that I was a free man. Slowly the extacy subsided. I lay on the bed, but now for a time*

I was in another world, a new world of consciousness. All about me and through me there was a wonderful feeling of Presence, and I thought to myself, "So this is the God of the preachers!" A great peace stole over me and I thought, "No matter how wrong things seem to be, they are still all right. Things are all right with God and His world."

William Wilson never had another drink. He had yet to attend a meeting or practice any of the twelve steps (likely due to the fact that he hadn't created any of these things yet). Bill started his recovery with what would later become the 12th step. He had but one spiritual experience, brought on by delirium tremens (DTs), sleep deprivation, and a potion of hallucinogens that was administered hourly for more than two consecutive days. What stopped Bill W. from drinking wasn't his famous group or its rituals, it was a powerful hallucinogenic trip. His *spiritual awakening* is one that is part of many individual journeys on the way to achieving what we now know as California Sobriety.

The reason Bill W.'s psychedelic experience caused him to never drink again is the same reason that it has worked for many others in the past century. His recollection of the experience is identical to that of countless others on their road to becoming California Sober. He had a spiritual awakening brought on by psychedelics that showed him his true potential and erased his urge to drink alcohol almost completely. After 18 years of being a blackout drunk, one psychedelic experience stopped Bill Wilson's alcoholism in its tracks. He was cured. Although the urge to drink returned on his deathbed, as I would suppose it may have many times, the founder of Alcoholics Anonymous never took another drink.

The Thirteenth Step - A Friend of Bill W.

While Bill W. went on to create the most famous recovery system of the 20th century, he never forgot the one true moment that saved him from his addiction. He invented twelve steps to help guide other recovering alcoholics to the spiritual experience he credited with his recovery, not yet realizing that his experience was brought about by 50 hours of orally administered hallucinogens. After years of promoting his path to recovery, Wilson realized that he had yet to find a consistently successful way to bring all of his A.A.s to the same awakening. That fact changed due to the help of his new friend Aldous Huxley, author of *The Doors of Perception*.

In the winter of 1943, the founder of Alcoholics Anonymous took his wife, Lois, on a cross-country road trip to check out some of the A.A. groups that had formed since his *Big Book* was published just four years prior. He and his spouse toured the country with stops in Chicago, Denver, and the Grand Canyon. At the end of his journey, Bill W. found himself in California. That's where he met Gerald Heard and Aldous Huxley, with whom he became fast friends. The men invited Bill and his wife to Heard's 300-acre spiritual retreat, known as Trabucco College, to spend New Year's week.

A decade later, Aldous Huxley requested a dose of mescaline from psychiatrist Humphry Osmand. Osmand had been studying the effects of both mescaline and LSD on schizophrenic patients and had discovered their potential for mind-expanding experiences. In May of 1953, Osmand traveled to Los Angeles for a conference. He brought the Mesc and supervised Huxley's first trip, which inspired Aldous to write *The Doors of Perception* (1954). His buddy Gerald also tried mescaline the following year and they began using LSD in 1955, information they quickly decided to share with Bill W.

Fate had brought the A.A. founder full circle and on August

29, 1956, in California, Bill W. had found what he had been searching for since it was revealed to him those many years ago. After nearly 22 years of sobriety, Bill Wilson took his first dose of LSD, and it brought him back to that fateful winter of 1934. His LSD experience was identical to the *spiritual awakening* he had at Towns Hospital, the experience that saved him from his alcoholism. He was immediately convinced of the potential for LSD to help alcoholics have the *awakening* they so desperately needed in order to *see the light* and stop drinking. The experience didn't break his sobriety, it simply reinforced his beliefs and gave him a map that he could now give others to follow to that moment of clarity.

Bill W.'s first Acid trip was done under the supervision of Dr. Sidney Cohen (who was later appointed by Richard Nixon in 1968 as the first director of the NIMH's Division of Narcotic Abuse and Drug Addiction), and Gerald Heard. From Heard's notes we learn that Bill first reported *a feeling of peace.* A couple of hours later, he spoke of feeling *an enormous enlargement* of everything around him. Not long after, Heard quoted Wilson as saying that he thought that *people shouldn't take themselves so damn seriously.* It's not until he returned home that Bill began to write to Heard, giving him updates on the results. In his first letter, dated September 26, 1956, Bill, after recounting some bouts of exhaustion, says *I do feel a residue of assurance and a feeling of enhanced beauty that seems likely to stay with me.*

He continued singing the praises of his new treatment in the coming months and didn't stop for several years afterward. In a second letter to Heard in December of 1956, some 4 months after his first Acid trip, Bill W. wrote *My reaction to things totally, and in particular, have very definitely improved for no other reason that I can see.* This is Wilson's testimony to the long-term awakenings that LSD and other psychedelics promote. William Wilson was a new man, once again, and he couldn't stop raving about it.

He would later write that *it is a generally acknowledged fact in spiritual development that ego reduction makes the influx of God's grace possible. If, therefore, under LSD we can have a temporary reduction, so that we can better see what we are and where we are going - well, that might be of some help. The goal might become clearer. So I consider LSD to be of some value to some people, and practically no damage to anyone.*

The outstanding residue seem to be these: all of the assurances of my original experience were renewed, and more. The sense of the livingness of all things and a sense of their beauty has been considerably heightened and restored... I can report this in spite of the fact that on my arrival home I had a severe reaction of anxiety, weakness, lack of focus and the like. But this time, the depression was pretty much absent. Bill W. not only saw his newest way to that awakening was a benefit to alcoholism, but that it had lessened his depression.

Wilson was so sure of his new remedy he decided to continue his treatments. On February 16, 1957, Bill had his first group session with LSD in which the *therapists* and *patients* all took the hallucinogen. Betty Elsner, an American psychologist, and pioneer in the use of hallucinogens in psychotherapy, was one of the participants. It was Betty's idea, as she wanted to see what would happen if everyone took LSD, blurring the lines between patient and therapist. She proposed a conservative dose of 25 micrograms and made the pills accordingly. 35 minutes later, she reported, Bill was stirred by the music. She also noted that Bill *looked much younger* (which may have been due to the fact that she also ingested some LSD).

In her autobiographical account of her career, Remembrances of LSD Therapy Past, Betty Eisner wrote that *Alcoholics Anonymous was actually considering using LSD. Alcoholics get to a point in the program where they need a spiritual experience, but not all of them are able to have one. Tom Powers was Bill Wilson's right-hand man in this. Tom had been through hell with alcoholism, so he brought Bill Wilson out to meet with us. Sid and I thought it might be a good idea to try a low dose together, but when I met Bill, I thought, "Uh-oh, this is going to be his therapy session." And that's one of the things it turned out to be. We each took 25 gamma, except for Bill. Sid offered him several pills, and Bill said "Don't ever do that to a drunk," and took two. But the rest of us just took one.*

Bill W. was so taken by the powers of LSD that he convinced his wife Lois, his secretary Nell Wing, and his spiritual advisor Father Dowling all to take the psychedelic substance. A year after his first experience with Acid, Bill wrote a letter to Sam Shoemaker in which he confessed that he had taken LSD several times and that the *material is about as harmless as aspirin.* He is also quoted as saying *they do open the doors to a wider perception.* In a letter to Heard in 1957, Bill W. wrote *I am certain that the LSD experiment has helped me very much. I find myself with a heightened colour perception and an appreciation of beauty almost destroyed by my years of depression... The sensation that the partition between 'here' and 'there' has become very thin is constantly with me.*

Wilson continually spread word of the success he was having with his ongoing use of Acid. He wrote to Swiss psychologist Carl Jung, on March 29, 1961, informing him of his continued experimentation with LSD to treat Alcoholism. *Some of my AA friends and I have taken the substance frequently and with much benefit,* Bill wrote, adding that LSD induces *a great broadening and deepening and heightening of consciousness.* Not long after, it appears that old Bill was intrigued by the possibility of joining forces with the most famous (or perhaps infamous) name in psychedelics, a man that John Lennon wrote the Beatles *Come Together* as a gubernatorial campaign song for.

In a letter to Timothy Leary dated July 11, 1961, Bill Wilson wrote the following.

Dear Mr. Leary;

> *It was most pleasant to have your letter of June 30th, along with the suggestion that we may have a number of mutual interests... A number of A.A.'s here in NY* [including Bill himself, his wife, his secretary, and his priest] *have been part of the development of the LSD possibilities. Our chief contact has been Dr. Humphry Osmand of Saskatchewan, whom we consider to be the greatest authority in this whole area. He is very close to Aldous and if you don't know him, you certainly should.*

> *Though LSD and some kindred alkaloids* [like mescaline and psilocybe] *have had an amazingly bad press, there seems no doubt of their immense and growing Value. Indeed it seems to make out a statistical case, as of now.*

> *Perhaps, too, you will find some interest in Alcoholics Anonymous – its principles and mechanisms.*

Wilson ends by informing Leary of his schedule in the hope of finding a way to *come together* before summer's end. He even instructs Leary in a postscript to contact his gatekeeper, Nell Wing, whose name he underlined, saying she *will know my whereabouts.*

Bill W. continued his use of Lysergic Acid to treat alcoholism and depression at least into the 1960s, and likely the rest of his life. You see, Bill began to hear gossip floating around about his newfound cure. Wilson was then informed (likely by his foundation) that A.A. members were violently opposed to his experimentation with a mind-altering substance. At first, he wrote a letter defending his psychedelic use to the board, to which he had relinquished control of A.A. in 1955, to no avail. He also asked Dr. Sydney Cohen to try to keep his name silent when it came to the papers the doctor was writing on the subject. Once the board made up its collective mind that A.A. was going to distance itself from mind-altering substances, Bill Wilson silenced himself on the matter.

On his deathbed, Bill Wilson, the founder of AA, asked for three shots of whiskey on Christmas of 1970. That request was denied by his nurse. He asked again on January 2, January 8, and January 14, 1971, each time being denied. Ten days later, on January 24th, 1971, Bill W., arguably the most famous Alcoholic in history and founder of Alcoholics Anonymous, passed away. While his caretakers may have had a no-alcohol policy, or his medications may have been affected by alcohol, I see no reason to deny a dying man his last request, even if it would break a 36-year sobriety streak. Addiction is defined by its harm to the life of the user. Bill's last drink could have done no more harm to his life than not having one and, quite possibly, may have been of some relief.

Chapter 2 - Education for Recovery

Substance re-education is one of the ways that California Sober can help people to understand the difference between an addictive substance and substances that have little to no chance of getting them hooked. Most non-users tend to squeeze all mind-altering substances into a single category that they call *drugs*. Others, both the abstinent and users alike, further break substances down into two subcategories, what they call *light drugs* and *hard drugs*. They misclassify these substances based on the current drug scheduling system, which has been flawed since its misguided and intentionally misleading inception.

Knowing which substances are addictive and which pose the least amount of harm to users is one of the major keys to understanding addiction. There are many addictive substances, and each affects the user in different ways. Some are highly addictive and have a high potential for overdose. Others are only addictive to those with a predisposition to addictive behavior, be it genetic, learned, or a form of self-medicating. There are even mind-altering substances that pose no threat of addiction or overdose. By learning which substances fit into which of these categories we learn which substances pose the greatest threat to our abstemiousness.

The biggest problem in our society, in relation to addiction, is the lack of education about what addiction is, what substances are addictive, and how to avoid becoming an addict. Simply repeating blanket statements to our youth, such as *drugs are bad* and *just say no* to all mind-altering substances, we rob them of an education that may save their lives. At the same time, alcohol is not put in the same category as other mind-altering substances, thus allowing many to believe that it is not a drug simply because it is socially acceptable and comes in the form of a beverage. This hypocrisy leads to the belief that because *everybody* does it, alcohol is not that dangerous of a substance.

In addition, we allow laws and government to teach our youth which drugs are more harmful than others, rather than scientific fact. The issue with this, especially on a federal level, is that the lawmakers are just as uneducated on the subject as our children are. That's because they were tricked, like most, by the American propaganda machine of the late 1960s. Before this starts to sound like some grand conspiracy, let's explore why there is a federal controlled substance list to begin with, who put it in place, and why no one questioned that the list went against all known science of the time. Before we do that, however, we need to understand what made it possible to fool the American public and, subsequently, the world. For that we need a brief history lesson.

Independence Limited
The American Revolution and the creation of the machine

We all know the story. The colonists of the Americas got sick of paying taxes to a corrupt and unfair government that didn't have their best interests in mind, so they created a new government based on equality and freedom. More beautiful words were never spoken, and the story is true and can be shoved down the throat of the common man so that he may believe that he is in the best place ever created and, again, this is true. But telling the truth while never revealing certain nuances is no different than a lie, so let's tell that story again, this time adding the details that we left out.

The rich white males were sick of paying taxes to a government that didn't treat them as well as they did the rich white males in the mother country, so they spread the idea of freedom in an attempt to set up a better government, which they did. The problem here is that that idea didn't apply to everyone. Not just yet. They knew they had some awesome ideas and they made laws that were ambiguous enough that they would eventually apply to everyone, but not in their lifetime. What they wanted in their lifetime was freedom for rich white men. Poor people, women, and anyone who's skin wasn't opaque, would still be inferior and, for all intents and purposes, treated as property and pets. Freedom was doled out, and it wasn't free.

For generations new ideas were welcome in tiny morsels and, even then, under protest. Anyone who complained was a traitor. After all, those ingrates were blessed to live in the greatest country that had ever existed with more freedom than any other. So what if that freedom was on a sliding scale that increased with wealth, gender, and skin tone. At least you were better off than you were anywhere else, so be happy you got what you got and be loyal to those who gave it to you, or else. Believe what we tell you and regurgitate it like gospel, for it's the American way.

When America was done kicking the British's asses in the 1770s, she did it again in 1812. Then, she turned her *freedom* fighters on the American natives in order to take the rest of the continent, to spread this *free America* across the land.

Next, she fought the Mexicans to expand those virtues south. Once she had all of the land she wanted, she fought herself on whether or not to give a tiny piece of that freedom to men (and only men) whose skin was darker than the majority. Not the same freedom that the white man enjoyed, just the freedom to not be owned (at least not all the way owned, as those of different ethnicities still had to do what they were told or suffer the consequences).

Throughout these battles, America continually beat the idea into the head of its children, generation after generation, that if they were not on board with the communal idea of what America stood for, they would be traitors. By the time this country passed its first century anniversary, American propaganda was so instilled in the hearts and minds of every red-blooded American boy and girl that the hive mind was nearly complete. This wasn't the act of any sinister plan, yet it was the result of generation upon generation of promotional brainwashing by the government. It was a mostly positive sentiment that made everyone feel a kind of kinship across gender, race, and status, if only in an US against them way.

Meanwhile, the Moral Majority continued shaping America's view of right and wrong by attempting to, and briefly succeeding in, making laws to banish extra-marital sex, alcohol, and substances that gave the country a less wholesome image. These laws never stopped anyone; they simply gave those in power the right to lock up whoever they saw as degenerate. It was easy to clean the streets of the unsightly when you could simply arrest them, and it gave them a way to keep the morally questionable in line, at least for a while.

Welcome to the Machine

At some point, every citizen was born into this American way of life. Schools, churches, and every other institution that teaches children how to think and what to believe, were promoting the idea that America could do no wrong, that we were the freedom fighters of the world, and no corruption could exist in our realm. To further hasten programming of the youth, comic books began promoting that same America with the very first superhero, Superman, who fought for *Truth, Justice, and the American Way*. This reenforced that the three ideas were one and the same. Truth and Justice *were*, in fact, the American way, and any other way of life was a threat to our own.

The Great American Propaganda Machine was now a fully developed and self-perpetuating part of the American way of life. It knows where you've been, provides you with toys to fill your time and occupy your mind so it never wanders into free thought of new ideas, it even told you what to dream. You might buy a guitar to punish your mom but, in the end, you'll always end up at the same idea, the same thought, the same concept that was drilled into you from day one, America. The land of the free and the home of the brave. Trust in her, she knows what she's doing, and protect her at all costs.

So, to protect America's idea that our way of life was the only way of living, she decided that she would protect any nation that shared that idea in the face of hostilities from those that thought differently. In other words, if you thought like US, we had your back, if you had any other idea that wasn't capitalist and democratic, watch the fuck out. To spread our values to the rest of the world, it was time again to prove we were willing to step outside of our national bubble to defend not a nation, not an ally, but the American way.

America was no longer fighting off an attack on our country, she was fighting an idea that didn't align with her own. With no physical threat, she felt the need to fight an idea that was perceived as a threat to the American way of life. America began her fight against communism, the idea that everyone in a particular country should share wealth, in opposition to America's idea that one should be able to obtain as much wealth as possible while others suffered starvation on the next block. A compromise of the two ideas may be the best solution (which happens to be the *new* American way), but I digress.

And so, America entered the conflict in Vietnam, in 1954, with the hope of liberating democracy and defeating communism. In the 1960s, under the Kennedy administration, her participation escalated from under a thousand military advisors to 23,000 soldiers. The Great Propaganda Machine ensured that no one would question America's intentions. There could never be a corrupt American government, the government built on freedom, democracy, and the will of the people, the government that fought for truth, justice, and the American way of life. There could never be a corrupt American government in the eyes of the pupils of the machine, the American public.

While the government was busy fighting this perceived threat, more and more Americans began experimenting with classic psychedelic substances and their ability to rewire the brain to accept and reenforce new ideas, although that experimentation was done on a relatively small but ever-increasing scale. For a decade this practice of using Cannabis, Peyote, Mescaline, and LSD to expand the mind, break the cycle of conformity, and come up with new ideas, inoculated small pockets of the American youth, growing in small circles throughout the nation but never truly threatening the popular idea that America was still apple pie and fairness, with smiling subservient women, children, and minorities falling in line behind the men who carried these ideas to promote their rule over the land.

The following presidential administration of Lyndon B. Johnson further escalated America's participation in the Vietnam conflict to 184,000 U.S. troops. Simultaneously America's children, eyes opened wide by new ideas and the use of psychedelics, began to question the governments sincerity when it came to having their best interests at heart. Everything came to a head when the next president, Richard M. Nixon, reinstated the draft in 1969, forcing America's recently enlightened youth to fight a war that they didn't believe she should be in in the first place. Those small, inoculated pockets of open-minded young men and women had spread to colonize the country, its fruiting bodies popping up everywhere, questioning, protesting, and flat out refusing to participate in what they saw as an injustice.

Rather than keeping America's promise to listen to, hell, to succumb to the will of its people, rather than creating a dialog between the holders of each view, rather than aligning truth and justice with the American way, rather than even considering the will of its people, the American government, under the power of Richard M. Nixon, started yet another war. Worse, Nixon began the deadliest war this country would ever see, a civil war that would be fought against its own citizens for more than 50 years with no true end in sight as of the writing of this text, amassing more casualties and prisoners of war than any war in the history of the world. On October 27, 1970, President Richard M. Nixon signed the first declaration of the War on Drugs, The Comprehensive Drug Abuse Protection Act of 1970 which includes the federal Controlled Substance Act.

I know what you're probably thinking. *Why would someone who is promoting a scientifically proven way to beat addiction be against drug laws and the War on Drugs?* Hear me out. Addictive drugs are made by cartels and pharmaceutical companies and very few of the addictive drugs that are killing people and destroying lives are on the top of the list of controlled substances. The highest level of controlled substances is reserved for *drugs* that are, read this carefully, non-addictive with no proven potential for abuse. Even more astounding is that these *controlled substances* are plants and fungi. I'll get into that more in a little while. First let me present the facts with a quote from Dan Baum, the Assistant to the President for Domestic Affairs (the guy who assists the President on matters relating to citizens of the U.S.A.) of then President Richard M. Nixon.

The Nixon campaign in 1968, and the Nixon White House after that, had two enemies: the antiwar left and black people. You understand what I'm saying? We knew we couldn't make it illegal to be either against the war or black, but by getting the public to associate the hippies with marijuana and blacks with heroin, and then criminalizing both heavily, we could disrupt those communities. We could arrest their leaders, raid their homes, break up their meetings, and vilify them night after night on the evening news. Did we know we were lying about the drugs? Of course, we did.

Am I saying that all drugs should be legal, and everyone should have access to them to use freely as they please? Maybe not. Maybe. That's a question for someone else. I can, however, say that drug laws have never stopped anyone from doing drugs and that there is absolutely no need to outlaw anything that is provided to us by nature. It the words of the leading scientific expert on the subject, Hamilton Morris, *no plant should be illegal, and the war on vegetables is insane. Nothing of use will ever be achieved by making plants illegal.* It is our birthright, if nothing else, to cultivate and freely use all that nature has provided us and no person, country, or civilization has the right to deny any natural creature the right to all that is natural. Still, the world's governments, in an outright attempt to control the masses, have taken it upon themselves to tell us what we can and cannot ingest.

What I am telling you, if I may clarify, is that the corrupt government of the late 1960s and early '70s, and the only president to ever resign (due to the exposure of his corruption), outlawed many substances that it knew helped facilitate anti-war sentiment, substances that are of absolutely no harm to anyone, but are believed to be by most Americans of the time and many Americans today, all due to the highly successful and self-perpetuating Great American Propaganda Machine. Welcome, my friends. Welcome to the machine. And now that its spell is hopefully broken, at least for a minute, let me further enlighten you as to what happens when we blindly believe that anyone in power has our best interests in mind. The Controlled Substance Act of 1970.

War Pigs

The Controlled Substance Act of 1970

In the United States there are five schedules of controlled substances signed into law by the Nixon Administration under false pretenses. Substances are classified by their assumed risk of dependence, in addition to their potential to be medicinal. Alcohol, like many other mind-altering substances, is not on the five schedules of controlled substances, thus promoting the falsehood that it is not as harmful as other substances that have made the list. To understand the harm caused by miscataloging substances we need to first explore the five schedules and what they represent.

Drug Scheduling 101

The Drug Scheduling System and how Nixon's war on Drugs failed
America for more than half a century, so far...

The Drug Enforcement Administration's first tell in their misdirection of the public is that their Schedules are scientifically proven to be misleading and hypocritical. Substances are supposedly categorized by their potential for abuse and addiction, Schedule 5 being the least addictive and having the least potential for abuse and Schedules 1 and 2 being the most addictive and having the most potential for abuse. Schedule 1 is reserved for substances that not only have the highest potential for abuse, similar to schedule 2, but these substances are also said to have no accepted medical use and are proposed to be unsafe, even under a doctor's supervision.

According to the DEA's website, *Schedule I drugs have a high potential for abuse and the potential to create severe psychological and/or physical dependence. As the drug schedule changes-- Schedule II, Schedule III, etc., so does the abuse potential-- Schedule V drugs represents the least potential for abuse.* Using that rationale we should see, logically, that the potential for dependence and abuse is highest for Schedule 1 drugs and lowest for Schedule 5, yet no science was used in the creation of the Controlled Substance Act of 1970, the schedule that is still used today. Instead, the leading factors contributing to the scheduling of these controlled substances were racism, their potential to promote anti-war sentiment, and *immorality*.

In fact, the majority of *drugs* on the first Schedule of the Controlled Substance Act are actually the least addictive and have the least potential for *abuse,* as it is defined today. It wasn't that these substances were addictive or prone to being abused that caused them to rise to the top of the list, only that they contributed to a revolution that that government was not ready to understand, and that they were used by minorities. The summer of love, and the free-thinking *hippy* youth that ushered it into existence, were considered a threat to the American way of life. The government wasn't ready for this type of change, and so it outlawed what it deemed the cause, when in reality the cause was that same government's own misdeeds. With that in mind, let's explore the Schedules, and some of the substances they seek to control.

Schedule 1

On the first and, in their logic, the worst Schedule of controlled substances you would hope to find the most highly addictive and abused drugs of all time. If your thoughts go to Fentanyl, Crack, and Crystal Meth, you'd be mistaken. While they are the most abused and deadly substances in the country, other than alcohol, they don't make this most notorious of lists. That would make too much sense. Instead, the authors of these Schedules chose to reserve this highest level for some of the least harmful, non-addictive substances that they were sure were going to ruin the nation and, more importantly, its efforts abroad. Heroin is on this list, as maybe it should be, but Heroin is not nearly as addictive as Fentanyl, which resides in a lower class.

Those who sought to control the nation's youth reserved their worst drug list for substances like Marijuana, which is only addictive in less than 10% of users and causes less harm than many of the drugs on Schedule 2 through 5. Cannabis (marijuana) has been proven to have many medical benefits and is only now (with legislation passed in November of 2022) approved for scientific testing. To this day, Cannabis is one of the most notorious *drugs* on the governments Schedule of Controlled Substances and is federally illegal to possess or cultivate in any quantity, although it is medically legal in 37 states, 4 out of 5 territories, and the District of Columbia (our nation's capital) It's also, as of this writing, recreationally legal in 21 states. While the majority is supposed to rule, the federal government refuses to bend to the will of its people, or even its states.

LSD, Peyote, Psilocybin and Psilocin are also on the highest Schedule. While they are infamous in fables and urban legends, those are just tales and propaganda used by the government of the 1960s to dissuade the youth from joining those pesky hippies. That government viewed the counterculture movement, as well as the drugs they used to expand consciousness, as a cultural threat to American values and the Vietnam War effort. The result was to designate these natural medicinal plants and fungi as Schedule 1 controlled substances in an effort to stop the hippies from infecting America's youth with their peace and love values. The truth of their effects is far more benign, and extremely beneficial in many ways.

LSD, as I have mentioned earlier, was used by the founder and most famous member of A.A. in order to aid him in revisiting his spiritual awakening, and to help him maintain his sobriety and lessen his depression. Many studies were done in the 1950s and 1960s showing LSD's effectiveness in treating alcoholism, the combined results of which are published on the government's National Institute of Health website, which I will discuss in further detail later. LSD is, for all intents and purposes, completely nontoxic, has zero potential for addiction, and almost no potential for abuse. This is due to the very nature of the substance itself.

While LSD is one of the most potent hallucinogenics, an immediate tolerance is achieved with one dose. To experience the same effects in a subsequent session on the following day, a user would have to double the dose. To trip again with the same intensity, on day three a user would have to quadruple his original first dose, and so on. Because of this, daily use is nearly impossible or, at the very least, a complete waste of time. In addition, users are generally not interested in going through such an intense experience all that often. One experience can be beneficial in treating Substance Use Disorder, anxiety, depression, and many other conditions for several months without the need for repeated doses.

A lethal dose of LSD was approximated (in 1973) to be over 140 standard doses. However, this approximation was disproven when a 46-year-old woman who took morphine for chronic pain accidentally snorted 550 times the average dose of LSD (55 grams as opposed to the standard dose of 100 micrograms) and didn't even require hospitalization. As a result, she was able to reduce her morphine dose significantly and, by micro dosing LSD subsequently, was able to come off morphine without withdrawal symptoms.[4]

Psilocybin and Psilocin are the active alkaloids in Magic Mushrooms, another non addictive substance that has little to no potential for abuse. It works on the brain in a similar manner to LSD and can have a similar, and in some cases better, result. The largest study to date, which we will explore later, boasted an 80% success rate in reducing alcohol consumption in participants with Alcohol Use Disorder, as well as other forms of addiction and various mental health disorders. This remarkable mushroom grows naturally on nearly every continent in the world and has been ingested by humans recreationally and medicinally for millennia, almost certainly since before our species evolved.

Peyote, a cactus containing mescaline, is another Schedule 1

---

[4] LSD Overdoses: Three Case Reports - Haden and Woods - Journal of studies on Alcohol and drugs - January 2020

drug that has no potential for addiction and low potential for abuse. It has been used for at least 5,000 years with no reported overdoses. Like the previously mentioned psychedelics, its spiritual sessions are beneficial in many ways. Studies of its use in the Native American Church show it's instantaneous and lasting aid in the reduction of alcohol consumption in participants with Alcohol Use Disorder, as well as many other disorders, similar to the above-mentioned mushrooms. Peyote has also been shown to be beneficial in Cocaine Use Disorder.

These *drugs* were put on the DEA's first Schedule of Controlled Substances for one reason, and one reason alone, to stop the Counterculture Movement in the United States and preserve an outdated mentality. The government failed in this mission, as can be plainly seen by new state laws reversing the Federal attempt to interfere with mind expansion and spiritual enlightenment. When did you ever turn on the news and hear about a Magic Mushroom epidemic or someone knocking off a convenience store for money to score some Peyote? Still, we are told that these drugs are the worst of the worst by the laws enacted to control their use. Since they are the worst of the worst, let's take a look at the supposedly *less harmful drugs* further down the list.

Schedule 2

Cocaine and its highly addictive free base form, Crack, reside on the DEA's more lenient Schedule 2, along with Crystal Meth, Fentanyl, and Opium. The second Schedule is supposedly reserved for drugs that, while highly addictive and highly abused, have some medicinal value. I defy you to find a medicinal use, or the need for a prescription for, say, Crystal Meth or Crack. It's no small wonder that our children are confused when they try a Schedule 1 drug and realize that they have no harmful effect. This leads them to believe that something on a lesser Schedule must be just as harmless. Without reeducation, this problem can't help but persist.

Schedule 3

The third Schedule still contains opioid medications, the most highly addictive substances on the planet, but at lower doses and in mixtures containing acetaminophen (Tylenol). It's not hard to simply take more of them to achieve higher dosages and feed, or even die from, an opiate addiction. Still, the DEA considers these drugs safer. Ketamine, or special K (which has similar qualities to PCP), is also on this list along with Steroids. These drugs are proven to be more harmful, and have more potential for abuse, than the Schedule 1 substances that I mentioned previously.

Schedule 4 - Mother's Little Helper

All the way down the list on Schedule 4, we find what the Rolling Stones dubbed *Mother's little helper* on their 1966 album *Aftermath*. Xanax, Valium, and Klonopin are all highly addictive with a high potential for abuse, yet the DEA has determined that they are not as notorious as the non-addictive psychedelics on Schedule 1. This misinformation causes users to think they are as safe as aspirin, leading to a high level of abuse among minors and adults alike. I know many people who have a decades long addiction to Xanax who would rather throw away their lives than give up their little friend. Those who want to quit can be helped by the California Sober method of recovery, but many are so in love with these highly addictive substances that they simply prefer to remain addicted. You have to have a desire to quit for any method of recovery to work. Still, even for those who prefer to stay on these medicines, the California Sober method can help the user limit their use to their prescribed dosage and original reason for use, such as anxiety.

Schedule 5

Schedule 5, the lowest of all potential for abuse (according to the Act), still contain opioid medications. We have all heard of the opioid epidemic and yet here we are, at the bottom of the list, still reading about *medicines* containing them. There has never been a class of drugs with more addictive properties than opiates. They cause physical dependence that results in potentially deadly withdrawal, yet here they are on the lowest Schedule of Controlled Substances, while much safer psychedelics find themselves on the strictest top tier. What's worse is that two of the deadliest, most addictive, and by far the most abused drugs on earth haven't even made the Schedules. They are advertised on television and downplayed by movies and TV shows while your children watch and learn.

Unscheduled

While we, as a society, have known of Alcohol's potential for abuse and addiction since the dawn of society, it somehow makes none of the Schedules of Controlled Substances. According to the National Institute of Health, another government agency, 15 million Americans 18 and over had Alcohol Use Disorder in 2019 while only 900,000 Americans had even used heroin in 2020, with only 691,00 having Heroin Use Disorder. That means that Heroin addicts are but 4.666% as numerous as Alcoholics in the United States. Still, alcohol is not even on any of the schedules of controlled substances. According to the government's National Institute of Alcohol Abuse and Alcoholism, an estimated 95,000 people die from alcohol related causes annually. That's 95,000 more than die from eating psychedelic mushrooms, or any other psychedelic for that matter.

Tobacco is reported to be more addictive than Heroin. It's sold over the counter in gas stations and convenience stores across the country with almost no regulation. It is the leading cause of the deadliest forms of cancer and yet it's allowed to be openly used in public. Obviously, drug laws don't teach our youth, or adults for that matter, which drugs are bad for you, so it's time we start educating the public. Until the government makes a new and more comprehensive drug Schedule, we cannot use their bogus guidelines as a reference any longer.

Say No to What?

As if the previous administrations hadn't done enough damage by misrepresenting the items on their Controlled Substance Schedules, the Regan administration further convoluted the subject by introducing a slogan that would confuse the public, while simultaneously incentivizing the youth to rebel against it, a slogan that would become that administration's mantra, a blanket statement that would undermine their (hopefully) true intent to educate the youth about the harms of addiction.

Just Say No to Drugs. You say it and it feels so right. That's because its meaning is subject to interpretation. In the hearts and minds of every individual who chanted Just Say No, it meant say no to what that individual's belief of what *drugs* were. Everyone can get behind a slogan that has such a broad spectrum. Every adult in every state, city, town, and village, knew what that meant, at least to them. To some, it meant say no to heroin and cocaine, to others it meant say no to what they had been programmed to believe were drugs by the Controlled Substance Act of 1970

The Regan administration was telling the public to Just Say No, but they didn't bother to educate themselves or others on what said drugs were, or to put any thought into what that statement meant. In reality, Just Say No doesn't make any sense. What were we saying no to? A drug is defined as any substance, other than food, that when ingested produces a physiological effect. But even that definition is too broad and confusing. On one hand, an alcoholic beverage can be a food. If liquids are not foods, is fruit juice a drug? What definition of food should we go by? If we use that definition, considering that all plants can be foods, no natural substance is a drug.

In addition, *just say no* only works prior to the user ever ingesting a harmful and addictive substance. Once the user has ingested a *drug* it is already too late to simply say no thank you. An addict would love to *just say no* to their substance of choice. If it were that easy, every addicted individual would simply no longer do the *drug* that is ruining their life. Unfortunately, that's not how addiction works. Otherwise, addiction would be a non-issue. It is hard to overcome addiction. Fortunately for those that are already addicted, California Sober has a way that can make recovery as easy as just saying no.

Just Say No is irresponsible and detrimental to its own core value. It simultaneously means everything and nothing, and that drugs can be anything from aspirin to coffee and everything in between. By creating the *Just say no* movement without any guidance on what it means, the administration further muddied the waters of drug education by leaving the definition to the individual. While all children should say no to anything not medically necessary, everyone needs guidance on what substances are addictive and cause harm versus which substances can be beneficial. When drug education isn't present, addiction is the result. That's when most users find themselves with only one option, the outdated standard model of recovery.

Chapter 3 - The Science of Recovery

Issues with the Standard Model

In the past, recovery was based less on science and more on asking the addict to turn their will and life over to their deity of choice, proclaiming that they, as individuals, have absolutely no power over their addiction. In addition, most recovery programs require that the addict abstain from any and all mind-altering substances, regardless of what it is the person in need is addicted to or the potential benefits of the substances shunned by these methods. The problems with this model are substantial and, in many cases, detrimental to the mindset needed for recovery.

First, one would have to subscribe to the notion that such a deity exists and to truly believe that said higher power intentionally interferes in the will of mankind. While this is not a problem for many, a large percentage of people simply do not buy into this way of thinking. A 2019 survey found that around 30% of Americans are non-religious, making it difficult for these individuals to get past the initial steps necessary to succeed in this recovery model. The same study also found that up to 15% of Americans don't believe in a higher power, thus excluding them from this version of recovery entirely. A treatment plan should be all-inclusive, and not rely on one's belief (or lack thereof) in a religion or a higher power.

To cope with the rapid increase in secular society, twelve-step programs have attempted to alter the definition of the *higher power* to include a variety of entities, both plausible and nonsensical, that these non-religious individuals can pray to for help. Some are progressive and all-inclusive such as humanity, love, the Laws of Nature, the Laws of Science, Music and the Arts, and the Universe. Others are hypocritical to their own purpose, such as EGO and Self-Will (according to DrugRehab.com). It's not difficult to understand why it would be discouraging for the intellectual addict to be told that they need to turn their will over to self-will. It would be equally mystifying for them to have to find a way to dissolve the EGO by turning their will over to the EGO.

This third step has the additional issue of removing all responsibility for success and/or failure from the individual. By turning your will and life over to a higher power you are also turning over responsibility for all of the results of your efforts, be they positive or negative. Our brains are designed to reinforce the positive and negative results of our accomplishments. If we truly feel that these accomplishments are not our own, the reward center of the brain will not react in quite the same manner as it would if we acknowledge the fruits of our own labor and take credit where it is due. We are making this journey, despite the obstacles on the path in front of us, whether or not we choose to believe a higher power is helping us along the way.

The second issue with the twelve-step model of recovery is the very first step in which one is asked to admit that they are completely and utterly powerless over their addiction and that their life has become unmanageable. This step is simultaneously both genius and ridiculous, and for multiple reasons. Its genius comes from the fact that one has to believe they have a problem in order for any form of recovery to work. Its uselessness lies in the fact that seeking treatment for addiction, in and of itself, is an admission that you are both out of control and that your life has become unmanageable, unless of course that user has been forced to seek help, in which case recovery almost never works.

Next comes the paradox of being powerless. If you are truly powerless over addiction nothing you do can ever help you to recover. One may be powerless when it comes to attempted control over the continued use of their substance of choice, but no one is powerless when it comes to discontinuing the use of that substance altogether. By admitting that one has no power over their addiction, one not only builds a psychological barrier between themself and their addiction that cannot be broken, that admission then gives that user another excuse to fail. While asking a user to take control of his actions, we are hypocritically telling them that they don't have any control to begin with, again compounding the psychological barrier between the patient and their recovery.

We all have some degree of control over our actions and, while addiction can lower that level of control (sometimes to a negligible amount), time away from said substance of choice leads to a significant degree of improvement in that control roughly equal to the time spent away. In other words, the more time one spends not consuming the substance they have trouble abstaining from, while focusing on their desire to refrain from its use, the more control, or will to abstain, one gains. Success starts with the realization that you can stop using, while controlled use may be out of the question. California Sober gives one the tools they need to abstain from their substance of choice long enough to see that they can have the power to refrain from its use.

Still, for some managing pain with the use of opiates or anxiety with the use of benzos that they are addicted to, the California Sober method of treatment has been proven to help them to achieve a middle ground. While it is almost never a good idea to attempt to continue using your Substance of Choice, some instances require that you do. Chronic illness can mean that the substance you are addicted to is the only relief you can find from unbearable pain, anxiety, and other illnesses. In those cases, the California Sober method of recovery is the only proven way to reduce the abuse of a necessary medication.

Another issue with traditional recovery is that it demands that an individual abstain from any and all mind and body altering substances (and often sex), other than socially accepted substances like caffeine and tobacco. This condition comes with the stipulation that one cannot use other medications to help control one's addiction, even though studies prove that the use of medicinal substances can increase the chance of success. To compound the damage done by these theories, lack of understanding of what constitutes a drug can be detrimental to the recovery of some patients. Many users of stimulant substances, such as cocaine, crack, Adderall, and crystal meth, use alcohol to come back down from the aftereffects of their high. In these users, a caffeine high can be a trigger for this craving for alcohol. Some people need to abstain from caffeine until they find a way to control these cravings.

Abstinence from all mind-altering substances may even be detrimental to solving one's problem with addiction. Studies show that the use of certain psychoactive alkaloids can be beneficial to those suffering from addiction to alcohol and other substances. Psychedelics like LSD, Psilocybin and Psilocin found in Magic Mushrooms, Peyote and other psychoactive cacti containing Mescaline, and Ketamine have been proven to reduce depression, treat addiction, and cause neurogenesis. In laymen's terms, they have the ability to create new brain cells and pathways, resulting in a new way of thinking. They cause the patient to be both introspective and extrospective, providing them with a form of self-therapy that has been proven to treat depression, addiction, and other conditions of the mind, a single dose acting for several months or longer.

While these claims can appear outlandish to those indoctrinated into the ways of standard recovery, the science speaks for itself. While most systems of recovery are a leap of faith that bear little fruit, the California Sober method of recovery is backed by science that spans 100 years, with studies that have proven its success for more than a half century.   The only reason that the California Sober method has not been publicized sooner is that the Nixon administration had shut down all research for the last 50 plus years and subsequent leadership didn't bother to question the prior administration's authenticity. That regime has finally given way to the people's will, allowing testing to resume, if only at a limited capacity. That said, enough testing has been done to prove California Sober's methods of treatment to be far superior to all other methods of addiction recovery treatment.

The Science of Recovery

Since the 1950s and as recently as today, trial after trial, study after study have proven that the California Sober system of addiction treatment is by far the best method of helping addicts recover from their addictions. While some still cling to the outdated notion that a *drug* is a *drug*, and that only abstinence from all mind-altering substances is the only road to recovery (hypocritically allowing for substances they consider socially acceptable), we know that these treatments work, and work well. Why then are we subjecting everyone that needs help to the same twelve steps that addiction specialists (and NPR) say have but a 5-10% success rate when California Sober methods have a proven success rate of almost 90%?

When used individually, each of the California Sober treatments is shown to have a 49% to 83% rate of success. When multiple treatments are applied, such as psilocybin and meditation treatments in addition to therapy, the success rates can be even more astounding. Still further, the California Sober method can be combined with the 12 steps of Alcoholics Anonymous, as the founder of A.A. discovered when he underwent the LSD treatment in the late 1950s and petitioned to incorporate it into A.A.

You wouldn't go to a doctor that closed his eyes to new innovations that were proven to work while sticking to what may have been the cutting edge a century ago. That would be like using ether and chloroform instead of anesthesia, or electroshock and insulin shock therapies for mental illnesses. In 1936, the year between Bill W.'s recovery and his publishing of the Big Book of Alcoholics Anonymous, doctors performed the first prefrontal lobotomy (a.k.a. the ice pick lobotomy) as a treatment for depression and sleeplessness. You wouldn't even consider these treatments today. Why then do we stick to a recovery program that hasn't been updated in just as long? While the indoctrinated refuse to loosen their grip on outdated rituals, the clinical trials and studies speak for themselves. It's time for a 21st-century treatment. One that is proven effective in treating substance use disorders, depression, OCD, and much, much more.

An Accidental Miracle
LSD - A Brief History

Lysergic Acid Diethylamide, or LSD, was first synthesized by

Swiss chemist Albert Hofmann at Sandoz Laboratories on November 16, 1938. His work was aimed at purifying the alkaloids in a fungus known as Ergot, which had been used for centuries by midwives, and some doctors (it was mentioned in a Nuremberg manuscript from 1474 and in a book by German physician Adam Lonicer in 1582), to cure the *uprising and pain of the womb*. Another German, Joachim Camerarius the Younger, wrote in 1586 that sclerotia of ergot held under the tongue would stop bleeding.

Albert Hoffman's boss at Sandoz, Arthur Stoll, had already isolated ergotamine, the alkaloid responsible for blood vessel constrictions that hastened childbirth and staunched bleeding post-partum. It's still used today to cure the symptoms of migraine headaches. When Hofmann asked Stoll if he could continue this research, he had no idea that he was about to change the world and become one of the most famous chemists of the 20th century.

Hofmann began working to rebuild the alkaloid ergobasine by starting with its nucleus (or base chemical) Lysergic Acid and adding the amino alcohol propanolamine. His experiment was a complete success. The excitement drove Albert to an attempt to improve ergobasine, which he did with his new substance Methergine, but why stop there? He was on a roll, and so Albert Hofmann continued to make lysergic acid-based compounds whose chemical structures, he hoped, could result in compounds with interesting pharmacological properties.

Hofmann's 25th such compound, which he simply called LSD-25, was made in the hopes that it would be a respiratory stimulant, due to the fact that it was structurally similar to a known analeptic called nicotinic acid diethylamide (Coramine). During testing, it was noted that it had about 70% of the effect of ergobasine on the uterus. It was also noted that the animals tested became restless in their cages.

With no other notable qualities observed, LSD-25 was shelved, as Sandoz pharmacologists and physicians had no interest in further testing of the compound at the time. From these experiments, two other substances, Hydergine (a treatment for mood and memory disorders such as dementia) and Dihydergot (a migraine medication), were developed. Still, Hofmann could never get the *relatively uninteresting* LSD-25 out of his mind. It bothered him that the substance *could possess properties other than those established in the first investigations.*

Almost five years later, in the hope that his instincts were right, Albert Hofmann went back to work on his pet project and once again synthesized LSD-25, making only a few centigrams (hundredths of a gram) for further analysis. He was sure that his creation would have properties that earlier testing had missed. That day, unlike any other in his career, Albert stopped work early due to the sudden onset of *unusual sensations.* Restless and dizzy, he hurried home to lie down. Albert would soon find that he had made a life-changing discovery that would forever change the course of human history. The following excerpt is from his report to Arthur Stoll:

Last Friday, April 16,1943, I was forced to interrupt my work in the laboratory in the middle of the afternoon and proceed home, being affected by a remarkable restlessness, combined with a slight dizziness. At home I lay down and sank into a not unpleasant intoxicated-like condition, characterized by an extremely stimulated imagination. In a dreamlike state, with eyes closed (I found the daylight to be unpleasantly glaring), I perceived an uninterrupted stream of fantastic pictures, extraordinary shapes with intense, kaleidoscopic play of colors. After some two hours this condition faded away.

Hoffman assumed that he must have somehow gotten a very small amount of his new compound on his fingertips. He surmised, due to the average toxicity of ergot, that the amount his body absorbed must have been about 250 micrograms (mcg). He began self-experimentation at that dose, which he soon discovered was 3 to 5 times the dose needed to have a full LSD experience. Albert knew that LSD provided a miraculous experience that could deliver years' worth of therapy in a single session. He continued his self-experiments with LSD, and later began testing other hallucinogens that he called *Mexican magic drugs* like Psilocybin mushrooms and a species of Mexican morning glories. Albert Hofmann continued taking small doses of LSD-25 for the rest of his life, always knowing that it would one day be put to good use. That day is on the horizon.

LSD - the Studies

The study of LSD's medicinal value was halted by the Nixon Administration's anti-counterculture movement, also known as the War on Drugs, in the late 1960s. Its designation as a Schedule I Controlled Substance directly contradicted decades of scientific and medical research. By the time it was outlawed dozens of studies had already been conducted between LSD's creation by Albert Hofmann and it's prohibition by the Nixon administration. From ending addictive behaviors and lessening the chance of relapse, to relief from anxiety and depression, study after study suggested that LSD had the ability to re-shape the mind in a way that had never been seen before, or since.

Recently, scientists have merged those studies to examine the combined outcome. The results were published in the Journal of Psychopharmacology. In a retrospective analysis, researchers found that of 536 participants, 59% of the people who received the LSD reported lower levels of alcohol misuse. Promising results lasted through follow-up visits at two and three months, and again at six months. There were no significant results at 12 month follow ups, suggesting that treatment should be recurring.[5]

In a 2020 study titled Therapeutic Use of LSD in Psychiatry, published in Frontiers in Psychiatry, researchers noted that "...LSD is revealed as a potential therapeutic agent in psychiatry; the evidence to date is strongest for the use of LSD in the treatment of alcoholism." In addition, the study's authors commented on the safety of psychedelics, writing that "As a recreational drug, LSD does not entail physical dependence as withdrawal syndrome, as do most of these substances (opioids, cocaine, cannabis and methamphetamine). Its frequent or long-term use can lead to tolerance, and after a single dose, emotional, physical, and mental stability is quickly recovered. Likewise, classical hallucinogens in general, and LSD in particular, exhibit very low physiological toxicity, even at very high doses, without any evidence of organic damage or neuropsychological deficits associated with their use. Their safety has recently led to considering LSD as one of the safest psychoactive recreational substances."[6]

While the retrospective analyses speak volumes, the actual studies that were going on in the 1960s are equally impressive. Doctor after doctor, scientist after scientist, were astounded at the remarkable success that LSD treatment provided. The biggest problem critics had was that it was impossible to do a blind study because it was obvious, not only to the patient but to the doctor, who received the LSD and who got the placebo.

---

[5] Krebs TS, Johansen P-Ø. Lysergic acid diethylamide (LSD) for alcoholism: meta-analysis of randomized controlled trials. Journal of Psychopharmacology. 2012;26(7):994-1002. doi:10.1177/0269881112439253

[6] Fuentes JJ, Fonseca F, Elices M, Farré M, Torrens M. Therapeutic Use of LSD in Psychiatry: A Systematic Review of Randomized-Controlled Clinical Trials. Front Psychiatry. 2020 Jan 21; 10:943. doi: 10.3389/fpsyt.2019.00943. PMID: 32038315; PMCID: PMC6985449.

To give you an example of the rates of addiction recovery that they were finding, the following results were pulled from various studies of the time.

In a review of studies, published in the Canadian Psychiatric Association Journal Vol. 14, No.1, 1969, author C.G. Costello wrote that "An unpublished report by the Saskatchewan Bureau on Alcoholism ... indicated that 69 (47.6%) of 145 alcoholics improved after LSD treatment." The period of the study was from 1957-1962 and the intervals between treatment and follow up varied from two months to five years, most cases having had the last treatment between two and four years prior to their follow up. 50 of the 69 improved cases were "totally dry," meaning they had not had any alcohol since their treatment.

Of the remaining 19 "their relapses are becoming fewer and of shorter duration, e.g., one day of intoxication compared to previous bout pattern of one week; gainfully employed as compared to former chronic unemployment." He goes on to say that improvement for the six studies "average from 50% to 93% with a mean of 75%. This would suggest that LSD therapy is indeed a worthwhile method of treatment..."[7] Considering 12-step programs average a less than 10% recovery rate for all that make the attempt, an average of 75% of patients improving drastically is unheard of.

Another study, from June 1963, had impressive results with the most hard-core addicts that could be found. Most of the patients treated had been referred by another Alcoholic Counselling Center whose policy had been to refer their most severe or chronic cases to the Saskatchewan Hospital. As a result, those treated were all patients who would be considered to have a very serious addiction by all ordinary

---

[7] AN EVALUATION OF AVERSION AND LSD THERAPY IN THE TREATMENT OF ALCOHOLISM C. G. COSTELLO, Ph.D. 1969

means of evaluation. 87% had tried and failed with Alcoholics Anonymous at least once and 57% had received some type of psychiatric treatment at least once prior. Their age ranged from 24 to 65, and the average age was 39.3.

Of 70 patients receiving the full treatment, including LSD therapy, and followed up between six and 18 months after discharge, 39 (56%), "had remained dry continuously since discharge or had been dry apart from a short "testing" bout of drinking immediately after discharge." Out of the 55 patients in the control group who received individual psychiatric treatment alone, only 8 (14%) remained sober. "A chi-square test showed that significantly more of the alcoholics treated with LSD were dry or improved at the time of follow-up, than patients receiving group therapy alone or of the controls."[8] In this group where 87% had tried and failed with Alcoholics Anonymous at least once, we have 56% of the group totally sober at 6 and 18 months after LSD therapy. Where Anonymous groups fail, California Sober methods prosper.

In his book, The Use of LSD in Psychotherapy and Alcoholism, Dr. Harold A. Abramson, M.D. edited the minutes from the Second International Conference on the Use of LSD in Psychotherapy and Alcoholism, held in May of 1965, where a group of investigators in the field of psychiatry met at South Oaks Hospital, in Amityville, New York. According to his notes, *the purpose of the meeting was to exchange information and discuss problems regarding the use of a remarkable drug that has been a focus of research in psychiatry for more than twenty years.* That substance was LSD-25, commonly known as LSD.

At the conference of nearly 50 doctors who had tested LSD on patients, all were aligned by one fact. "The scientific literature . . . is singularly affirmative. Every worker who

---

[8] TREATMENT OF CHRONIC ALCOHOLISM WITH LYSERGIC ACID DIETHYLAMIDE - S. E. JENSEN, M.D.' AND RONALD   RAMSAY, B.A.

studied LSD's use for treating alcoholism is in unusual agreement." The unusual agreement was that they all found LSD to be a success. On the subject of relapse, Doctor Abram Hoffer remarked that "Had they been given 200 mcg or more (of LSD), with a therapeutic objective, in a therapeutic setting, by therapists interested in the therapeutic experience, and had they used the community resources, including A.A., perhaps at three-and-one-half years about fifty percent or more of their subjects would have been sober."[9]

The work done by Betty Eisner, with Bill W. and others (mentioned earlier), was remarkable and way ahead of its time. She was so excited about her discoveries that she wrote of her work to her role model, founder of analytic psychology and Swiss psychiatrist, Carl Jung. Betty couldn't wait to tell Mr. Jung of her success in using the LSD treatment with her patients. "For the past six to nine months," she wrote in a letter dated August 2, 1957, "I have been engaged in an absorbingly interesting pilot study of the therapeutic aspects of lysergic acid (LSD-25). ...LSD unlocks the door to an individual's unconscious. ...{there} are levels of the unconscious available which have been described heretofore only by the mystics and poets. ...when taken under proper circumstances and with the proper preparation and dosages, {LSD} accomplishes in a handful of sessions the process of discovering one's place and function in life and the universe which you call individuation."

One month later, on September 3rd of the same year, she sent another note explaining more of her research. "It appears that the individual man experience what is most necessary {through the use of LSD} -- and to the amount he can take," she said of her weekly sessions with patients taking increasing doses each week. "We have also observed that at times it is

---

[9] The Use of LSD in Psychotherapy and Alcoholism - Copyright © 1967 by Harold A. Abramson - THE BOBBS-MERRILL COMPANY, INC. A Subsidiary of Howard W. Sams & Co., Inc. Publishers-Indianapolis New York Kansas City

possible to slip past the areas of difficulty of the Ego... Woe to the person who does not do his utmost to integrate the insights he gains under LSD into his every-day life!" She ends by saying "I have never experienced anything which has helped me more than LSD in the process of attempting to free myself from the limitations, conditionings, and ego-centricities-- on the many levels-- which prevent us from being the loving individuals which we were all created to be."

From the many studies on its benefits toward reducing addiction, to renowned author, researcher, and psychologist Betty Eisner's work (among many others) in psychotherapy, LSD has been proven to treat many debilitating issues, from depression to alcoholism, and more. Had it not been for the misguided Controlled Substance Act, countless studies could have been performed that would show its benefits in many other areas of psychiatry, similar to that of Psilocybe Cubensis mushrooms, peyote, mescaline, and even Cannabis. Though more studies will be done in the future, as its benefits are too apparent to ignore, one fact remains. LSD has the ability to stop alcoholism and other addictions in their tracks.

In one of the first LSD studies since the 1960's, researchers found that LSD also significantly decreased state and trait anxiety in terminal patients (fear of death and related consequences) at 2 months and sustained that reduction for 12 months.[10] In other words, terminally ill patients facing the end of their lives found relief from their worries, both mentally and spiritually, through the use of LSD-25. This study confirmed what the studies of the 1950s and 60s had shown. LSD is a remarkable psychiatric substance that can have lasting benefits across the spectrum of psychiatric issues, in addition to its remarkable rate of success treating

---

[10] Safety and Efficacy of Lysergic Acid Diethylamide-Assisted Psychotherapy for Anxiety Associated With Life-threatening Diseases - Peter Gasser, MD, Dominique Holsten, PHD Yvonne Michel, PhD, Rick Doublin, PhD, Berra Yazar-Klosinski, PhD, Torsten Passie, MD, MA, and Rudolf Brenneisen, PhD - The Journal of Nervous and Mental Disease - July 2014

addiction.

Godflesh

The Magic of Mushrooms

Psilocybe - a brief history

Perhaps the most complex unadulterated gift of Nature that this planet has to offer, Magic Mushrooms grow wild on every continent (other than Antarctica). Psilocybe-containing mushrooms first appeared on the scene about 5.3 million years ago, about the same time that our ancestors dropped out of the trees and started walking on 2 feet. It's much more than likely, considering 22 primates (including ourselves, which alludes to our ancestry) eat mushrooms, that we have been consuming these gifts of nature since before we evolved into the intellectual creatures we are today. Some theories suggest that these mushrooms were one factor in that evolution. We trip; therefore, we are, but more on that in a minute.

Proof of their use in antiquity dates back to about 12,000 years ago when Psilocybe use was depicted in the Mushroom-head art of the Bradshaw rock paintings. Interestingly, these Australian rock paintings bear striking resemblance to figures drawn by the Sandawe of Southeast Africa, some 6,000 miles across the Indian Ocean. In these ancient paintings, humanoids are depicted with craniums that are shaped like the caps of these mind-altering fungi, offering that the Psilocybe containing mushrooms that they were consuming went straight to their heads, altering their perceptions and curing conditions of the mind, as the following studies show they do. Whatever beneficial effects these mushrooms were having, one thing is for sure. These Mushroom-heads were definitely mushroom heads.

Psilocybe mushrooms have also been depicted in cave art in the Sahara Desert as early as 9000 years ago. A Paleolithic cave painting in Tassili, Algeria depicts natives running or dancing toward the top of a hill with Psilocybe mairei in their hands. Parallel lines drawn from the hands that hold mushrooms to their brains imply that the fungi are affecting the mind. At the front of the line and top of the hill, the leader of the group appears to be harvesting the psilocybe. Also at this site, there is a mural of a bee-faced Shaman standing in a dominant pose, mushrooms growing out of every surface of his body. The two remarkably unique depictions show that these magic mushrooms were used both medicinally (as we can see from the Shaman image) and recreationally (as is shown by the happy line of festive harvesters).

Just a few thousand miles north, and a quick hop across the Strait of Gibraltar, 6000-year-old pictographs in the Selva Pascuala cave in Villar del Humo, Spain, depict a row of 13 Psilocybe hispanica mushrooms, the magic mushroom native to that area. What I find most interesting here is that of over 700 sites of prehistoric rock art of the Iberian Mediterranean Basin, also known as Levantine art, the artists drew no landscapes and almost no vegetation. The art focused on humans and the animals of the area, both hunted and potentially domesticated, with the only real depiction of a nonanimal being the magic mushroom native to the area, Psilocybe hispanica.

To put the timeline of this art into perspective, civilization as we know it was only formed five to six thousand years ago. That means that humans were recording their psychedelic experiences with Psilocybe mushrooms on rocks across the globe thousands of years before our ancestors came together to form society. Before towns, before rulers, before law, people were ingesting mushrooms to expand their consciousness and alleviate the symptoms of countless disorders of the mind. It's more than probable that humans have been ingesting these medicinal wonders since before they split off into a unique evolutionary branch. In other words, our ancestors were eating Magic Mushrooms since before modern humans walked the earth.

Then, in the 1500s, Spanish missionaries tried, and nearly succeeded, to destroy all records and evidence of the use of what the Native North and Central Americans called teonanacatl, or God's flesh (a name the Celts in Europe gave one of their magic mushrooms as well), in the name of religion and *morality*. The missionaries would have succeeded in wiping America's history clean of these magic mushrooms if it were not for a Spanish Franciscan friar and historian who mentioned the psychoactive fungi by its native name in his writings. Those who kept this tradition alive hid their medicinal and spiritual magic mushroom ceremonies for centuries afterward, until scientific research in the 1950s brought a renewed interest in this miracle of Nature.

Psilocybin has been shown to create new brain cells, a process called Neurogenesis, and causes hyperconnectivity between brain networks, altering thought pathways. In his book Food for the Gods, author Terence McKenna presented a hypothesis that human evolution was driven by the addition of Magic Mushrooms into the diet of Homo Erectus, causing them to be better hunters, more sexually promiscuous, and more creative. This, he surmised, led to the development of musical expression, language, and religion. From there, philosophy and science were the eventual outcomes. McKenna called his thesis the Stoned Ape theory. Considering that fMRIs show the creation of brain cells and changes in neural pathways when these mushrooms are consumed, this hypothesis is not just possible, it's likely.

Psilocybe Trials

98

Like its manmade cousin LSD, research shows that Magic Mushrooms are a miracle treatment for a host of disorders including, but definitely not limited to, Alcohol and Cocaine Use Disorders, anxiety, depression, nicotine addiction, obsessive-compulsive disorder, migraines, and many other conditions. As of this writing, there are hundreds of articles on the subject on the National Institute of Health's website, including more than 60 clinical trials that the NIH oversees, researching psilocybin's therapeutic effects.

Albert Hofmann, the pioneer of psychedelic science who synthesized LSD-25, first identified Psilocin and Psilocybin as the *active ingredient* in Magic Mushrooms in 1958, extracting pure Psilocybin from P. Mexicana mushroom in 1959. The following year Timothy Leary began his research into its use in psychotherapy, specifically in regard to lowering recidivism rates. Recidivism is the tendency to slip back into a previous condition or mode of behavior (also known as relapse). This is one of the ways the California Sober method of recovery prevents addicts from relapsing. Leary continued his research until he, and his research partner Dr. Richard Alpert, were suspended from their jobs at Harvard University for their work with psychedelics.

All Psilocybe research ended in the United States in 1970 (at least until recently). Its designation as a Schedule I Controlled Substance contradicts almost 65 years of scientific and medical research and thousands of years of safe medicinal use worldwide. New studies began in the 1990s but were slow due to the red tape of working with a Schedule I Controlled Substance. It wasn't until 2018 (and a few more times since) that the FDA gave Psilocybin a *Breakthrough Therapy* designation, allowing it to be studied for its benefits in alleviating Major Depressive Disorder. Since then, a multitude of studies and articles have been published showing that Psilocybe containing mushrooms have the key to *fixing* conditions of the mind.

Since the psychedelic re-awakening of the 1990s, studies have shown that Psilocybin is astoundingly effective in every psychological issue it is tested for. When administered to subjects with obsessive-compulsive disorder, all patients showed improvements within 24 hours of treatment, yielding a 23%-100% decrease in Yale-Brown Obsessive Compulsive Scale score.[11] For Anxiety and Depression in patients with advanced-stage cancer and reactive anxiety, Psilocybin significantly reduced anxiety one month after treatment, and depression was significantly lower at 6 months.[12] When used for quitting smoking, 80% of the trial participants were abstinent at a 6-month follow-up.[13] [14] Significant decreases in drinking behavior for up to 9 months were shown when Psilocybin was used to treat Alcohol Use Disorder.[15] In Major Depressive Disorder, the Mushrooms significantly decreased depressive symptoms for up to 6 months.[16] Anxiety and depression related to life-threatening cancer was significantly decreased at 7 weeks and sustained for 6.5 months[17] with another study duplicating the results showing significant decreases in anxiety and depression at 5 weeks with effects

---

[11] Moreno FA, Wiegand CB, Taitano EK, Delgado PL (2006). Safety, tolerability, and efficacy of psilocybin in 9 patients with obsessive-compulsive disorder. J Clin Psychiatry 67: 1735–1740

[12] Grob CS, Danforth AL, Chopra GS, Hagerty M, McKay CR, Halberstadt AL et al (2011). Pilot study of psilocybin treatment for anxiety in patients with advanced-stage cancer. Arch Gen Psychiatry 68: 71–78

[13] Johnson MW, Garcia-Romeu A, Cosimano MP, Griffiths RR (2014). Pilot study of the 5-HT2AR agonist psilocybin in the treatment of tobacco addiction. J Psychopharmacol 28: 983–992

[14] Jones G, Lipson J, Nock MK. Associations between classic psychedelics and nicotine dependence in a nationally representative sample. Sci Rep. 2022 Jun 22;12(1):10578. doi: 10.1038/s41598-022-14809-3. PMID: 35732796; PMCID: PMC9216303

[15] Bogenschutz MP, Forcehimes AA, Pommy JA, Wilcox CE, Barbosa PC, Strassman RJ (2015). Psilocybin-assisted treatment for alcohol dependence: a proof-of-concept study. J Psychopharmacol 29: 289–299

[16] Carhart-Harris RL, Bolstridge M, Day CMJ, Rucker J, Watts R, Erritzoe DE et al (2016. a). Psilocybin with psychological support for treatment-resistant depression: six-month follow-up. The British Association for Psychopharmacology Summer Meeting. 17–20 July, Brighton, UK; Abstract

[17] Ross S, Bossis A, Guss J, Agin-Liebes G, Malone T, Cohen B et al (2016). Rapid and sustained symptom reduction following psilocybin treatment for anxiety and depression in patients with life-threatening cancer: a randomized controlled trial. J Psychopharmacol 30: 1165–1180

sustained for 6 months.[18]

As if those statistics aren't convincing enough, on August 24, 2022, a Jama Psychiatric article laid out the results of the largest-ever trial of psilocybin, the active alkaloid in magic mushrooms, in the treatment of alcoholism. About half of the participants, all of whom were alcohol-dependent for an average of 14 years, were given psilocybin while the other half were given an antihistamine as a placebo. Both groups were also given psychotherapy. The results were astounding. Not only did the psilocybin group reduce their heavy drinking days by 83% (compared to about 50% in those who received the placebo), the number and frequency of drinking days as well as the number of drinks they consumed were also significantly lower. Eight months later, close to half of the Psilocybe group had stopped drinking altogether.[19]

Other studies found naturalistic psychedelic use to be independently associated with significantly reduced odds of subsequent daily illicit opioid use among a community-based sample of people who used substances. "These findings align with growing evidence that psychedelic use may be associated with detectable reductions in subsequent substance use including illicit opioid use,"[20] and that "psilocybin use was associated with [30% reduction in the] odds of [Opium Use

[18] Griffiths RR, Johnson MW, Carducci MA, Umbricht A, Richards WA, Richards BD et al (2016). Psilocybin produces substantial and sustained decreases in depression and anxiety in patients with life-threatening cancer: A randomized double-blind trial. J Psychopharmacol 30: 1181–1197

[19] Bogenschutz MP, Ross S, Bhatt S, et al. Percentage of Heavy Drinking Days Following Psilocybin-Assisted Psychotherapy vs Placebo in the Treatment of Adult Patients With Alcohol Use Disorder: A Randomized Clinical Trial. JAMA Psychiatry. 2022;79(10):953–962. doi:10.1001/jamapsychiatry.2022.2096

[20] Elena Argento, M. Eugenia Socias, Kanna Hayashi, JinCheol Choi, Lindsay Mackay, Devon Christie, M-J Milloy, Kora DeBeck, Psychedelic use is associated with reduced daily opioid use among people who use illicit drugs in a Canadian setting, International Journal of Drug Policy, Volume 100, 2022, 103518, ISSN 0955-3959, https://doi.org/10.1016/j.drugpo.2021.103518. (https://www.sciencedirect.com/science/article/pii/S0955395921004369)

Disorder]."[21]

Here we have Psilocybe Mushrooms reducing substance dependence and use disorders in nicotine, alcohol, and opiates, with several new trials aiming to discover their use in combatting Cocaine Use Disorder. I suspect, due to the success of other classic psychedelics and other hallucinogens (such as Peyote, Ayahuasca, Ketamine, and more), they will have similar results. One of the reasons that psychedelics work towards changing one's *bad* behaviors, other than the *rewiring* of the brain, is the trip itself. It can take years of therapy to get a patient to open up about and truly reveal, the underlying cause of their substance use disorders (SUDs), to change their outlook on the future, and to discover their ability to change and realign their priorities to suit their best interest. Psychedelics can facilitate years of breakthroughs in a single session.

Psilocybin, as with other classic psychedelics, realigns the user's outlook toward the future so that long-term benefits outweigh immediate desires. At the same time, it reinforces the user's belief that they have the ability to quit their Substance of Choice, thus allowing them to change their priorities and values. This results in the realization that using their Substance of Choice is not as important as what they are losing. As a result, quitting the substance that is destroying their life is an option they can facilitate. Because the addict comes to this realization on their own, they are less likely to rebel against the idea or excuse themselves from it as being powerless. The fact that they have a new outlook and confidence allows them to follow through.

The Psilocybe treatment is one of many beneficial ways that California Sober helps people find their way to recovery from

---

[21] Jones, G., Ricard, J.A., Lipson, J. et al. Associations between classic psychedelics and opioid use disorder in a nationally-representative U.S. adult sample. Sci Rep 12, 4099 (2022). https://doi.org/10.1038/s41598-022-08085-4

addiction and mental conditions. It is, so far, the most tested and well-researched psychedelic and is proven beyond the shadow of a doubt to aid in the recovery of these conditions. The success rate of magic mushrooms and their active ingredients are astoundingly high and, when combined with other California Sober methods of recovery, guarantee the user's best chances of success.

Lophophora Euphoria

Peyote - A Brief History

Peyote has been used by ancient Americans since the first humans wandered the deserts of southwestern Texas and Mexico. Oral records recall the use of peyote by indigenous peoples such as the Huichol of northern Mexico and many Native American tribes in Oklahoma and Texas. Its usage was also recorded among many Southwestern Athabaskan-language tribal groups. The Tonkawa, the Mescalero, and Lipan Apache were the first known practitioners of peyote religion in the regions north of Mexico. They also introduced peyote to the Comanche and Kiowa from the Northern Plains. The religious, ceremonial, and healing uses of peyote date back at least 6,000 years.

Two archaeological specimens of Lophophora williamsii, better known as Peyote, found in Shumla Cave No. 5 on the Rio Grande, Texas, were radiocarbon dated to 3780-3660 BC. The peyote buttons still contained mescaline, the active ingredient that makes one embark on a psychedelic journey, in the amount of 2% of the total dried weight. According to an article published in the journal Scientific Reports, "The two peyote samples appear to be the oldest plant substance ever to yield a major bioactive compound upon chemical analysis. The identification of mescaline strengthens the evidence that native North Americans recognized the psychotropic properties of peyote as long as 5700 years ago."[22]

Peyote only grows wild in the southern United States and Northern Mexico. Its habitat is one isolated region that encompasses both countries, with the majority of area in Mexico, only 20% spilling over into Texas. Due to its small range, Peyote is an endangered plant species. Its endangerment is further increased by the Controlled Substance Act, which makes it illegal to grow in the United States, and by the laws of many other countries that follow the same outdated and misguided falsehoods. The proponents of these laws would rather let a plant go extinct than admit the federal schedule of controlled substances is not scientifically accurate, or the will of the people.

Another mescaline rich cactus, although it has far less of this *active ingredient* than Peyote, San Pedro has been used since at least 8600 B.C. in Peru, according to archeological evidence of it being intentionally introduced to a cave in Cueva del Guitarrero. This source of the sacred substance, mescaline, is a less popular, faster growing, non-endangered, legal cacti, further proving that Peyote is not illegal simply because it contains mescaline, but because of its popularity as a mind-altering substance of the counterculture of the 1960s. Had the Nixon administration known there was a backup plan for attaining the altered state that peyote delivers, San Pedro would have been on the #1 Schedule of Controlled Substances along with its psychedelic cousins. Luckily, however, it is not.

Peyote - the trials

Studies by the Native American Church that have been

---

[22] El-Seedi HR, De Smet PA, Beck O, Possnert G, Bruhn JG. Prehistoric peyote use: alkaloid analysis and radiocarbon dating of archaeological specimens of Lophophora from Texas. J Ethnopharmacol. 2005 Oct 3;101(1-3):238-42. doi: 10.1016/j.jep.2005.04.022. PMID: 15990261.

conducted from 1977 to the present suggest that the use of peyote therapy significantly reduces the alcohol consumption in its members, and that these members fare better than those who participate in Alcoholics Anonymous.[23] Because Peyote is a controlled substance (for anyone who is not a member of the Native American Church), studies are mostly limited to the observations of the Church and its members. However, it became obvious to the observers of the church's studies that Peyote, like every other classic psychedelic, has a significant benefit in the reduction of alcohol in those suffering from alcoholism.

While Peyote and other psychedelic cacti are less studied than other psychedelics like Magic Mushrooms, studies have been conducted in recent years showing that Peyote lowered the odds of Cocaine Use Disorder, reducing the odds of CUD by over 50%[24], and that peyote use is associated with lowered odds of nicotine dependence.[25] From these studies, which mimic those of LSD, Psilocybe, and other hallucinogens, we can surmise that Peyote is on par with its cousins when used to treat other addictions. One can also safely assume that San Pedro would have similar effects, due to it containing the same *active ingredient*, though in smaller quantities.

My self-experimentation with mescaline, and that of my colleagues, has shown it to be equal to Psilocybin and LSD in its effects. As with Psilocybin and LSD, Mescaline, the active ingredient in Peyote and other psychedelic cacti, is a serotonergic hallucinogen and an agonists or partial agonists at brain serotonin 5-hydroxytryptamine 2A receptors. While

---

[23] Curing Drug and Alcohol Addiction with Peyote - Is the cure for alcoholism and other addictions locked up in hallucinogenic drugs? By John Horgan Discover Magazine Jan 11, 2009, http://discovermagazine.com/mind/curing-drug-and-alcohol-addiction-with-peyote

[24] Jones, G.M., Nock, M.K. Exploring protective associations between the use of classic psychedelics and cocaine use disorder: a population-based survey study. Sci Rep 12, 2574 (2022). https://doi.org/10.1038/s41598-022-06580-2

[25] Jones G, Lipson J, Nock MK. Associations between classic psychedelics and nicotine dependence in a nationally representative sample. Sci Rep. 2022 Jun 22;12(1):10578. doi: 10.1038/s41598-022-14809-3. PMID: 35732796; PMCID: PMC9216303

each psychedelic has its own nuances, all of the ones listed herein take the participant on a journey to self-awareness through dissolution of the Ego. That dissolution of the Ego allows the user to *find* a new way of thinking about their addiction (or other life problem) that realigns their priorities and heightens their confidence in making the changes that will better their lives.

Beyond the Gateway
The Wonders of Cannabis

Cannabis - A brief history

Cannabis has been cultivated since at least 8200BCE where, of all things, the flowers, or buds (the part with the highest concentration of its *active ingredient*, for anyone left that doesn't know) were found at an archeological site in the Oki islands near Japan. Marijuana with high concentrations of THC, obviously cultivated for its psychoactive properties, was found to be burned in wooden braziers on at least 10 burial sites at Jirzankal Cemetery in Western China. But what I find most interesting is that around 6000-5000 BCE buds were found in Romania (Frumusica site, Onecti) and in Switzerland (Thayngen-Weier site). In other words, humans were cultivating and distributing Cannabis around Eurasia for at least 7,000 years (and likely indefinitely longer). Cannabis is also mentioned in one of the worlds earliest medical texts, the 3500-year-old Papyrus Ebers.

Cannabis - The Studies

Cannabis has been notoriously called the gateway drug since the early days of the War on Drugs, and I tend to agree. However, I offer that Cannabis is the gateway one can use as an exit from addiction, rather than the entrance. Cannabis use prior to the use of alcohol, cocaine, opiates, or other addictive substances makes the addict less likely to use, or less likely to use as much of, their Substance of Choice. This is due to Cannabis having a similar effect, although not as pronounced and not as long lived, as the thought process brought on by classic psychedelics. While it works on the mind in a strikingly different way, marijuana promotes introspection. It enables the user to reflect on their actions and consequences more immediately than an addict normally does prior to using other substances.

When an addict wants to use their Substance of Choice they generally fight, and often push away, the thoughts that tell them that they shouldn't. Marijuana's introspective qualities cause the user to think about the consequences of their addiction in real time. While one might seek out their substance of choice out of habit under normal circumstances, even rationalizing and minimizing those consequences, the same person, under the influence of marijuana, tends to see the problem more clearly. In addition, Cannabis lessens the desire to consume other substances. In other words, when one ingests Cannabis, they often don't feel the need or desire to drink or abuse other substances.

While the other psychedelic treatments boast long-term effects with no need to re-medicate, Cannabis (A.K.A. weed, pot, and marijuana) works as more of an immediate acting daily preventative. Studies show that on days when alcoholics ingested Cannabis, they consumed 29% fewer drinks and were twice less likely to binge drink.[26] Both regular users and those who used only in an effort to not drink had similar results in regard to daily consumption. The results show that when

---

[26] Karoly HC, Ross JM, Prince MA, Zabelski AE, Hutchison KE. Effects of cannabis use on alcohol consumption in a sample of treatment-engaged heavy drinkers in Colorado. Addiction. 2021 Sep;116(9):2529-2537. doi: 10.1111/add.15407. Epub 2021 Jan 26. PMID: 33464670; PMCID: PMC8286984

addicts use Cannabis for the purpose of abstaining from other substances, they reduce their consumption.

In another study published in the International Journal of Drug Policy, 973 patients were questioned about their alcohol use before and after receiving medical marijuana treatment. 44% reported drinking less frequently on a monthly basis and 34% drank fewer drinks per week. In addition, 8% said they drank no alcohol in the last month of the survey.[27] These studies, along with my personal observations of colleagues and some self-experimentation, show that Cannabis can be used to lessen the desire for ones Substance of Choice while pursuing other methods of maintaining abstinence and realigning one's long-term goals.

Because Cannabis is safer than alcohol and other harmful substances, it's use as a replacement and/or as a deterrent is more than justified. I say this because, unlike the classic psychedelics mentioned previously, a small percentage of the population can develop Cannabis Use Disorder. Some studies have suggested that 9% of people who use marijuana will develop Cannabis Use Disorder,[28] [29] with those numbers rising to about 17% in those who start using in their teens.[30] [31]

---

[27] Philippe Lucas, Susan Boyd, M-J Milloy, Zach Walsh, Reductions in alcohol use following medical cannabis initiation: results from a large cross-sectional survey of medical cannabis patients in Canada, International Journal of Drug Policy, Volume 86, 2020, 102963, ISSN 0955-3959, https://doi.org/10.1016/j.drugpo.2020.102963. (https://www.sciencedirect.com/science/article/pii/S0955395920303017)

[28] Anthony JC, Warner LA, Kessler RC. Comparative epidemiology of dependence on tobacco, alcohol, controlled substances, and inhalants: Basic findings from the National Comorbidity Survey. Exp Clin Psychopharmacol. 1994;2(3):244-268. doi:10.1037/1064-1297.2.3.244

[29] Lopez-Quintero C, Pérez de los Cobos J, Hasin DS, et al. Probability and predictors of transition from first use to dependence on nicotine, alcohol, cannabis, and cocaine: results of the National Epidemiologic Survey on Alcohol and Related Conditions (NESARC). Drug Alcohol Depend. 2011;115(1-2):120-130. doi:10.1016/j.drugalcdep.2010.11.004

[30] Anthony JC. The epidemiology of cannabis dependence. In: Roffman RA, Stephens RS, eds. Cannabis Dependence: Its Nature, Consequences and Treatment. Cambridge, UK: Cambridge University Press; 2006:58-105

[31] Hall WD, Pacula RL. Cannabis Use and Dependence: Public Health and Public Policy. Cambridge, UK: Cambridge University Press; 2003

That said, Cannabis is far less addictive and remarkably less dangerous to one's health than the substances that it can help one refrain from.

Stigma

Recent polls suggest that 28% of Americans have tried one or more psychedelic substances in their lifetime.[32] Still, psychedelics have been stigmatized by urban legends, other recovery methods, ignorance, and by 1960s government propaganda. While both of former are easily refuted, some older people may remember the videos that were put out in the 1960s and 70s demonizing psychedelics with outright falsehoods, such as the myth that one may *never come back* from a trip. These fables have the potential to scare away patients that might be otherwise successful in California Sobriety.

Yet another stigma exists among some alcoholics in traditional recovery systems. Because alcohol is socially accepted, many alcoholics don't see themselves as drug users, going as far as seeing users of other substances as a lower class of addict. *I may be an alcoholic but at least I'm not a drug addict* is an all too familiar mantra in strictly alcohol-based recovery systems when, in fact, alcohol is a drug, and the most highly abused one at that. Many alcoholics pride themselves on never sinking to the use of *drugs*. Meanwhile, their substance of choice is one of the most harmful and abused worldwide.

In addition, traditional recovery methods demonize the use of any and all mind-altering substances, save for a few that they

---

[32] Results, interactive data, and methodology on American opinion on psychedelic drugs from a July 22-25, 2022, YouGov survey

enjoy themselves. They blindly repeat the old falsehood that a drug is a drug, allowing only for medications that don't cause the user to *feel* anything. They claim that all *mind-altering* substances are harmful while disregarding the harm of many substances prescribed by a physician, even though pharmaceuticals are the most commonly abused substances. They don't consider the science behind the California Sober method of recovery, science that was downplayed for decades and that is just now becoming recognized and embraced, science that shows California Sober as the most successful method of reducing and dismantling addiction.

For those who have stigmatized *drugs* in their mind, the first obstacle in California Sober Recovery is the acceptance of the fact that there are different classifications of substances, and that substances that have been miscategorized by previous generations are not harmful and are beneficial in recovery from substances that cause harm. Lumping them all into the category *drugs*, or separating alcohol into a category all its own, can be detrimental to one's healing and long-term success. Still, there are options in the California Sober system of addiction treatment that require no mind-altering substances whatsoever.

Just Say OM

Meditation – History

Meditation is at least as ancient as our species and, according to at least one study, quite possibly the reason we evolved to be human. Campfire rituals of focused attention, combined with the natural selection of those in whom this practice enhanced working memory, helped our ancestors evolve into the enlightened creatures that we are today. Without meditation, we might have ended up as just another group of primates, fumbling about the planet with the rest of the animals in blissful ignorance. Through the process of meditation, we formed better memory and focus on past, present, and future events, enabling our species to be the self-conscious and self-aware beings that now decide our own destinies.[33]

Meditation has since been used to transcend consciousness and to focus energy and mood in ways that have been shown to alleviate stress, anxiety, depression, addiction, OCD, and other conditions of the mind. Ancient peoples created religions and ritualistic ceremonies around the practice with great benefit to the human condition. There is no shortage of ways that meditation promotes wellbeing in our minds and bodies, heightening our ability to focus while releasing endorphins in our brains, resulting in elevated mood and heightened awareness. Meditation centers the mind, helping us to focus not only while we are performing the practice, but working the *muscle* of focus to be stronger whenever we need it otherwise.

In today's fast paced world of 30 second video clips, our minds are no longer trained to hold attention for long periods of time. Meditation is the art of focus and the enemy of distraction. If your mind is easily stolen from its desired intention, meditation is the exercise that strengthens your ability to keep your mind set on a single goal. In addition to its primary function of holding your attention, meditation has the added benefit of mind and mood altering through several brain processes that take place when we are in a meditative state. As the mind focuses, breathing patterns self-regulate, the heart slows, blood pressure drops, and a calm takes hold over our body and mind. The neurons in the brain change the frequency in which they oscillate (or spin), and the brain releases certain endorphins that trigger our pleasure and

---

[33] Rossano, M. (2007). Did Meditating Make Us Human? Cambridge Archaeological Journal, 17(1), 47-58. doi:10.1017/s0959774307000054

reward center. When done correctly, and with some practice, meditation causes a natural high.

Contemplation, transcendence, and mindfulness are but a few of the techniques one can follow in their practice of meditation. Each is used to overcome the shortcomings of our human selves, the very nature of our addiction, anxiety, depression, and obsessive-compulsive behavior, and other conditions of the mind. Meditation can help to center the mind in order to get past these natural transgressions. The mind's plasticity is encouraged by the use of meditation in the same way that it is furthered by exercise and, as mentioned earlier, the use of classic psychedelics. Each of these natural wonders promotes neurogenesis that in turn allows us to *change our minds* about addiction and other conditions of the mind.

Meditation - The Studies

In a similar way to psychedelic treatments, Meditation can help its practitioners transcend the self, thus achieving a oneness with the *Universe*. With some practice, meditation can relieve physical and emotional pain, anxiety, depression, and addiction. It can also help those of us that react without thinking (as many addicts do) to take a step back from a situation and calm our thoughts in real time, as problems confront us. While this may sound like the rantings of a hippie cult leader, or some other spiritual self-help mumbo jumbo, meditation is scientifically proven to work by altering the oscillation of neurons in the brain, specifically in the frontal midline regions.

A study from the University of Utah, published in the journal Science Advances October 12, 2022, has shown that Mindfulness Meditation, in conjunction with therapy, significantly reduces the use of opioids in long-term users by changing their state of mind in a way similar to psychedelics, without ingesting a single substance. In the largest neuroscience study of Mindful Meditation to date, lead author and Professor Eric Garland has had undeniable success in treating addiction with his Mindfulness-Oriented Recovery Enhancement (MORE) treatment.

The study revealed that Mindful Meditation takes the brain out of its default mode (where automatic behaviors like reaching for substances are done out of *habit*) and increases theta waves (the waves associated with REM sleep). Research has found that people with low theta waves tend to have trouble concentrating and have wandering minds. They also tend to dwell on (often negative) thoughts about themselves. Low theta waves are associated with a loss of self-control as the brain slips into DMN or default mode network. Garland's MORE treatment more than doubled frontal midline theta brain activity.

In simplified terms, default mode is when you are so absorbed by thoughts that you do things without consciously thinking about them, whereas high theta activity quiets the mind allowing you to become less focused on yourself, causing you to get lost in whatever it is you are doing. Think of high theta waves as when you're *in the zone*, be it while shooting a game of pool or playing a sport, and default mode as when you're worrying about something, and you realize you just went to the fridge and opened a beer or poured a glass of wine without even knowing you did it.

In a randomized clinical trial that originally included 250 adults with both chronic pain and opioid misuse, 45% of those who completed Garlands MORE treatment were no longer misusing opioids 9 months later, compared to just 24% of patients in the control group. What is more amazing is that the trial participants suffered from chronic pain and as a result did not have the option to quit opioids altogether. The

MORE group not only learned to control their addiction, while still using opioids for pain management, they reduced their normal dose and had less cravings and less emotional distress. The trial was published in the April 2022 issue of JAMA Internal Medicine.[34]

Earlier studies also showed that meditation increased the likelihood of abstaining from alcohol and other substances. A 2018 study, published in the Journal of Substance Abuse Treatment, demonstrated that those who practiced Transcendental Meditation (TM) were more than twice as likely to remain abstinent from alcohol than the control group (25% vs. 59%) and while half of the control group went back to heavy drinking, none of the TM group did.[35]

Breathe

Breathing is one of the few things that we can do both consciously and unconsciously. Controlling your breath can provide a link between both realms of the mind and also help regulate emotions. A breathing method called cyclic breathing can be a quick method of regaining composure in stressful situations, or just elevating your mood. In this simplified method of meditation, all you need is five minutes to promote more positive feelings, fewer negative ones, relieve anxiety, and lower your heart rate and blood pressure, while producing some of those feel-good hormones that we all love.[36] Best of all, it can be done anywhere that breathing

---

[34] Garland EL, Hanley AW, Nakamura Y, et al. Mindfulness-Oriented Recovery Enhancement vs Supportive Group Therapy for Co-occurring Opioid Misuse and Chronic Pain in Primary Care: A Randomized Clinical Trial. JAMA Intern Med. 2022;182(4):407–417. doi:10.1001/jamainternmed.2022.0033

[35] Gryczynski J, Schwartz RP, Fishman MJ, Nordeck CD, Grant J, Nidich S, Rothenberg S, O'Grady KE. Integration of Transcendental Meditation® (TM) into alcohol use disorder (AUD) treatment. J Subst Abuse Treat. 2018 Apr; 87:23-30. doi: 10.1016/j.jsat.2018.01.009. Epub 2018 Jan 16. PMID: 29471923.

[36] Brief structured respiration practices enhance mood and reduce physiological arousal Balban, Melis Yilmaz et al. Cell Reports Medicine, Volume 4, Issue 1, 100895

is allowed.

Cyclic breathing is a simple method that many of us have unknowingly practiced before. Start by inhaling slowly through the nose until your lungs are full. When you think you're done inhaling, inhale one more quick breath and hold it, expanding the lungs to maximum capacity. After a brief hold, slowly exhale through your mouth. Repeat this method of breathing for about five minutes or so. In addition to its mind enhancing benefits, this method is also a good workout for the lungs and helps to keep them young and healthy. This can be done in combination with any of the other methods contained in the California Sober lifestyle. For most of us, there's no easier way than breathing to find peace.

Move

Physical activity, especially cardio which increases heart rate, is shown to help in the treatment of addiction. This is likely due to the fact that exercise increases dopamine levels in the brain, stimulating the same reward center that alcohol and other mind-altering substances trigger. When we exercise, we make more of those feel-good hormones that our brain's crave, reducing the need for external substances to supplement them. Exercise can curb cravings and lower anxiety levels while simultaneously increasing the dopamine in the brain.

According to one study by Frontiers in Psychiatry, published on the National Institute of Health website, "...exercise was shown to influence many of the same signaling molecules and neuroanatomical structures that mediate the positive reinforcing effects of drugs."[37] In another study, rats were

---

[37] Smith MA, Lynch WJ. Exercise as a potential treatment for drug abuse: evidence from preclinical studies. Front Psychiatry. 2012 Jan 12;2:82. doi: 10.3389/fpsyt.2011.00082. PMID: 22347866; PMCID: PMC3276339

given a dispenser with various substances including morphine and amphetamines. The rats who used a wheel to exercise hit the dispenser far less than the rats that didn't exercise at all. This study has been repeated several times with similar results.[38] [39]

Studies also show that Yoga increases levels of gamma-aminobutyric acid (GABA), a chemical in the brain that helps one manage anxiety and stress.[40] Yoga's intense breathing patterns are shown to release endorphins. Endorphins are the body's natural pleasure inducing rewards. The word endorphin is a portmanteau, or two words squished together, consisting of endogenous (from within) and morphine. It stands to reason that the body's own natural spike of endorphins from yoga and exercise would help in curbing cravings by giving the addict a natural fix.

These studies are but a drop in the bucket of studies done on the California Sober methods of recovery. A complete list of the studies that prove that California Sober works would fill a library and are not the main focus here. Our focus is to recover from addiction and other conditions of the mind using the methods contained within. If one desires, a simple search using keywords such as *classic psychedelics* and *use disorder* yields enough results to keep one busy for weeks. The point here is to provide the reader with a small sample of the scientific backing that California Sober has, and to show the remarkable success rates of our methods.

---

[38] Lacy RT, Strickland JC, Brophy MK, Witte MA, Smith MA. Exercise decreases speedball self-administration. Life Sci. 2014 Oct 2;114(2):86-92. doi: 10.1016/j.lfs.2014.08.005. Epub 2014 Aug 14. PMID: 25132360; PMCID: PMC4175302.

[39] Kanarek RB, D'Anci KE, Jurdak N, Mathes WF. Running and addiction: precipitated withdrawal in a rat model of activity-based anorexia. Behav Neurosci. 2009 Aug;123(4):905-12. doi: 10.1037/a0015896. PMID: 19634951; PMCID: PMC2786257.

[40] Streeter CC, Whitfield TH, Owen L, Rein T, Karri SK, Yakhkind A, Perlmutter R, Prescot A, Renshaw PF, Ciraulo DA, Jensen JE. Effects of yoga versus walking on mood, anxiety, and brain GABA levels: a randomized controlled MRS study. J Altern Complement Med. 2010 Nov;16(11):1145-52. doi: 10.1089/acm.2010.0007. Epub 2010 Aug 19. PMID: 20722471; PMCID: PMC3111147.

Sleep - The Art of Brain Washing

Sleep is a necessary part of recovery and helps to minimize a host of conditions of the mind. Lack of this necessary brain reboot can irritate those conditions, limit our ability to make good decisions, and worsen an addiction to substances. When you sleep, the mind takes a break from all of the problems of the world, but it also does all of the work it cannot do while you're busy using it all day. In the same way that your devices need to be rebooted every now and then to avoid malfunction, your brain too will malfunction if it doesn't get the reset it needs. A third of our lives are spent sleeping. Many of us try to lower that amount, with disastrous results. Knowing what happens when we sleep can help us to reconcile the lost hours as truly productive parts of the day.

Brain Washing

Every good cult needs a fair amount of brainwashing before everyone is inevitably on the same page. The good news is that California Sober is not a cult, it's a science-based system of recovery from addiction and an excellent remedy for a host of conditions of the mind. The brainwashing that we recommend is a process that your body regularly performs, naturally and autonomously, every time you sleep. Without sleep, your brain will break, everything starts to malfunction, paranoid hallucinations push aside normal patterns of thinking, and you may even die, eventually. There's no way around the fact that the brain needs to sleep. Now let's explore why, and what happens when we do.

For millennia, conscious beings have wondered why we sleep and what that unconscious state even does, as far as the brain is concerned. It turns out that while your consciousness takes a well-needed break, the night shift comes in and does all of the things the brain doesn't have time to do while you're awake. Clerks begin sorting all of the memories of the day, filing some in permanent storage and discarding the ones that seem of little value, while the cleaning crew takes out the trash, mops the floors and cleans the windows.

As if there aren't enough tasks for the night shift to perform, the movie crew has to write, direct, and present several performances of a twisted version of reality, blending the memories of past and present events with possibilities of future events, starring character's you know, some you don't, and even ones you may have invented, for your viewing pleasure (although it has been suggested that these are simply trips to the great beyond or an alternate universe). The more you sleep, that is to say the more complete sleep cycles you go through in a sleep period, the more work gets done and the more refreshed you feel upon waking.

It's only recently that scientists have found that sleep is important for storing memories. In addition, studies suggest that toxic molecules accumulate in the space between brain cells, refuse that the brain has put out for the garbage crew all day long. While we slumber, the space between brain cells changes (increasing by 60 percent between conscious and unconscious states), literally changing the cellular structure of the brain, allowing it to flush out toxins that build up while we are awake. In a plumbing system called the glymphatic system, brain cells known as glia control the flow of cerebrospinal fluid (CSF), a clear liquid surrounding the brain and spinal cord, by shrinking or swelling. This allows this fluid to flow rapidly through the brain, cleansing itself of toxic molecules. In simplified terms, the brain's plumbing system opens up and washes the garbage out of our brains.[41]

---

[41] Xie et al *Sleep initiated fluid flux drives metabolite clearance from the adult brain.* Science, October 18, 2013. DOI: 10.1126/science.1241224

Either through the natural course of your circadian rhythm (that's the pesky biological clock that lets you know when it's bedtime), or due to hours of tedious mental tasks, you start to feel tired. You may even begin to nod out (microsleep), missing the end of your favorite show or, worse, everything your boss said in that important meeting you and your co-workers were called in for. That's your body's way of telling you that the brain needs a reboot. If you're smart, you listen to your brain and find your way to a comfortable place to get some much-needed rest. Otherwise, you fight the forces of nature in a futile attempt to finish less important tasks. In any case, you will eventually succumb to the desire to close your eyes and drift into the wonderful world of unconsciousness. That's when the fun begins.

Sleep is divided into two main categories, NREM (No Rapid Eye Movement) and REM (Rapid Eye Movement) The NREM is further broken down into 3 stages called N1, N2, and N3. Each stage has its purpose, with some tasks overlapping, and the length of each stage changes with every cycle of sleep you complete. While a decent nap can be one complete sleep cycle of an hour and a half to two hours, a good night's sleep consists of 4 to 6 cycles, each cycle putting more emphasis on the dream world, a place of the most vivid hallucinations one can experience, where suspension of disbelief is a rule that cannot be easily broken.

The first stage of sleep is the N1 stage (active sleep), often called the gateway stage of sleep. In this stage our unconscious and conscious minds blend a bit, leading to ridiculous (or possibly genius) fleeting thoughts and spontaneous dreams. Beta waves are replaced by Alpha waves when we are still partially awake but fully relaxed. In the N1 stage, Alpha waves are combined with Theta waves (as in the earlier meditation study) in an equal mixture (50/50). Muscles are still active and may move or jerk (known as a hypnic jerk). The eyes slowly roll, and we may even have the feeling of falling, causing us to react and jerk ourselves awake (I happen to have a love hate relationship with this phenomenon). The N1 stage lasts from 1 to 7 minutes and comprises 2-5% of sleep.

The next stage of sleep, known as N2, is a deeper sleep. Alpha waves are excessively diminished or even completely stopped. Your heart rate and body temperature drop (an anti-aging technique when done properly). Powerful bursts fire from neurons throughout several regions of the brain, etching new memories (and reinforcing old ones) in the fabric of our minds. These are known as sleep spindles.

Long Delta waves called K-complexes, the longest and most distinct brainwaves, and the largest event in healthy human EEGs, keep us asleep through external stimuli that are deemed non-dangerous while simultaneously aiding the sleep spindles in consolidating memory. K waves are why we can sleep with the television on, or while listening to the cars drive by on a busy street and will still wake up if we smell smoke or hear an intruder breaking into our homes. This stage can last for around 30-60 minutes and comprises about half (45-55%) of our sleep cycle. Dreams in N1 and N2 are both short lived and intense.

From here, we enter the deepest non-REM sleep stage known as N3 (formerly called N3 and N4 sleep and known as slow wave sleep or deep sleep). The delta waves take the lead making this session the hardest stage to awaken from, some people sleeping through noises of more than 100 decibels (think motorcycles, bulldozers, even a rock concert). External stimuli are barely noticed, if at all. You are completely removed from consciousness and the world that we often refer to as reality, your mind and body becoming almost separate entities. What happens to the physical body doesn't (always) happen to the self.

This is the stage of sleep where strange things, if they are going to occur, begin to reveal themselves. While the body is basically shut off, there is usually no movement in the eyes or muscles during N3 sleep, sometimes mobilization occurs. Those who wake up screaming in the night, known as night terrors, do so at this stage of sleep. If you're going to wet the bed, the time for that is also now. Sleep walking and sleep talking are also done in this unusual stage of sleep, which is strange in that this is the time when the brain exhibits the least amount of neurological activity (a phenomenon I refer to as the Peripheral Consciousness Paradox [near death cardiac patients also seemingly have mind activity without brain activity according to a study] which is something I will get into at a later time).

As your brain falls deeply into this long-awaited bliss, your neurons switch off, needing less oxygen to keep them alive. Heartrate, breathing, and brain wave activity all reach their lowest levels, and the muscles are as relaxed as they get (other than during paralysis). Even dreams are short lived and nearly halted. While your brain only turns completely off when you are dead (but don't forget the earlier mentioned study that suggests that the mind may still be active when the brain is off), N3 sleep is the closest it gets to off while you're on this side of the dirt. This is the opportune moment for *brainwashing* to begin.

The blood drains from your cranial cavity while simultaneously being replaced with a watery liquid called cerebrospinal fluid (CSF). Rhythmic, pulsing waves of CFS begin the process of washing your brain, flushing away toxic, memory-impairing proteins[42] while low-frequency high-amplitude Delta brainwaves lull us deeper into this restorative state. This brainwashing session may also aid in rinsing out many of the harmful substances we have used to alter

---

[42] Fultz et al *Coupled electrophysiological, hemodynamic, and cerebrospinal fluid oscillations in human sleep*. SCIENCE, 1 Nov 2019 Vol 366, Issue 6465 pp. 628-631 DOI: 10.1126/science.aax5440

ourselves while we are awake, bringing us back to the best versions of ourselves imaginable. Our minds have left the building while these micro custodians and maintenance engineers try to restore us to the vibrant selves we were not that long ago. The N3 stage lasts for 20 to 40 minutes and makes up about 15-25% of our sleep cycle. (Note: when N3 was further broken down into N3 and N4, N3 was categorized by 20-50% Delta waves and N4 was known for having greater than 50% Delta Waves)

After N3 is complete the brain goes back to N2 (and sometimes N1) as a transition into the final stage of sleep, which is as perplexing as the NREM stages. This last stage is known as REM sleep due to the Rapid Eye Movement that occurs during the phasic microstate, and also known as paradoxical sleep because it involves seemingly contradictory states of an active mind and a sleeping body. While it's interesting that REM can be broken into two distinct microstates, which I will briefly discuss as not doing so would leave too many open questions, for our purposes I will later refer to it as the singular state of REM sleep.

REM can be broken down into the microstates of phasic and tonic REM. During phasic REM the eyes jump around, muscles twitch, and external stimuli, such as sounds, are almost unperceived by the brain. During tonic REM the eyes and muscles lie dormant and external stimuli can trigger a response from the brain. These microstates are momentary, switching between each other in a way that allows us to be both conscious and unconscious at virtually the same time, likely a way for us to be able to survive potential predators while we are roaming the unconscious realm. While our brain is more active during phasic REM, our responses to external stimuli are greater during tonic REM.

During REM sleep we react to what we see as if we are awake. We truly cannot tell the difference between our dreams and reality, as strange as dreams can be. I often wonder why, when the strangest things happen in dreams, we never question the reality of it until the dream ends and we awaken. In any case, this is why the brain disengages most of our motor function (a process known as muscular atonia), otherwise we would act out our dreams. The body stops regulating temperature during REM, letting us drift towards room temperature, and REM is associated with enlarged penile and clitoral tissue. At this stage of sleep our brain activity is the same as when we are awake, when compared to NREM stages. Breathing becomes erratic and irregular, pulse and blood pressure also vary, and we can sometimes awaken spontaneously.

In the first sleep cycle our REM is only a few minutes, but as we go through further sleep cycles REM time gets longer and longer, eventually lasting for up to an hour. We slowly transition deeper and deeper into the world of dreams, never questioning the odd laws of our new home's physics, eventually falling in love with our new lives that seem to last forever, and when they don't, we grasp at their fading memories fleetingly, clutching at dust in the wind.

We go into REM about every 90 minutes. Lack of REM lessens the ability to learn complex tasks. When we deprive ourselves of it, all we think of is sleep due to the fact that if we don't get enough of that magical restful experience, repeating the day's chores becomes torturous. If we achieve the goal of getting everything done and are lucky enough to reward ourselves with a few hours, or sometimes minutes, of *me time* to do what makes us happy, we usually try to extend that free period as much as possible, even if it interferes with the time we need to rest and reconfigure.

While our brain undergoes this much-needed maintenance during sleep, our bodies rebuild muscle and bone tissue in order to repair anything that was damaged in the course of our daily adventures. For this reason, attention should be paid to when we sleep and for how long. Depriving ourselves of this much needed time to rebuild the body and mind can have grave consequences. Lack of rest can also contribute to addiction and other conditions of the mind. It is as important that we sleep well as it is to exercise and eat right, all of these things contributing to a healthy mind and body that craves less exogenous chemicals to feel at peace. Sleep is the key to health, and robbing ourselves of this much needed rest and repair session is the downward spiral to our bodies and minds failing.

Chapter 4 - The Components of California Sober -
Transcendence and Changing Your Mind

Changing Your Mind

California Sober is a way to change your mind about anything
from addiction to who you are as a person and anything in
between. Once we have truly decided it is time for a change,
making that change can be one of the hardest things we ever
do, but it doesn't have to be. Putting in the work can be as
painful as shedding your own skin or as easy as a leisurely
stroll in the park on a warm summer's evening. It's really up
to you. I found these changes to be nearly impossible until I
was truly ready to make them. At that point, it was as simple
as breathing fresh air. Like finger cuffs, the more you fight it,
the more it hurts and the harder it is to break free. The other
option is to simply relax and allow yourself freedom.

Like many suffering with addiction, my childhood was rough.
I was physically, mentally, and verbally abused from day one
by parents who were a mess and could barely keep their own
shit together, let alone help me with mine. I was bullied by
most kids and accepted by few. My family moved around

often, making finding a steady set of friends impossible and learning truly a challenge. Due to my changing schools several times by the time I was in first grade, I didn't read at the same level as other kids my age, the embarrassment of which made me not want to participate, compounding the problem.

A poor long-haired boy with ripped jeans and Black Sabbath prominently displayed across my T-shirt, I was profiled by teachers, police, employers, and society in general. When school was no longer bearable, I decided to try my odds at living without the benefit of even a high school education. It was hard to get work in the most menial of jobs, as even minimum wage employers would take one look at me and tell me that the job had been filled or that I didn't have enough experience for an entry level position. Life chewed me up and spit me out so many times that my skin eventually became tough as leather.

I fought that first change. I wanted the world to be peaceful and happy. I wanted everything to be fair, and just, and pleasant. I refused to toughen up because I thought the world was the problem and the solution should simply present itself to me through my own sheer will, or karma, or as a gift from God, but that's not the way the world works. Not immediately at least. So, I cried, I kicked my feet, and I yelled *it's not fair* to anyone who would listen. The response I got was *toughen up, kid. Life ain't fair. You gotta kick it in the balls and make your way through*, and so eventually, and under protest, I did just that.

The only way to survive was to get tough, and so I did. I built up walls and defenses that nothing could get through and I held them strong, even when whatever was trying to get in was positive. My reaction to anything that got in my way was the same. Make it stop at all costs. People in the streets, bosses, friends, family, even the dog, they all had to learn that

I wasn't taking any more shit from anyone. I was the nicest guy and would give the shirt off my back until I sensed the slightest disrespect, at which point I would bite so hard that I'd leave a mark they wouldn't soon forget. Survival at any cost, even if it meant I had to punish the ones I loved until they submitted.

If my work was pristine and still the boss felt the need to discipline me for being frequently late or absent, *fuck you, I quit* was a ready response. If I was loyal and respectful and still the woman in my life complained that I was lazy and broke, *fuck you, leave then* was tossed off as if I didn't care. If the dog was let out and yet still felt the need to shit on the floor while I slept, her nose was rubbed in it, and she was tossed outside by the collar. If she felt the need to run away, she was dragged home walking on her back legs as I held her fronts in the air by the scruff of her neck. If the kid locked her bedroom door in defiance, my fist went through it so that I could unlock it from the other side.

But somewhere in there came a time when my defenses were no longer necessary, or at least not *as* necessary. Nothing was left in my way but me. Still, the slightest attempt to go against me was met with fierce and violent anger. Don't get me wrong, I never really struck anyone that didn't truly have it coming and, even then, only in self-defense. I just made them think that I might. That's no way to treat a family, innocent civilians, or those who employed my services, so it was definitely time for another change. Somehow, though, I didn't get the memo. *If they would just fucking listen*, I told myself, *I would be the perfect man, the perfect dad, the employee of the century, the superhero citizen that gave the little I had to the poor and rescued kittens born in alleyways.* I had nothing but good intentions, but good intentions pave the way to hell.

Alcohol and substances made my already short fuse almost

nonexistent. At some point in life rage is no longer self-defense, you're just an asshole. I'm glad I was able, with the help of my girls, to see myself through their eyes, the eyes of the child that I once was, the innocent victim that only needed love. At some point you have to stop blaming those that mistreated you and take a long hard look at what you have become. You have to find the person you started out as, now that those who broke you are long gone, discarded as the waste of time that they turned out to be. The problem is you can't teach an old dog new tricks. People never really change, right? Not after 40-50 years of being the monster of their own creation, made to guard themselves from the evil of the world, even if that threat minimally exists, if at all. It's not so easy to change your mind, to change who we are or have become, but there is a way.

Relief from addiction, or any part of yourself that is no longer necessary in order to cope, is as easy (and often as complicated) as changing your mind. Unfortunately, this does not mean that simply deciding not to do drugs or deciding to be a better person will immediately make you someone new. The brain gets used to the elation that alcohol and other addictive substances provide. When we use exogenous substances to trigger the reward center of the brain on a regular basis, the brain self-regulates and makes less of the chemicals that give us these feelings naturally. When you stop feeding the brain these substances, it needs time to start producing its own. In addition, your brain craves the easy and more effective externally administered reward. This is addiction. You can't simply decide you're not addicted. Still, when you are ready, you can change your mind.

In the same sense, it's hard to undo the years of hardship that made you the person you no longer wish to be. Your brain has wired itself to react in certain ways to certain situations. It's muscle memory or, in this case, subconscious reaction.

The only way to stop doing the things that you have wired your brain to do or stop the bad habits that you've wired yourself to depend on, is to rewire the brain. The California Sober method of recovery does just that. You can, with the right intentions, use these methods to become the person you want to be, the person you may have once been, or the person that you know you were meant to be.

From magic mushrooms to mindful meditation, all of the treatments in the California Sober method of recovery have one thing in common. They *rewire* your brain, literally changing your mind.[43] Evidence shows that psychedelic substances cause neurogenesis. When ingested they create new neural pathways, rewiring the brain to be in tune with a higher level of consciousness. At the same time, psychedelics, and meditation each dissolve the ego allowing the practitioner to feel a oneness with nature, transcending consciousness and rediscovering the feeling of higher purpose. When taken with the right intentions, psychedelics can create new patterns of thinking that align with the person you're trying to become, without changing the things you love about yourself.

Humans have known the benefits of transcending one's sense of self and feeling connected to something greater for millennia. Hominids have used psychedelic substances and meditation for this purpose since before modern humans walked the earth. Some researchers believe that doing so is the reason we evolved such complex brains, emotions, and rituals.[44] Archeological evidence shows that humans have

---

[43] Psychedelics and Neuroplasticity: A Systematic Review Unraveling the Biological Underpinnings of Psychedelics - de Vos Cato M. H., Mason Natasha L., Kuypers Kim P. C., Frontiers in Psychiatry Vol 12. 2021
https://www.frontiersin.org/articles/10.3389/fpsyt.2021.724606
DOI=10.3389/fpsyt.2021.724606   ISSN=1664-0640

[44] Psychedelics, Sociality, and Human Evolution - Rodríguez Arce José Manuel, Winkelman Michael James - Frontiers in Psychology Vol 12 2021
URL=https://www.frontiersin.org/articles/10.3389/fpsyg.2021.729425

consumed various psychedelics for well over 10,000 years. It wasn't until the Crusades that these rituals were systematically erased from many cultures. After millennia of finding and learning about these sacred plants, that great knowledge was stolen from society less than 1000 years ago in the name of morality, and further hidden from our view by the Controlled Substance Act of 1970.

With scientific advances and a cultural revolution that is slowly making these miracle substances normalized again, we can finally reap their benefits and destigmatize their use in modern society. The proof is here. Psychedelics, meditation, and exercise, in conjunction with therapy, lower and often eliminate addiction. By following the California Sober method of recovery, the chances of overcoming addiction more than quintuple that of traditional twelve step programs while having the plasticity to be used in addition to the twelve steps, as Bill W. learned for himself as far back as the late 1950s.

From Alcohol Use Disorder and Substance Use Disorder to Anxiety, depression, PTSD, and OCD, California Sober methods have the ability to rewire the brain to promote new ways of thinking. California Sober's transformative effects also work on a host of other conditions of the human mind. Recovery isn't only from addiction. Our methods can help you out of any rut you find yourself in. California Sober can give you a new way of thinking about things, whether your issue is with your job, your relationships, or just life in general. If it's time for a change, California Sober makes it as easy as changing your mind.

DOI=10.3389/fpsyg.2021.729425 ISSN=1664-1078

Balance - The Key to Everything and the One True Law of the Universe

Balance and Duality

Without darkness, light has no meaning. Without cold, what would be warmth? I could go on, but the point is simple enough. The world we live in requires balance. Newton's Third Law of Motion says it best. For every action, there is an equal and opposite reaction, and while Newton wasn't talking about getting drunk and high, or about the chemical reactions in the brain, his words apply here as well. Balance is unavoidable, and necessary to maintain the harmony of the cosmos. It's a fundamental truth in Nature. What goes up must come down.

The problem with addiction (and any mental health issue) is that it lives in a world of extremes and excess. No one can deny the elation of being on top of the world. It's that type of living that attracts most people to alcohol and other substances in the first place. When you're feeling down, they pick you up. But rather than settling for a little boost, we feel the need to climb higher and higher until we feel so good that we forget the ground even exists. We dance around in the exosphere while our problems, so far below, become but tiny, insignificant dots. They don't even matter, those silly little, tiny old issues. Why were we ever worried about them in the first place?

The problem with climbing so high is that when you eventually fall back to earth it's so much further. Down and down we go, lower and lower, until we feel the bone shattering impact of the floor where we once stood. With our noses pressed against the concrete, our eyes painfully struggling to roll back and look up at them, those problems towering above us look like they're tall enough to touch the heavens. They seem so enormous that, with the slightest of wrong moves, they could come down and crush us with such force that our lives would never be the same.

If we could simply stand on level ground, we would see that our problems, though some larger than others, are not as massive as we thought. They aren't as small as they looked from the exosphere, but definitely not as towering as they appeared from the floor. They range in size from something we wouldn't notice as it crushed beneath our feet, to a bit of a hurdle, maybe even a small climb. When you take a step back from them, looking at them from a small distance, they don't seem so overwhelming. From a level perspective, our problems are all manageable one at a time.

All highs are followed by lows. Remember, what goes up, must come down. That is the nature of the universe. When we let ourselves sink, it is with the knowledge that will have to climb back out of it. The lower we let ourselves go, the more overwhelming the climb will be and the harder we will have to work to pull ourselves back up out of it. Even when we let ourselves coast for too long down a slight incline, we will eventually find ourselves at the bottom of a valley that will take all of our strength to petal back out of.

The opposite is true of getting too high, although the same concept applies. The higher we get, the further we fall. It's really that simple. Even if it's a slow incline that takes us just a little higher each day, eventually we will see our world so far below that we know that we can't help but eventually crash back to that floor. Even when we only go up a little at a time, every step up brings us further and further from where we need to be. Grounded, with both feet planted on the floor so we can get over whatever obstacle is in our way. No matter which way we go, up or down, we should always be able to reach the middle.

The Balance of Recovery

For some substance users, for some alcoholics, for some suffering with mental issues, abstinence is that level and flat ground. They may have climbed too high at one point, they may have crashed really hard, but in the end, they find that as long as they don't ever leave level ground, they are ok. Their problem is simply that they like the view from above. Walking on level ground is fine and all. It's even quite lovely at times. Still, after a while they miss that awesome view and begin to forget the danger it carries with it. So, after a while of walking on level ground, they just say *fuck it* and run up the tallest hill they can find as fast as they can, until they fall off the cliff on the other side. They crash into a ditch, get all broken up about it, and then begin the slow climb on the road to recovery again.

For those people it might be a good idea to just stay on level ground, and a small percentage of them are really good at it, never so much as stepping on a brick, and for those few, abstinence truly works. But that's not true for everyone. Most people in traditional recovery can't get that awesome view out of their heads for very long and so they run up the hill, fall into the valley, climb out, and walk the level ground until the pain subsides. Then they run up the nearest hill again and the process begins anew. What they need is balance. They need a path that allows them to get the view without the sharp edge on the other side. That's one of the many benefits the California Sober method of recovery provides.

Others are not fortunate enough to be born on level ground. They have always existed at various levels, on the peaks and in the valleys, and are searching for the path that allows them to live among those who were lucky enough to be born at sea level. They have no choice but to look for ways to elevate and descend, sometimes taking paths on which they find themselves too high or too low, dealing with the dangers of each. Their highs and lows are naturally more extreme than the average person will ever deal with. For them, the California Sober method of recovery also has the tools to direct them towards the safest path with the least number of obstacles.

In both cases, traditional recovery doesn't allow for anything but walking on level ground or suffering the consequences. Those who attempt it are forced to endure extremes that most cannot. These people suffer because of rules that have no basis in science, while the California Sober method of recovery has scientifically proven ways to end that suffering. Many of us, as well as those who tread best on level ground, run back and forth between bouts of complete sobriety and binging their substance of choice. Sometimes it starts with a slow incline, but it always ends with a fall from a high place into a deep ravine. Some people cannot be purely abstinent from all substances. For those people, the California Sober method of recovery has a plan that can usher them up and down small hills and valleys, always spending the perfect amount of time on level ground.

That's not to say they can use their addictive substance of choice, be it alcohol or some other harmful substance, ever again. They cannot. They can, however, use less harmful and non-addictive substances to find the path they need to follow to true peace of mind. The balance they need is provided by the California Sober plan, rather than leaving them in a world where they must suffer the pitfalls and endure the constant ascension from holes they were left in by traditional methods of recovery, methods that blame them for their failures when that failure is incorporated into those types of recovery systems by design.

Balance and harmony are the key to the California Sober method of recovery, a system that is proven to have the most success in not only recovery from addiction, but a system that helps heal all types of conditions of the mind. From depression and obsessive-compulsive disorder to addiction, be it to alcohol or any other harmful substance, to simply being caught in a rut in life and needing a change, California Sober is the answer to many of life's problems, problems that are so complicated and yet only require a simple change of the mind, a change that can leave you with your favorite version of who you have always been or make you the person you have always wished to become.

The Components
What makes California Sober work

The path to betterment is as unique as the individual seeking relief from their addiction, or other condition. In the same way that not all antidepressants work on depressed individuals, some may benefit from one medication while others find relief in another, the regimen necessary for success depends entirely on what works for you. An alcoholic, as well as those addicted to opioids and other pharmaceuticals, may get remarkable results with Cannabis alone, other psychedelics with a less fuzzy and more pronounced experience, or some combination of each, while someone trying to fully abstain from (or ingest less) Cannabis would benefit more from psychedelics. All can benefit from meditation, diet, and exercise.

While these medicinal substances can have striking results on their own, group therapy (in the form of California Sober meetings) is recommended for all, especially if one is not currently in another form of therapy. It is important to seek help. Studies show that people who attempt to beat addiction alone have a lower success rate. While that most certainly does not mean that it is impossible, I know many who have overcome their addictions with one or more of the California Sober medicinal substance plans on their own, having support makes it that much easier to do. Someone rooting for your success may be all you need to get over that hump, while group therapy meetings with those in a similar situation will help others.

Psychotherapy, behavioral therapy, cognitive therapy, humanistic therapy, and other forms of one-on-one therapy are all shown to be beneficial. Which therapy works for you will depend on your personality. We are all individuals, and our problems are as unique as we are. Because of this, our treatment must be custom tailored to the individual. There is no cookie cutter, *one cure fits all,* in long term success. That said, each of the California Sober treatment plans individually have the highest success rate and can be used as a starting template that can be modified and built upon to meet one's personal needs.

Find a Meeting

The first thing anyone should do when seeking California Sober treatment is to find a CS group in your local area. New groups are opening up all over the country, in person and on social media forums. If you can't find a group, any one-on-one or group therapy can serve as a starting point. I would suggest that A.A. and N.A. meetings are beneficial, but the truth is that the truly indoctrinated in these groups shun those who openly participate in the California Sober method, even if it aids in their recovery (although times are changing, and some Anonymous groups support the California Sober method). The biggest complaint I get from new CSs switching over from one of these groups is that they were asked not to attend meetings or, more often, that their sponsor dropped them due to their belief in the California Sober methods of recovery.

If you're having a hard time finding a meeting, you can also contact California Sober to help find one near you. Our social media groups are full of helpful CSs that would love to bring you into the fold. If you are already experienced in running meetings in other forms of recovery, or you are successful in your California Sober recovery and want to help others, you can follow our guidelines to start your own chapter. If you are already attending some form of therapy, you are already on the right path. That said, this journey is always easier when you can talk to others like yourself who understand what you are going through.

Start your treatment plan

Another important aspect of California Sober is choosing a treatment plan that works for you. While all of the plan's components provide a high success rate immediately, some components of the plan have long term benefits while others last only for the duration of the substance's effect. For example, the cannabis component is an excellent way to thwart off cravings of an urgent nature, but it is dependent on one's ability to predict when their urges will begin and ingest their proper dose of cannabis prior to the urge taking hold. The Psilocybe component, on the other hand, has the potential to relinquish those urges for between 1 and 11 months from a single dose. While all the components are scientifically proven to promote recovery, the All-Inclusive Treatment, which I will get into later, has the most promising results.

The Cannabis Component

Let me preface this section by once again breaking down the myth that simply switching to weed from another substance is the core of California Sobriety. If it were that simple, every alcoholic and addict that ever smoked a joint would have been instantaneously relieved of their addiction. The truth is that the treatment has to be used with intention. In other words, the Cannabis treatment, as well as the psychedelic treatment, has to be followed with the express purpose of making a life change that includes freedom from addiction. If the plan is not followed with the intent of eliminating addiction, it can have limited results, or no benefit at all.

Studies show that when alcoholics and other addicts ingest cannabis products containing Tetrahydrocannabinol, cannabidiol, and other cannabinoids at least one hour prior to using their substance of choice (SOC), less of that substance is consumed. For alcoholics, consuming the proper dose of cannabis prior to drinking leads to less drinks consumed. For those addicted to other substances, the effects are similar. Consume edible cannabis prior to ingesting your SOC and the urge to use is decreased at the onset of the marijuana's effects. When an hour is simply too long to wait, and immediate relief is needed, smoking cannabis can create an instant relief. That said, smoking doesn't last nearly as long as edibles and has the drawback of having to smoke or vape. Smoking and vaping are harmful to the lungs, which is why we recommend edible forms of Cannabis.

Types of Cannabis and their effects

Cannabis has long been referred to as a gateway to other drugs. This was a falsehood that was promoted by those behind the *War on Drugs* to explain away the fact that they intentionally miscategorized Marijuana as a Schedule 1 Controlled Substance, in opposition to the well-known fact that Cannabis is harmless and, in most cases, non-addictive.

The truth is that most of the individuals who experiment with pot have already used alcohol, tobacco, caffeine, and even highly addictive substances before they ever tried marijuana. In addition, most people who try marijuana never move on to more addictive substances, and many addicts start with much harder substances than weed. We, in California Sober Society, believe that rather than the gateway to harder substances, Cannabis is more often the gateway leading to freedom from addiction.

In order to begin the Cannabis Treatment, one must first determine the type and dosage that works for them. As many cannabis users can tell you, different effects will be experienced depending on the type of cannabis ingested. While any active isolated ingredient, such as THC or CBD, will always have the same effect, cannabis is an alkaloid cocktail that works best when used with its natural constituents, due to the Entourage Effect. In laymen's terms, the mixture of alkaloids is more beneficial than any of the active ingredients alone. Because of its natural composition, different strains of cannabis have different effects. The simplest way to get ones most desired effects is to break cannabis into two distinct types, Indica and Sativa, thus creating two very different medicinal substances.

Sativas have more of a *head* effect that can be energizing and invigorating. They can relieve stress and increase creativity and focus. Sativas can alleviate depression and, for some people, provide relief from anxiety. Indicas have more of a *body* effect, being more relaxing and sedative. They can also help with anxiety and are great at treating insomnia. While a Sativa strain is good for when you want to get things done, an Indica strain is more of a couch weed. For most, both are beneficial. Sativa when things need to get done and Indica when you want to watch a movie that you don't mind possibly falling asleep to.

In some individuals, Indicas can have undesired side effects like paranoia and self-consciousness that Sativas do not. In others the opposite can be true. For most, both are fine. This is why experimentation with each on separate days is recommended, until you find which one (if not both) is right for you. From there, different strains have unique effects within these two categories. Once you know if you're an Indica, Sativa, hybrid, or all-around cannabis person, experimentation within these categories can help you fine tune your preference to what best suits your recovery.

Cannabis Dosage

If you are not a regular Cannabis user, the right dosage for you needs to be found. 5mg edibles are a good starting dose. They are sold as gummies, mints, chocolates, and even drinks (which are especially easy to fine tune dosage with). If you find 5mg to be too overwhelming, you can increase your tolerance by taking them nightly, just before bed, for a few days, or you can simply break them in half. Like most medicines, potency depends on body weight, tolerance, and personal brain chemistry. Over time, more may be needed until your tolerance plateaus. Once you find your perfect type and dosage, the treatment plan is easy to follow.

The Cannabis Experience

The Cannabis Component can be part of your California Sober plan and, like all of the other components of the California Sober method of recovery, that plan should start with therapy and support, which we will get into further on. While I dare not say that no one can do it alone, support is the cornerstone of any life change and not consuming your Substance of Choice is likely the biggest life change you've made since the changes you experienced when you first became addicted. Let's not kid ourselves, getting California Sober is a change for the better but it is still a change, and one that you have to dedicate yourself to. Everyone can benefit from help, and for most the lack thereof can be detrimental.

The Cannabis component is a preventative medicinal approach that is different from the other components in the way it is administered. At the onset of cravings, one takes their recommended dose of cannabis. If, after the effects become apparent, the patient still has cravings, another dose is taken. This is repeated until the patient no longer craves their Substance of Choice. This can be done alone, in conjunction with therapy, or with one's California Sober Mentor (CSM), while it is recommended that the patient do his first several sessions of treatment with a licensed therapist or a CSM. This is to guide the patient into focusing on why they are using the cannabis while under its effects. The Cannabis component can be undertaken alone, as long as it is done with the intent to refrain from harmful substances.

Intent is the key to the California Sober method of recovery. Taking these substances without the intent to be free from addiction, or the intent to overcome some other issue, is in no way going to free the user from their problem. One who takes these substances without intent is simply self-medicating and will likely go back to self-medicating with their substance of choice. Taken with the intention of freeing oneself from these issues is the only way that they work to produce the desired effect, freedom from addiction or some other condition of the mind. Without intent, the healing cannot begin.

The Cannabis component is an ongoing medicinal treatment that must be administered every time one has a craving that they feel they may not be able to control. It's ability to reduce or remove cravings is usually limited to the duration of the effects of the medicine and must be readministered as the effects begin to wear off and those cravings resume. That said, after several weeks of treatment users crave their SOC less often and the regimen becomes second nature. As the cravings subside, the Cannabis component can be lessened and eventually stopped, if so desired, although some CSs use Cannabis as part of a daily maintenance program that includes meetings, meditation, and other California Sober components.

Cannabis has the added benefit of being harmless, especially in comparison to ones Substance of Choice, and is usually benign in all other aspects of the user's daily life. Most people who choose to use Cannabis in their recovery report that their lives are better because of it. They find themselves having profound thoughts, being more kind and more empathetic, and even becoming more creative than they ever were before. Cannabis is also beneficial inasmuch as it helps the user to reflect on their life and what they hope to accomplish. Due to its psychological effects, patients using the Cannabis component often reflect on potential relapse scenarios with more determination to remain abstinent from their SOC than those in standard recovery programs. The Cannabis treatment makes it hard to simply forget your motivation and go back to using your SOC, as opposed to abstinence which often leads to Default Mode Network (when you do things out of habit without conscious thought).

The Psychedelic Components

The LSD Component

The LSD Component, as with the other psychedelic components, has a longer duration of effects between usage. The benefits of Lysergic Acid are shown to last up to 12 months, with the most pronounced results seen in the first month, decreasing slowly but steadily. Therefore, treatments are recommended as often as needed to bring consistent relief. Some patients may need weekly or monthly treatments at first, eventually leading to quarterly and yearly treatments, while others may not feel the need to use their SOC for several months to several years, if at all, after the first treatment.

The LSD experience can be intense for some users and has been equated to a lifetime of therapy in a single session. This intense therapeutic effect doesn't happen through micro-dosing, however. While micro-dosing has the benefit of causing neurogenesis, macro-dosing of 100 to 200 micrograms shows the most benefit in the reduction of use of alcohol and other harmful and addictive substances. While micro-dosing is great in that it helps relieve anxiety, depression, PTSD, OCD, and other conditions of the mind, macro-dosing is the key to the therapeutic results that promote ending addiction patterns and provides the best and longest lasting relief for all other conditions of the mind.

LSD is safe in that it has relatively no overdose potential. The dose it would take to kill someone is hundreds of times the dose needed for a full experience. Therefore, LSD is not something that one could, under normal circumstances, *accidentally* overdose on. In fact, it's potential for death by overdose in humans is purely hypothetical, as it has never occurred. As mentioned previously, a woman accidentally snorted 550 doses of LSD that she thought was morphine. She never required hospitalization, and was able to use LSD to wean off morphine, her SOC. Still, LSD is a powerful hallucinogenic substance and should be used under the care of a therapist who is experienced with the substance (preferably a CSM), or with someone who has had many LSD experiences and is able to guide the user towards their intention and away from any negativity, until the user has had many *trips* and is comfortable with the experience.

LSD Dosage

A study published in the Journal of Nervous and Mental Disease suggests that doses of 100 to 200 micrograms increase self-analytic behavior and positive social-emotional behaviors. It's recommended that those who have limited experience with psychedelics start with smaller doses of 20 to 50mcg, until they understand the journey further. Many opt to start at 100mcg. as their first experience. Those who have experienced LSD several times may want to begin their treatment at a higher dose, as the benefits are shown to increase with dosage, up to 200mcg. When Bill W., the founder of Alcoholics Anonymous, had his first LSD experience he ingested 50 micrograms. He wrote about the benefits of that experience for several months before deciding it was time for another.

The Psilocybe Mushroom Component

The Magic Mushroom Component, like LSD, has a long duration of effects between usage. The benefits of Psilocybe mushrooms are shown to last up to 12 months, with the most pronounced results seen in the first month and, again, decreasing slowly but steadily. As with LSD, treatments are recommended as often as needed to bring consistent relief. Some patients may need weekly or monthly treatments at first, eventually leading to quarterly and yearly treatments, while others may not feel the need to use their SOC for several months to several years, if at all, after treatment. The Psilocybe experience is a little less intense than that of LSD. Still, it has been equated to a lifetime of therapy in one session. This intense therapeutic effect doesn't happen through micro-dosing, although a small threshold dose of half a gram of dried mushrooms has been shown to stop a user from partaking in their SOC almost immediately. While micro-dosing mushrooms also has the benefit of causing neurogenesis, a dose of 2 to 5 grams shows the most benefit in the reduction of use of alcohol and other harmful and addictive substances. While micro-dosing can relieve anxiety, depression, PTSD, OCD, and other conditions of the mind, macro-dosing is the key to therapeutic results that promote ending addiction patterns.

At least one proponent of Psilocybe treatment has cured his chronic stuttering by using these mushrooms. Paul Stament, a man who is working with NASA to put mushrooms in space, is a self-taught mycologist who has even discovered new fungal strains. On a night when he ingested a large dose of these powerful medicinal fungi, Paul used intent to rid himself of a stutter he had had since he was a child. He has never stuttered since. He went on to become a world-renowned mycologist without a single class on the subject.

Mushrooms have no overdose potential. The dose it would take to kill someone is unknown because it hasn't ever happened. If you take too many mushrooms you will regurgitate them. Even the most intense Psilocybe trip is less than that of LSD, which is why I call it the starter psychedelic. Still, Psilocybe is a powerful hallucinogenic substance that should be used under the care of a therapist who is experienced with the substance (preferably a CSM), or with someone who has had many mushroom experiences and is able to guide the user towards their intention and away from any negativity, until the user has had many trips and is comfortable with the experience.

Psilocybe Dosage

Psilocybe can have almost immediate results from just half a gram of dried mushrooms, causing the taker to immediately abstain from their substance of choice upon the onset of effects, usually within 20 to 40 minutes. At that point, especially with higher doses, many substances are no longer felt by their user. This doesn't mean that these substances aren't working on the central nervous system and under no circumstances are other substances to be mixed with mushrooms or other classic psychedelics, with the possible exception of Cannabis. The fact that the user cannot *feel* other substances can cause a substance user to take more of their SOC, making the potential for overdose on any substance greater while under the influence of Psilocybe and other psychedelics.

The dose needed for a full psychedelic experience of Psilocybe mushrooms is between 2 and 5 grams of dried mushrooms. Beginners may want to start at the low end of this spectrum while experienced users may desire a more potent experience. They can be eaten dried alone or on pizza, or however else you like to eat mushrooms. Mushrooms can be eaten fresh, but fresh mushrooms are about a tenth as potent and that would make for a lot of eating. They can also be brewed into tea and drunk. However you wish to ingest them is fine, as long as it is orally.

Under absolutely no circumstances should any mushroom ever be injected. Mycelium has the ability to grow from pieces of their fruiting bodies, also known as mushrooms. A 30-year-old man boiled mushrooms into a tea, filtered it through a cotton swab, and injected the *tea* intravenously. Days later, he vomited blood and developed jaundice, diarrhea, and nausea. The mushrooms had grown in his blood and caused organ failure. He spent 22 days in the hospital, being treated with antifungal and antibacterial medications and was instructed to continue the treatment for the long term upon his release. Injecting mushrooms can, and likely will, lead to death. Pizza and tea are much better and non-deadly ways to get the full experience.

The Peyote Component

The Peyote Component, like LSD, also has a long duration of benefits between usage. The benefits of Peyote also last up to

12 months, with the most pronounced results seen in the first month and, again, decreasing slowly but steadily. As with LSD and Psilocybe mushrooms, treatments are recommended as often as needed to bring consistent relief. Some patients may need weekly or monthly treatments in the beginning, giving way to quarterly and yearly treatments, while others may not feel the need to use their SOC for several months to several years, if at all, after treatment.

The Peyote experience can be less intense than that of LSD, yet still it has been equated to a lifetime of therapy in one session. This intense therapeutic effect doesn't happen through micro-dosing, although a threshold dose has been shown to stop a user from partaking in their SOC almost immediately. While micro-dosing Peyote also has the benefit of causing neurogenesis, a macro-dose shows the most benefit in the reduction of use of alcohol and other harmful and addictive substances. While micro-dosing can relieve anxiety, depression, PTSD, OCD, and other conditions of the mind, macro-dosing is still the key to therapeutic results that promote ending addiction patterns.

Peyote has no overdose potential. The dose it would take to kill someone is unknown because, once again, it hasn't ever happened. If you take too much Peyote you will regurgitate it. Even the most intense Peyote trip is less than that of LSD. As with all classic psychedelics, Peyote is a powerful hallucinogenic substance that should be used under the care of a therapist who is experienced with the substance (preferably a CSM), or with someone who has had many Peyote experiences and is able to guide the user towards their intention and away from any negativity, until the user has had many trips and is comfortable with the experience.

Peyote Dosage

The dosage of Peyote can vary by how much of the mescaline alkaloid is present in the cactus. Dried Peyote usually contains about 3-6% mescaline with some plants having as little as a 1% alkaloid content. Because of this, a little guesswork is needed to find the threshold dose. The threshold dose of mescaline is 100mg, with an average dose of 200mg, a high dose being 300 to 700 mg. Using those figures, a threshold dose of Peyote would be between 1.5 and 10 grams of *dried* Peyote, with an average dose ranging from 3 to 30 grams. As with any psychedelic, starting at or around the minimum threshold dose and working up to the desired dose over time is smarter than the opposite.

The Psychedelic Experience

The Experience

Under the supervision of a licensed therapist, a CSM, or an experienced Psychedelic Coach or shaman, one takes their dose of their chosen psychedelic with the intent of finding freedom from their addiction, depression, anxiety, or any of the other previously mentioned (and likely many unmentioned) conditions. An experienced user may decide they prefer a solitary experience, as I often do. This is not recommended for anyone who hasn't undergone this type of session enough times prior in order to fully understand and master the experience. A guide, or an experienced partner, can help if a moment of personal crisis occurs. The object of the session is to have a transformative experience. This is easiest when one feels safe and taken care of. Best that it's done with someone the user trusts and in a place that promotes serenity.

Intent is of great importance. One should go into the experience with the intent to recover, while the session should not be used to dwell on negative experiences. Past issues can come up, and should be addressed if they do, but only in a way that promotes positivity. Dwelling on things we cannot change is counterproductive. These issues should only be acknowledged as behaviors we are working towards eliminating. We go into the trip with the intent to better ourselves. Once it begins, we go wherever it takes us and, with the help of our chosen guide, steer the trip toward a positive outcome.

Set, also known as mindset, is very important in the psychedelic experience. The user's mindset has a very pronounced effect on the outcome of the trip. A positive outlook will usually result in a positive experience while a negative mood can bring the experience to a place that the user may not wish to go. While negative emotions need to be addressed, going into the journey with a positive mindset will usually result in positive experiences. The most important part of the mindset is to be relaxed and open to the recovery desired. The intent to fix a problem is the most beneficial way to experience psychedelics and has the highest potential for recovery. Remember, it's your mind. There is nothing to fear.

The setting should be a place of comfort and safety. If you choose an outdoor setting, that setting should be easy to get to and without any dangerous aspects. Swimming, or even entering water of any depth, is discouraged. Central Park, in New York City, is an amazing place for an experience, as is any park setting, as long as you can tune out the people. Natural settings with little to no human distractions are best, if outdoors is the way you wish to go. If you choose to remain indoors, as many people do, a place that is clean, comfortable, and free of people not involved in psychedelic therapy is recommended.

The sounds of nature can bring one to a place of oneness and clarity rather quickly, while seeing and hearing nature have mental health benefits all their own. If an outdoor setting is not chosen, these sounds can be replicated indoors with all of the comforts of a soft couch or chair to relax in. Nature sounds can also be replaced with soothing music, windchimes, and any other sounds that the user prefers to hear. Music with deep lyrics that mean something to the user can evoke emotions but it's usually best, at least at first, to have audio that has no words so that the user can create their own mental dialog. A playlist of instrumental songs from all of one's favorite artists can also be used, as long as there is a progression of moods, and it doesn't jump from one tempo to another and back.

Visual stimulation is always abundant in a natural setting, allowing the CS to revel in the marvel of something they have probably taken for granted their whole lives. You might be surprised at what you see in something you've always dismissed, or simply not noticed before. Lighting, geometric patterns, and color can enhance the experience indoors. Dim lights are recommended, and candlelight can be amazing, as long as there is someone else with you that is not along for the ride. Video of geometric patterns and psychedelic swirls on a big screen can provide a pleasant background as well. Once the setting is determined, the mindset is positive, and intentions of what we are going to work on in this session have been set, it's time to start the psychedelic journey.

The onset of the effects of psychedelics begins within 20 to 90 minutes after ingestion in LSD and mushrooms while Peyote can take up to 2 hours (mescaline, Peyote's active ingredient, works much faster) and slowly increase for 6 to 15 hours (mushrooms lasting 5 to 6 while LSD can last from 8 to 12 hours). At first you may feel elated and unusually happy. Soon, colors will appear brighter, and you will begin to see shapes and patterns more clearly. Contrasting shades, such as a checkerboard pattern or stripes, may appear to move in and out of the plane they are on. For example, the black squares on a checkered floor may seem to descend as the white squares appear to rise only to drop again as the black squares rise. Optical illusions like this are common and nothing to worry about.

As the intensity increases, moving objects will appear to leave colorful trails that catch up to the object as its motion ceases. All senses are heightened, and everything is experienced anew. It's as if you never noticed things that you see every day. All colors are brighter, sounds are crisper, smells and tastes pop, and texture takes on new meaning. Everything you have learned to take for granted becomes amazing again all at once. Simply waving one's hand slowly can provide entertainment, and even distract from negative thought processes. It's like seeing the world through the eyes of a child, but with some enhancement.

As feelings of elation continue, one tends to experience a profound insight into themselves, their lives, and their view of the world. What is truly important in their lives becomes obvious to them and they begin to see what life can be without the addictions or other conditions of the mind that burden them. This is when the realization of new possibilities becomes so obvious that many wonder why they never came to these conclusions sooner, or without the use of psychedelics. This is the height of this form of treatment, the place where the CS realizes that they do not want, and more importantly do not need, the substance that has held them back for so long.

The intensity continues to increase until the climax, or peak, is reached. At this point, almost magically, the intensity abruptly gives way to normalcy and the ride is over. If psychedelics were sex, the peak would be the orgasm. When it's over, it's over, but you're left with an afterglow of effects that include an elated mood, a new sense of being, and a clarity of purpose. You may see a lesser version of those trails for a couple more hours. This is the time most patients use to reflect on the experience with their therapist, CSM, shaman, or just in their own minds.

Since the psychedelic treatment has the most benefits in the first month, it stands to reason that this treatment should be continued as often as needed. While some users do not need another treatment for several months, others might find it necessary to undergo monthly, bi-weekly, or even weekly sessions. Classic psychedelics have been shown to be harmless when done at these doses and in a controlled setting. The only consideration is the time and intensity of the experience.

Other Components
Stretch

The other components of California Sober are things many of us already do every day. For those of us who do not, a few minutes a day is all you need to reap the benefits of some simple procedures that will transform your life and help you to live longer. If you are not a regular practitioner of healthy behaviors (as almost no addict is when they are using) don't be overwhelmed. The key to life is to ease into everything, including health. Do a few minutes today, a few more tomorrow, and so on. By day two you'll be doing more than you were yesterday and before you know it, you'll be doing a lot more than you were last week.

Stretching is the easiest way for most to lean into health, no pun intended. Stretching releases toxins and lactic acid from your muscles, causing you to feel better after every session while promoting flexibility and range of motion that was likely lost to a lot of sitting around getting high. Stretching also causes the release of endorphins (the morphine within) which make us feel good and help to relieve the pain of life, both physical and emotional. A better you can begin with a simple movement that will make you feel better.

Start by stretching for 15 seconds per pose, increasing by 5 seconds a day until you are at 30 seconds. You can begin with one or two poses, adding a new pose daily until you are sure that you have chosen stretches that incorporate all parts of the body, and in every direction they move. On day one you can choose to just touch your toes from a strait kneed sitting or standing position. By day 30 you'll be opening up your hips and increasing your range of motion like a teenager. The more often you stretch, the easier it is, so it's less work the more you do it and once you're involved in stretching for a few weeks you never want to stop.

Diet

What you put into your body is as important as what you do not. Processed foods, fast foods, and things consisting of mostly sugar can put a drain on your consistent energy levels, causing you to feel the need for a boost when you are actually sluggish from your diet, and not simply the lack of your substance of choice. Sometimes these feelings can be confused, especially in cases of habitual use at a given time, namely dinner time. In addition, low blood sugar can act as a trigger, especially in the case of alcoholism.

I used to come home from work and reach for a beer, or whiskey (or whatever was readily available). I thought that I was craving alcohol and that it, or another substance, was the only thing that could make me feel right and relieve the pressure of the day. I never ate before that first couple of drinks because I thought I knew what my body was craving. One evening, after skipping lunch, I was surprised with a fully cooked meal waiting for me when I walked in the door. Instead of grabbing a beer, I decided to eat first. What happened surprised me and changed the way I looked at my after-work ritual.

After eating a full meal, I couldn't drink my beer as fast as I usually would. In fact, I sipped it for the first hour. That time was long enough for me to realize that my after-work cravings

153

were partially due to low blood sugar and hunger. I had been drinking before dinner for so many years that it never occurred to me that I was just hungry, and not really craving alcohol. The experience didn't stop me from drinking later in the evening, but it did slow me down. I'm not saying a good meal will make you quit alcohol or other substances, just that there are many triggers, and that hunger and low blood sugar can contribute to intense cravings.

I'm not going to tell you how to eat, I'm simply going to point out the simplest thing about nutrition, something that we as a species have all but forgotten. Everyone living today was born in a time in which the natural world is not a place where we exist. Many of us don't even realize that it exists, other than on the Nature channel. We live in a fantasy, created by our forefathers and enhanced and upgraded by every generation, where we are farther and farther from reality, living in a world that we didn't evolve to exist in. Our homes, our jobs, our hobbies, and even our problems are all man made, and this includes our diet.

In the age of go, go, go, a world in which we are in a hurry to make a living and stay ahead in the rat race, many people live on fast food, microwavable meals, and premade sugar products. Our idea of healthy eating is grabbing a protein bar on the way to work instead of our usual sugary cereal or baked goods and coffee. A donut for breakfast, fast food at lunch, and a TV dinner are all too common in our society. Most of us don't even read the ingredients or nutrition label on the foods that we consume. It's a fast-paced world and no time is left to bother thinking about what we ingest. I'm going to say something so simple that it should be obvious, still most people don't bother even attempting it. We should make 90% of what we eat from scratch.

I'm not saying that you can never eat a TV dinner, or that you can't run through a drive through once a week. I'm not saying that you can't have dessert. What I'm saying is that our bodies evolved for millions of years to eat what the earth provides, and the earth doesn't provide a McRib or a Cinnabon, or even lasagna. And while the earth does provide meat and vegetables, when you buy them premade, they are loaded with sugar, salt, and preservatives, and are leached of the nutritional value that they had before they were processed in a factory. Odds are, if you didn't make it from natural ingredients yourself, what you are eating is not something you should be putting into your body on a regular basis.

Other than the fact that eating healthy, and by healthy I only mean natural foods, increases longevity (you live longer), eating natural foods increases the release of endorphins. If you can simply manage to eat foods with only whole ingredients like vegetables, fruit, and meats that are not processed, your energy levels and endorphin levels skyrocket to their natural potential. This doesn't mean you can't eat out. Many restaurants cook meals from scratch and, as long as you tell them not to add salt (which is already in all natural foods), are just as healthy as what you might make at home. You can still eat what's in that TV dinner, and it will probably taste even better if you find a recipe and make it yourself while ensuring that the ingredients that you put in it are natural.

One of the largest problems may be your beverage of choice. We aren't meant to consume refined sugar, the main ingredient in most drinks (other than water). In fact, you should drink water more than any other beverage, if not exclusively. I grew up drinking soda with every meal, sometimes even for breakfast, and it was so common that I didn't ever drink water. Water was something that I had to get used to as an adult because no one ever told me that that was what you were supposed to drink when you were thirsty. For me, water was what you drank when you ran out of Pepsi or Coke.

I still have a soda now and then, but the longer I went without it, the more I lost my taste for drinkable sugar, which works in the same way as many substances. Foods and drinks with sugar cause a subtle high followed by a crash. Sugar withdrawal, much like caffeine, causes headaches, irritability, and cravings for the substance the body has become addicted to. On top of that, sugar use and its eventual crash cause heightened cravings for one's substance of choice in many addicts. I'm not saying you have to cut it out altogether, I'm simply advising that sugar should be a limited treat. To what extent is up to you.

Exercise

As I mentioned, we no longer live in the natural world that our bodies are designed to thrive in. Our jobs, since the industrial revolution, have little to do with the natural order of things. Mankind once lived without the careers we all strive for today. Before society, which is only 6000 years old, we walked the earth in search of food all day and worked to make shelters that would see us through the night. We ate what we found or killed and then walked on to find more. Hunting and survival gave us cause to walk, and often run. When the sun fell, we finished what we had started and then slept until it rose again.

Learning how to farm created the need to build even longer lasting shelters. In turn, wandering and scavenging gave way to working gardens and building homes and cities. This new life consisted of hunting, working the soil, planting, harvesting, building shelters and common areas, and sleep. Every daily task required some form of exercise. Mankind, being the exceptionally intelligent species that we are, was constantly thinking of new ways to make that hard life easier. Still, we labored from sunup to sundown in order to survive Nature's trials. It wasn't until a couple of hundred years ago that industrialization began.

At that point, in all of our genius, we found ways to make life easier. Survival of the fittest was no longer necessary. The inventors made it so that every person could survive, regardless of intelligence or strength. With every new invention came less work for most until those with the most possessions had the least to do. The rich had others to tend their fields and could buy their meat from those who hunted. They could pay to have their daily chores done and their shelters maintained. Those who could afford the luxuries of the time had no need for labor and exercise. Still, those who had less fortune still had to work hard to survive. With that, new needs were created that didn't exist in nature.

Today, most jobs have absolutely no meaning in the natural order of things. Unless you hunt, farm, or build homes, your job wouldn't have been necessary without the formation of modern society. You would have no use in the natural world. Our society has become such that no one is doing what they need to do to survive that natural world, we are doing what we need to do to survive in the ultimate dreamworld. It's amazing if you think about it. We conquered nature and now work not to survive but to gain more possessions. I'm not downing it; I only bring it up to make one point. We used to have to exercise to survive. Now we don't.

As mammals, our bodies have evolved for 170 million years to move almost constantly, from sunrise to sunset, in order to survive. As primates, we have evolved for over 50 million years in our basic configuration, 6 million years on our own two feet, and 300,000 as humans. That's a long evolution of constantly moving, walking, hunting, farming, and building. In contrast, we have only been sitting around on our fat asses for a couple of hundred years, and that's only the elite. In the last several decades, even the lowest classes of society are able to get by with jobs that don't require much exercise at all, in comparison. They say that necessity is the mother of invention. I say laziness is that mother.

After millions upon millions of years of evolving to move around continuously, sitting around can feel like a much-needed break. Unfortunately, that's not what our bodies are designed to do, and so it is literally killing us. Lack of movement causes back pain, high blood pressure, heart disease, obesity, and many other conditions that are much more common, and many that didn't exist in modern society. The life we evolved to live in hunter gatherer tribes is a lifestyle that is almost extinct in the modern world. We've gone from a species that migrated across the world on foot to one that won't go to the corner store without getting in a car.

Exercise is shown not only to increase our longevity, but to promote the release of endorphins. The more we move, the happier we are. Through exercise we gain strength, mobility, and even pleasure. Exercise is also shown to help aid in recovery from addiction to alcohol and other substances. It doesn't take a lot to make a difference either. If you take a 10-minute exercise break for every hour you spend sitting, there are remarkable results. If that's too much, try five. That's the number of minutes where the health benefits begin. Less than that can still help and, although studies recommend at least five, anything is better than nothing.

Our immune systems don't have a circulatory system. The lymphatic system pumps through the use of our limbs and, while we're at it, walking is the best exercise for many people. There is an ongoing perpetuation of the idea that we must reach 10,000 steps a day, but that's a goal, not a mandate. The truth is that half that number greatly increases your odds of survival. Any number of steps are better than none. Instead of driving to the corner store, take a walk. Walk around your neighborhood. Studies show that walks in nature help reset the brain and increase the odds of recovery.

There's no one size fits all for exercise. The key to life is doing a little more of what's good for you each day while doing a little less of what's not. Start with a 10-minute walk each day. Every day increase it by one minute, or even 30 seconds. Anyone can do 30 seconds more than they did the day before and, before you know it, that increase becomes 15 minutes in a month. None of us can change overnight but any of us can change over time, as long as we realize that the time to start is now and we make our best effort to not go backwards. Stick to it and you will feel like a new person in no time at all.

For those of us who use Cannabis in our recovery, it can also be a motivational tool (especially the Sativa strain) for exercise, stretching, meditation, and more. Low to moderate doses of classic psychedelics can also motivate the user to exercise. There's nothing like a walk in the park, and there's no experience grander than a walk in the park during psychedelic therapy or Cannabis therapy. When multiple aspects of the California Sober system of recovery are combined, the results are astounding. In addition, things that we tend to see as a chore can become a life changing and pleasurable experience.

Meditation for the soul

Believe it or not, many people are intimidated by meditation. Some believe that it takes a special kind of enlightened being in order to achieve results, while others think it's just some hocus pocus bullshit that only works in the minds of some hippie believers. Either of these ideas couldn't be further from the truth. Meditation is scientifically proven to reduce heart rate and blood pressure, reduce anxiety and depression (as well as other mental obstacles), and help addicts find their way to recovery. In fact, the results are astronomical for those who practice daily, and anyone can do it. It's as simple as you let it be and can help you overcome the problems of everyday life while controlling your emotions to a degree you may have never thought possible.

I was definitely a non-believer, a skeptic of the highest order.

I had tried to meditate with no success due to my impatience. I would attempt to meditate for a few minutes only to become restless and bored. Then one evening, when my mind just wouldn't shut off, I gave it a serious try. I concentrated on my breathing. When thoughts wouldn't stop racing through my mind, I concentrated on a sound that I had made up in my head. Every time a thought would start to appear in the foreground of my mind, I simply let the sound in my mind become more prominent than the thought. I ushered any *words* that entered my thoughts to the background. Before I knew it, I was at peace. I stayed there for about 20 minutes or so, until I was able to forget all of my problems and only feel happiness.

My makeshift form of meditation worked for me, but I've also found peace in mindfulness meditation and transcendental meditation. The truth is, any form of meditation has its benefits and, like everything else, there is no one-size-fits-all approach. Whatever works for the user is the right type of meditation for that individual, and I encourage everyone to try as many types of meditation as they can, even after you find the one that's right for you. There's no harm in trying another, and it might be even better than the last. I do different forms of meditation from time to time because each has its own use and because it's fun to switch it up every now and again. When I don't have the time it takes to reach the level I want, I either meditate for whatever time I do have or simply breathe.

Breathe

Breathing exercises have similar benefits to meditation and work when you don't have the time or place to indulge in the practice. Studies show that cyclic breathing can be more beneficial than mindful meditation when you only have five minutes or less to spare. It sounds a little cliche, *just breathe* or *take a deep breath* being phrases that are thrown around whenever someone is in a state of panic or distress. The simple truth is that that's why those phrases came about. Sometimes all you need to calm your nerves or rationally approach a situation that you are used to leaning into with anger or panic is a few simple breaths. Cyclic breathing takes that to a level that is scientifically proven to calm. When you feel the urge to thoughtlessly react to a situation, just breathe.

Stick to the Naturals

Stick to the naturals, an old friend of mine once said while we were debating which substances were okay to use regularly verses which were dangerous and prone to abuse. It was a saying that was thrown around by our ever-growing group of friends, a mantra that we lived by until some lines began to blur as we reached adulthood. We were not yet addicted to anything in particular (although I may have been an addict at birth), we were simply in an experimental phase of our youth. My friend was referring to the safety of Cannabis, mescaline, mushrooms, and LSD (as it is the cleanest synthetic substance and related, chemically, to LSA naturally occurring in Morning Glories), as opposed to pharmaceuticals, cocaine, or heroin. *Stick to the naturals and you'll be alright.* His words were inspiring, hauntingly prophetic, and way ahead of their time.

You see, there was no California Sober methodology promoted in the *Just say no* era. It was the 1980s and there were but two sides. The War on Drugs ensured that everyone had to pick one. There were the druggies, those who would experiment with anything and everything that would take them to a place far removed from this reality, some pioneering the final frontier of the human mind in an endless search for the answer to *who are we and why are we here,* lumped in with others who were just looking to escape, and then there were those who did not do any *drugs* at all, other than alcohol and other socially acceptable substances.

When looking for a mind-altering substance's potential medicinal value, I always go back to my old friends and their wise assessment. *Stick to the Naturals*, I remind myself. The reason for this is simple. Man has a natural desire to take apart whatever he sees, find out what makes it tick, and improve it. We tend to seek the knowledge of how things work, out of pure curiosity. Then, out of pure narcissism, we assure ourselves that we can do a better job than old Mother Nature herself. We think we can make everything better, yet all we ever seem to do is make things more powerful and addictive.

Take Opium for example. First, we found a medicine in nature that does things that absolutely no other plant on the entire planet can. It relieves even the most severe pains (from menstrual cramps to shattered bones), suppresses cough, increases happiness, promotes productivity, helps with sleep, and more, but that wasn't enough. For millennia, our species selectively bred the plant in order to increase the amounts of these *magic* alkaloids, making it stronger and stronger, until we were satisfied that nature had done about as good as she could. Then we took matters into our own hands.

We extracted Morphine, Opium's most active ingredient, and then Codeine, the former increasing Opium's strength 10-fold and making it possible to administer exact doses of the highest amount of the substance possible without causing death, an amount that increases with tolerance, but that still wasn't enough. In the guise of looking for a less addictive and less harmful substance, the scientific community created Heroin, and our friends at Bayer (yes, the aspirin company) marketed it as a non-addictive alternative to Morphine. They had to know they were wrong, as it only takes a few days to become addicted, but that never stopped Big Pharma. They were onto something that could make them rich, and they knew it.

Next, Bayer made Oxycodone and marketed *that* as a less addictive alternative. That's the same Oxy that Purdue Pharma has been charged with creating the current opioid epidemic with. Next came Methadone, then pethidine, then fentanyl (which you may not know has been around since the 1950s), and carfentanyl. At this point we are 10,000 times stronger than Morphine, but why stop there? The strongest opioid to date goes by its abbreviated chemical name of 4-F-Ohmefentanyl which weighs in at a whopping 18,000 times the potency of Morphine and at least 180,000 times stronger than Opium which, strait from the poppy, was good enough for the strongest of pain for the first several thousand years of society. `Not only are these substances more powerful than Opium, they are equally more addictive.

Still, pharmaceutical companies across the globe work tirelessly to *improve* upon the opioid's molecular structure, each time making stronger, deadlier, and more addictive synthetic opioids in the name of profit and greed. While strong pain remedies are needed for people with chronic illness, at some point we have to decide that something that can kill in dosages that can barely be seen with the naked eye is simply too much and that we have all the opioids we need, medically speaking. Pharma can, and will, bastardize every gift of nature to make a buck, and they aren't going to stop at painkillers.

Don't let them fool you. All of the substances that cause addiction, all of the poisons killing our children, are pharmaceutical in origin. The opiate epidemic, as I just mentioned, was started in 1874 with the heroin (also known as Diamorphine) they laughably called non-addictive, and it proceeded from there. Amphetamine was synthesized in 1887, methamphetamine in 1893, and methamphetamine hydrochloride in 1919. Germany began marketing meth over the counter in 1938 and it was used by the Nazis to keep their soldiers alert and awake for extended periods of time. Meth was even marketed in the United States as a diet drug throughout the 1950s and 60s, until it was put on Schedule II of the Controlled Substance list, still not considered by the government as worse than those pesky Schedule 1 substances like Cannabis and mushrooms.

Some pharmaceuticals align with the California Sober philosophy, although much care must be taken when they are used as a treatment (or recreationally) due to the fact that, unlike classic psychedelics, instead of building a tolerance that prohibits their daily use they accumulate in the system and multiple days of use can cause psychological side effects. They also demonstrate some potential for psychological addiction and can cause adverse reactions when taken with other substances. MDMA (also known as Ecstasy, Molly, or X), for instance, is now being used as a treatment for PTSD. MDMA has not been tested enough to determine its effects in recovery from Substance Abuse Disorder but has potential as a PTSD treatment. I only mention it because it is now falsely referred to as a psychedelic.

Quite a few other pharmaceutical psychedelics show great potential, one of which is at the center of California Sobriety. LSD is a synthesized (manmade) chemical, although it is derived from the ergot fungus and does have its cousin in nature, LSA, which is found naturally in the seeds of the Morning Glory flower. Unlike many pharmaceuticals, pure LSD is a clean pharmaceutical with little to no unwanted side effects and no potential for abuse or unintentional overdose. LSD is likened to the experience achieved by such natural substances as LSA, Peyote, Psilocybe mushrooms, and other classic psychedelics and is categorized among them.

Another potentially beneficial pharmaceutical is Ketamine, known on the streets as Special K. Seven studies conducted between 1997 and today suggest that Ketamine improved abstinence rates in Alcohol Use Disorder, Cocaine Use Disorder, and Opioid (Heroin) Use disorder. Ketamine is a derivative of Phencyclidine, also known as Phenyl Cyclohexyl Piperdine or PCP, and was developed as a safer anesthetic than PCP. I, myself, believe Ketamine to have great potential for controlling substance abuse due to my experiments with its parent substance, PCP, in the 1990s. In those experiments, I found that PCP could temporarily block cocaine, opioid, and alcohol cravings, yet the benefits only lasted as long as the effects of the substance remained.

The problems with ketamine are many. Ketamine is being marketed as a safe psychedelic when in fact it is neither safe nor a psychedelic, in the classic sense of the term. Ketamine is a dissociative anesthetic that happens to have hallucinogenic effects. Unlike psychedelics, which allow the user to experience external stimuli on another level while still experiencing reality (a sort of hyper-reality), ketamine, like PCP, can cause more of an out-of-body experience. That's where the *dissociative anesthetic* term comes in. On K, the user feels as if they have left their body, and reality for that matter, and the experience is more dreamlike, rather than the reality-based experience we have with classic psychedelics.

These substances can also cause personality shifts that are present only under the influence of the substance. One might be an entirely different person while under ketamine's influence than they are when they are not. The more often they take the substance, the longer that other personality takes hold and the more they lose their sense of reality. Ketamine is a dangerous substance when abused and, especially with these online companies sending users at home therapy kits that supply a year's worth of *medication*, it is easily abused. For those that it works for and who are able to refrain from abusing it, I hope that resilience lasts. For addicts, I don't think ketamine is a good idea.

The benefits are short-lived; therefore, it is recommended that you take the substance every few days, at least twice a week. When substances like ketamine build up in the system, the long-term benefit is less pronounced. Tolerance is formed and psychological addiction is reinforced while feelings of depression and other conditions of the mind may even become more pronounced. The problems that Ketamine once fixed are what it eventually causes with the slightest misuse, or a misdiagnosis or dosage mistake by these doctors whom the patient never actually sees in person.

Ketamine is now being marketed as a safe and natural psychedelic alternative to other medications, one with little to no side effects. While ketamine may have some benefit, I would take a step back from anything that companies have to lie to promote. Ketamine is a man-made substance that, as I mentioned, is a derivative of PCP. There is no ketamine treatment that is sourced naturally. Again, ketamine is a dissociative anesthetic, not a classic psychedelic. Rather than give you that lasting feeling of oneness with nature, ketamine can make us feel like we are out of place in the universe and removed from the natural world. As it builds in the system, emotional problems can get worse instead of better. Classic psychedelics are a cleaner journey with no chemical toxins left behind.

In addition, what usually costs a veterinarian (or a street user) $20 is now being sold for hundreds of dollars through companies that let you do at home ketamine therapy for a couple of thousand dollars a year. Ketamine has become big pharma, and that means big business and fortune for a lot of people, strong motivation for them to push it *legally*. Always be wary of a 10,000% mark-up in the interest of *medicine*. Natural medicines, while they will be expensive once they are legalized, can be grown in bulk in the comfort of your home for less than the cost of a single dose.

My point is this: If you *stick to the Naturals* (and LSD) the guesswork is taken out of the equation. There are no side effects from LSD, Psilocybe Mushrooms, or Peyote and other mescaline containing cacti that last beyond the experience itself and, therefore, classic psychedelics are the cleanest way to rewire the brain to think differently about addiction and other conditions of the mind, and to refrain from the use of the substance that has taken over your life. While other substances show potential, no substances (or any other method of recovery) outperform the California Sober method of recovery.

Know Your Source

There are many unscrupulous characters in this world, those that would disregard human life in the name of profit and greed. For this reason, it is important to be able to trust the source from which you obtain the substances mentioned herein. Since this book deals mostly with natural substances, I always suggest that one grow their own materials. This has the benefit of ensuring that your materials aren't tainted with drugs such as fentanyl or other harmful substances aimed to cause addiction or cheaply enhance inferior quality product.

Growing your own also has the added benefit of saving you tons of money. One seed can grow a pound of Cannabis saving the user a minimum of $4000 and $40 worth of materials can grow $5000 worth of Psilocybe mushrooms, for instance. You save money, you don't have to deal with illegal sales, and you don't end up with tainted substances that can harm you.

Be Wary

Be wary of all of the experts that are jumping on the psychedelic bandwagon. It wasn't but a few years ago that they were on the other side of the same topic. With new treatments come new fortunes to be made. Therapy can be expensive, and well worth the price. Medicine, however, should be affordable, especially when that medicine comes from nature. As soon as ketamine was approved for depression, medical companies began off label prescribing and it showed up for sale by these companies on all of the social media platforms. Never trust an expert that hasn't had dozens of years of experience. Without these decades of observation and self-trials they are but novices with a medical degree.

While the world changes rapidly, those who change their advice based on what is popular and socially acceptable are but frauds trying to make a buck at the expense of those who will let them. In the 80s and 90s, those who used Cannabis and Psychedelics were considered burnouts and were said to be killing brain cells. Now, those same experts agree that psychedelics help form new neural pathways, creating the brain cells they were said to destroy. While many of us have always known of the healing potential of these medicines, take care in who advises you on their use, that they themselves have undergone the treatments and understand their value on a personal level.

California Sober for Mental and Physical Health

The Therapeutic Aspect

Similar to other recovery groups, California Sober groups meet and talk about their issues with substances and alcohol, as well as other issues in their lives. Group therapy of this type is recommended but, if you find that after several weeks of trying, that this is not for you, other forms of therapy can be just as beneficial. The main reason we recommend groups is that they work well and provide some comradery and support in alleviating addiction. One on one sessions with a therapist who believes in the treatment can be just as helpful, and sometimes more so. A combination of group and one on one therapy is the most beneficial, for those who choose to do so.

In addition to therapy, support of friends and family who do not share in your addiction and are understanding of the California Sober method is a great way to stay on track. If you have these types of people in your world, use them as an anchor. If you do not, the groups can provide this stability. While there is success in going it alone with the help of a therapist, someone you can call when you hit a low point in your treatment can be the difference between another day away from your addiction and relapse. That's why having a California Sober who has long term success as a California Sober Mentor (CSM) is one of the most beneficial parts of the plan.

In addition to meetings and one on one sessions, psychedelic therapy opens doors that traditional therapy can take years to accomplish. By psychedelic therapy, I am referring to not only using classic psychedelics in a therapy session, but to solo and group psychedelic experiences. Nothing can help you dive as deeply to the core of your problems and reinvent your way of thinking about them as classic psychedelics can. When used in a controlled environment with the intent of solving a problem, be it addiction or any other condition of the mind, psychedelic therapy outshines other methods and allows the user to decide their fate. Remember, psychedelics can rewire the brain when used with the intent to do so, and usually surprise those who take them without conscious intent, giving them answers they didn't know they were looking for.

The Health Aspect

From a bad mood to a bad back, everything we deal with in

life can trigger addiction. One of the best ways to combat addiction is to lower the amount of physical, mental, and emotional pain you have to deal with in any given day. That is why lifestyle alteration and an interest in self-improvement, including better health and quality of life, can be the nudge you need to stick with the program and control your cravings. Fitness elevates mood by boosting your natural endorphin levels and alleviates certain types of pain that are caused primarily by sedentary behavior. Any addict who was at their weakest can attest to the physical pain that comes with it.

It doesn't take much to alter your routine to include some basic movement, and that's all it really takes to keep yourself from becoming old and rickety before your time. Yoga, stretching, calisthenics, mobility exercises (like standing from a sitting position or squats), keep your body flowing in motion, rather than becoming a huge pain. As we get older, we move less than when we were children. The less we move, the harder it becomes to do so. Fortunately, the more we move, even after the stiffness sets in, the more we can move. This eventually leads to a full rejuvenation of the body and mind.

The California Sober lifestyle can promote the desire to stretch and exercise while creating new neural pathways and enhancing creativity and peace of mind. When all of the components of the California Sober method of recovery are incorporated into one's life, the physical and mental health benefits begin to appear, seemingly without effort, almost instantaneously. And while the all-inclusive plan has the highest rate of success, incorporating any one (or more) of these components into your everyday existence has more success than any other program. You just have to ask yourself, *am I ready to change?*

Chapter 5 - The California Sober Method of Recovery

Now that we have gone over the basics of what the California Sober method of recovery is, the science of what makes it tick, and how the world was robbed of these traditions and medicines, it's time to go over the plan and how it applies to you. By incorporating the following into your routine, you will have the ability to change your mind and rewire it in order to achieve your goal, returning to or discovering the best version of yourself, the true you. Once you decide where you want the path to take you, the California Sober method will guide you on that journey. The final destination can, and often will, change with time. That's a discussion for later. For now, we only need to know in what direction we are headed.

The Questions

Real-life changes are major shifts in lifestyle that can be anything from an alteration of your everyday routine to a transformation of who you are. While change can be easy when the individual is truly ready for that change to occur, it can be overwhelming if one attempts to change without first questioning their own motivation. Once our true intentions are revealed by asking ourselves a few simple questions, that intention can be focused to drive our will and keep us on the path to our desires. Sometimes the questions reveal to us that the change we thought we wanted is not what we really need, and new intentions are discovered. Before we proceed, we need to ask ourselves three questions.

Do I really want to change?

The first question you must ask yourself before embarking on any form of recovery, or any life altering adjustment, is *Do I really want to change*? I know it sounds silly. If you didn't want to change, why would you be reading this?   Why would you seek out help or enter some type of program? It seems logical that these types of actions would only be initiated if one was truly and undeniably ready to change, to become a better version of themselves. Unfortunately, this is not always the case. Either consciously or often subconsciously, the desire to change is to appease some outside force, such as someone else's desire for you to change, or your desire to circumvent a consequence of the actions you're trying to refrain from.

While these can be valid reasons to desire a change, unless these reasons truly make you *see the light* and want that change for yourself, and you wouldn't rather continue the lifestyle you're leading and simply avoid the consequences, they may not be enough to make you take the leap necessary to make that change stick. In other words, you have to want the change for yourself, regardless of whether or not that change remedies the issues that you feel your problem is causing. Many times, I had been asked, even told, to change. I wasn't ready. I was happy doing what I was doing regardless of the fact that everyone else saw it as a path to my own destruction. I didn't want to change and so, as much as I *tried*, I couldn't. The truth was, I was going through the motions to appease someone else's vision of what I needed to be doing. You have to truly want to change for that change to happen, which leads us to our next question.

Why do I want to change?

Ask yourself this question and see what you come up with. The answer varies greatly from person to person and the same answer can motivate individuals in completely different ways. *A person in my life can't stand my behavior and if I don't alter it, they will no longer be a part of my life* is a popular reason one may have to want to change. This motivational factor is a dangerous one to reckon with as it often leads to a relapse of unwanted behavior, whether it be substance abuse, or the fact that one is a bit of a slob, or anything else that can be a deal breaker. The problem here is that you'd only be changing your behavior in order to avoid punishment or consequence.

Imagine you are walking along a trail with headphones on. You're listening to music, swaying left and right, spinning around, having a great time. You're not paying attention to a fucking thing, without a care in the world, when suddenly you find yourself on a bridge over a deep ravine. The bridge is long and narrow without any type of guardrail and the ravine is hundreds of feet deep. Any misstep and you'll surely fall to your death. This is a serious situation and so you focus your attention, steady your balance, and carefully cross that bridge. It's a little scary, but you got this. You pull your shit together, turn off the music, straighten your back, outstretch your arms, and cross that bridge like it's the thing to do.

You feel great. You feel accomplished. The fear has subsided and morphed into a sense of pride and satisfaction while the endorphins cause elation. You feel awesome and so you crank up the tunes and go back to having a good time. You're swaying about, spinning around. Shit, now you're even walking backwards with your eyes closed. And why not? The threat is gone and there's no danger in sight. This is the time to party like never before because you never know when you're going to find yourself in a dangerous situation again. Enjoy life while it lasts and you'll just cross that bridge when you come to it, right?

The problem with changing your behavior in the face of a negative consequence is that you only need to keep up the good work until the threat has passed. Once that family member, life partner, or friend is no longer upset with your behavior, it's very easy to slip right back into old ways and enjoy yourself until the next problem arises. When it does, you just make the same adjustments until it passes and move on, never taking a second to see that you're never truly out of danger. Straitening up to cross the bridge isn't a big deal until the day you miss a step and fall to your death. You won't stop apologizing until that person refuses to answer your calls or ever see you again. And that's why you have to want the change for yourself, regardless of the consequence.

If you're always paying attention to where you're placing your feet, you'll never fall, but you won't pay true attention to where you put your feet until you have fallen, broken a leg, and nearly died. At that point, you may have already lost what it is that made you want to change in the first place. Harder lessons have never been learned, but easy lessons don't stick. Before you make a serious change, you have to want that change to occur, regardless of the outcome, to make a better version of yourself in *your* eyes, and nobody else's. You have to want to be the person who's always got their eyes open, and not just when you think you have something you need to see, but because you don't want to miss a thing.

The only way to stop ingesting harmful substances, or change any behavior for that matter, is to visualize yourself without that problem and like who that person is. Even further, you have to experience life as that version of yourself and want that life more than the one you currently have. You won't do it for someone else. You won't do it for a job. It's not that you can't. You just won't. You have the ability to be whoever you want to be. It's much harder to be whoever *they* want you to be. If, deep down, you like what you're doing now, that's what you'll continue to do until you don't like it anymore.

That said, the California Sober method of bringing about that change can open your eyes to who you truly want to be, even if you can't see it yet. You may go into it thinking you want to keep going the way you are going, only to find that you have a better idea of who you want to be than you thought. It's a true awakening, if you allow it to be, and once your eyes are fully open to the possibilities, the next step is to figure out how to facilitate that change and become the you that you see, that you want to be, instead of trying to be the you that they want you to be.

What would it really take for me to be able to change?

Once you've figured out which direction you want to start heading, it's time to map out a path. For that you need to ask yourself, *what would it really take for me to be able to change?* What are the roadblocks? What, other than yourself, is standing in your way? Some obstacles you can go around, others you'll have to completely remove, and some you can simply step right over. You'll have to decide which ones are which, and that's a heavy task because you probably love a great deal of them. The right treatment, some hard thinking, and a bit of trial and error will help each of them to reveal to you what type of obstacle they are and how they are to be dealt with.

For instance, a loved one can be an obstacle. They may even have the same problem as you, going as far as telling you that you can't change because they don't want to have to change themselves or adjust to the new you. What type of obstacle this is depends on how it affects you. If their continued behavior is something that will have no effect on your success, you can simply step over them. If it is to have very little effect, you can go around them. If their effect will make it impossible for you to be successful in your change, you'll have to remove them entirely, as much as that would hurt, in order to guarantee your success.

It's nice to think you can just step over them or go around them, but bear in mind that once you do, you will have to continually step over and go around them every time you find them in your way. You probably won't have the ability, at least for several years, to be in the company of someone who is using your SOC. The more you are in their presence, the higher the odds that you will give in and join them. The only option, if they are respectful of your problem, might be to only see them when they are not using. Going around them like this can be tiring and wear you down until, ultimately, they become an obstacle that just has to be removed altogether or, if you have the strength, you can just keep taking the long hard way forever, going over and around these obstacles that you can't bring yourself to remove, increasing your chance of relapse drastically.

The bad news is that it's easiest to simply remove any obstacles from your life altogether. The good news is that once you have cleared your path of all obstacles and the road ahead becomes easy to navigate, you can then (after several months of success) revisit an old obstacle that was once blocking your path and see that it is now easily stepped over and, therefore, can once again be in your path without a problem. The more you tend to your path, the easier it is to assess which obstacles are worth the trouble of climbing over and which become too much of a burden. It's your path. Only you can find the balance between the beauty an obstacle brings verses the trouble it causes. No one's path is level and strait, yet walking it daily and cleaning it up regularly builds the strength needed to walk it with ease.

The Plan

Gotta break these shackles gotta break these chains,

and the only way to do it is if we use our brains [45]

Now that you have decided that you want to change, and only because you truly want to be the best version of yourself (and not simply to avoid some consequence or ultimatum), let's figure out how to make that change happen for you in the same way that it has for so many others. Let's explore the best course of action to truly make that change stick. Each of us has our own path to follow and, although most find the all-inclusive method best for them, you need to choose your own path to California Sobriety. The way to do that is to first understand what each path holds and then to choose the right one for you.

There are many components to the California Sober system of recovery. Each works in a unique way to bring about the same result, a change of mind. Through diet, exercise,

---

[45] We Gotta Know – Harley Flanagan / John Joseph / Parris Mayhew – 1986 © Universal Music Publishing Group

meditation, and proper sleep habits, we strive to keep our mind and body healthy and focused on our long-term goal of living without substances of abuse. We keep our bodies and mind strong in order to combat whatever life may throw at us. Life has no shortage of unpredictable obstacles but as long as we remain strong and grounded, we can overcome whatever it is that falls into and blocks the path to our eternal wellbeing.

These practices keep our heels dug into the dirt to help us maintain our mental health while pushing forward through the day-to-day barriers we find in our way. Remember, while California Sober methods can help us to refrain from harmful substances, they also work well against a world of mental and emotional issues that are far too often left handled by the over-prescribing of the pharmaceutical *magic pill*. That's not to say that there is no need for medication, just that we may be able to live a lifestyle that makes the need for medication less, and often negligible.

We may use Cannabis to thwart off cravings of an immediate nature, cravings that would otherwise cause us to use a more harmful and addictive substance. We may also use it to self-medicate in situations of high stress or low mood, when that remedy would help us to refrain from other more harmful substances that we formerly used to combat those same conditions. Cannabis can be a preventative, used to keep our addictions at bay, or as a substitute for pharmaceuticals that we want to avoid. It can lift the spirit, encourage productivity and creativity, and alleviate depression, anxiety, and many other conditions.

When you're in a state of mind brought on by the Cannabis component, quietly reflecting about getting high on your substance of choice is met with negativity towards that idea. Cannabis can stop you in your tracks and remind you of all of the harm that your Substance of Choice has done to you and your life. In direct contradiction, when you're completely abstinent (or worse, drinking alcohol), thinking about your substance of choice can easily lead to your brain's default mode and relapse. The addition of Cannabis helps the CS to remember their goals that can be otherwise forgotten in a moment of craving.

Cannabis not only reduces cravings, but it can also help in the transition from addiction to California Sobriety. People that have a long history of substance abuse have a hard time *settling* for what others may call normalcy (abstinent sobriety). One of the reasons traditional recovery is so unsuccessful where California Sober thrives is that many addicts are so used to being on their Substance of Choice that abstinence can be like living in someone else's skin (or like not having any skin at all). The body is uncomfortable while the mind races to negative thoughts until living without those substances feels like torture. California Sober methods relieve that torture and ease the addict's breakup with their SOC.

Other individuals simply prefer life enhanced. They can't see a future for themselves in which they have no ability to feel better than they do without substance. They've seen another side of life and, while they know they can never use their SOC again, they prefer to live a life with occasionally altered perception. Now that the genie is out of the bottle, they refuse to put it back. Cannabis, as well as other California Sober components, removes that longing that an addict feels while promoting a positive outlook that makes California Sobriety as easy as hitting the reset button on life. All you have to do is follow the plan, which can include Cannabis if that's what is right for you.

Psychedelic therapy is more of a long-term way to prevent cravings for one's SOC and relieve many other conditions. Like Cannabis, psychedelics can be used in low doses to prevent immediate urges, control anxiety, depression, OCD, and more. The true marvel of psychedelics, however, is their proven ability to help with these same issues for up to a year from a single dose, when that dose is at the proper level. Considering that psychedelics show up to a 90% success rate in the first 3 months (as opposed to less than a maximum success rate of 12% with traditional recovery programs), they are the highest performing method of recovery known today.

Meditation and breathing exercises work to calm the mind while helping us to learn to control our thoughts and cravings. They take some practice but can be learned easily and relieve not only addiction, but many of the same problems we use the other California Sober methods to alleviate. By working the focus *muscle*, we strengthen the ability to calm our minds and bring ourselves to a place of peace. With that in mind, once you have mastered the techniques, meditation and breathing can be used on their own, or while experiencing the effects of psychedelics or cannabis.

By incorporating all of the aspects of California Sober, or as many as we choose to, into our daily lifestyles, we create a better version of our true selves. Through exercise, meditation, music, and psychedelic therapies, we enhance our inner being and nurture the best part of ourselves while simultaneously discarding the parts of ourselves that lead us down dark paths to destructive behaviors. We are mindful of the things that make us the people that we truly love and, maybe more importantly, we are mindful of what makes us the people we no longer want to be.

In the all-inclusive California Sober method of recovery, the person desiring change explores all of the different components, each having an astoundingly high success rate on its own, and incorporates them into their life. The California Sober components address first the mind, then the body, and finally the spirit, which is the you that you want to return to, or the version of yourself that you want to become. This can take some time to get used to and may seem overwhelming. That is why I encourage you to take it in small bites. Micro-dose each method, if you will, at least at first.

As much as you want to jump right in and become the best version of yourself today, it's easier to start with what you need to survive the moment, then the day and, ultimately, the rest of your life. If you are able to incorporate just one of the California Sober methods into your routine each week, even just a small version of each method to begin with, before you know it you will be on the all-inclusive plan without any effort at all. For a few of us, it can take some time to integrate all of the methods while others may find it effortless. While true change comes slowly, stopping the use of your SOC can be immediate and long lasting if you follow the path.

Phase 1 - California Sober Remediation Therapy (CSRT)

The first phase in the California Sober method of recovery is to stop using your Substance of Choice. The fastest way to accomplish this in the short term, and in the case of an immediate need for intervention, is with remediation therapy (RT). Remediation therapy is the process of meditating and/or ingesting Cannabis, or a threshold dose of one of the Classic psychedelics, in order to *change your mind* about using your SOC in the immediate future. This practice has the ability to halt default mode behaviors, ranging from a passing thought about using to finding yourself putting your shoes on to go out and find your SOC. The need for relief is immediate and you need help now. California Sober Remediation Therapies give you that help immediately.

Cannabis Remediation Therapy (CRT)

If you are choosing Cannabis for your remediation therapy, you have to first know the dose that is right for you (see cannabis dosages in chapter 4). As soon as you have the slightest inkling that you may want to use your SOC, immediately take your proper dose of Cannabis. In the case of the need for immediate remediation, more is better than less as a mild dose may not have enough of an effect. While I always recommend edible forms of Cannabis to prevent the harms caused by smoking anything, if you think that you may obtain your SOC before the edible has a chance to work, smoking Cannabis has an almost immediate onset and may be necessary in this extreme case. Eating an edible form of Cannabis prior to or just after smoking ensures the effects last through the craving.

Once the Cannabis has produced the desired effect, most people find that they no longer want their SOC. In some cases, intense thoughts of the negative consequences that would follow the use of ones Substance of Choice are brought on by the Cannabis. In other cases, the desire to use one's SOC is simply lifted. The urge to use that harmful substance simply gives way to better thoughts of how to spend that time more productively. Occasionally, the Cannabis therapy may just cause you to forget what it was you wanted to do in the first place, and so you find yourself doing something more productive, or just watching a movie. In any case, the problem is temporarily solved.

Psychedelic Remediation Therapy (PRT)

For those who wish to use classic psychedelics for their RT, the basic outline is the same with a few minor differences in the details. There are different doses of psychedelics for different uses. Micro-doses are doses where you feel very little (if any) effect from the psychedelic of choice. These doses are generally used for daily maintenance and show promise in promoting neurogenesis (the creation of neurons a.k.a. brain cells). While micro-dosing may help some people who suffer from anxiety, depression, and bi-polar disorder, most studies show that a threshold dose or more is most beneficial. While it may have benefits in other areas, micro-dosing is significantly less effective in preventing the use of alcohol and other substances.

For PRT, one must then find their threshold dose. This is the dose where you just begin to feel the effects of your chosen psychedelic (more on dosing can be found in Chapter 4). As with cannabis, the moment you feel the need to use your SOC, immediately take your threshold dose of your chosen psychedelic. Most people choose Psilocybe Mushrooms, due to their mild nature, while others prefer mescaline (peyote) or LSD. In the case of the need for immediate remediation, a little more is better than less, as too mild of a dose may not have enough of an effect.

This is where it is important to discover your threshold dose, as too much will take you on a full psychedelic experience. While that's not a bad idea if you're in a safe place and don't have anywhere to be for several hours, it's not the best idea if you have any responsibilities to tend to in the immediate future. For Psychedelic Remediation Therapy the threshold dose is all you really need in order to not want to use your SOC in the short-term future. It's also an excellent dose for relieving anxiety, depression, OCD, and many other issues.

Once the psychedelic of choice has produced the desired effect, most people find that, as with Cannabis, they no longer want their SOC. At the onset of the psychedelic effect, the desire to use one's SOC is replaced by feelings of peace. The urge to use that harmful substance gives way to creativity that leads to more productive use of one's time.   Even if the user tries to ingest their SOC, psychedelics often have the ability to prevent the desired effect. At this moment, the problem is again temporarily solved.

Meditative Remediation Therapy (MRT)

Meditative Remediation Therapy can be practiced independently or in conjunction with CRT or PRT. It is of great value to those who do not wish to participate in one of the other remediation therapies, but it is also essential for those who want to use meditation to center themselves and focus their intent during the use of CRT or PRT. This particular meditation aims to quiet the mind while directing us towards remaining California Sober. It can also help a new practitioner of the California Sober methods start to see the shape of what that version of themselves might look like. MRT is a customizable form of meditation that eases the beginner into meditation while allowing the seasoned practitioner room to expand.

The first thing to do is to get comfortable. If you are going to add one of the other Remediation Therapies, the time for that is now. Once you are ready, it is time to find a comfortable and quiet place to relax. What that means is subjective and up to you. Many people sit cross legged on a pillow on the floor while others use a chair or couch. I've found that lying flat on my back helps me to perform the techniques necessary to truly have an enlightened experience, without the burdens of posture and physical feelings invading my consciousness. That said, I will warn you of the dangers of this position in advance. More than once I have found myself losing time and drifting off to other worlds while meditating lying down. It's very easy to blur the line between Nirvana and naptime. While this isn't a bad thing when you have the time, if you are meditating lying down you may want to set a timer or an alarm.

Once we have found our comfort, we close our eyes and begin

our meditation with cyclic breathing. This begins our grounding process, calming our minds and centering ourselves as we settle into our meditation. Inhale smoothly through your nose until your lungs feel completely full. When they are at capacity, take one quick sharp breath, expanding the lungs a little bit more than you thought possible. Hold that last breath for 6 seconds and then slowly exhale through slightly puckered lips (as if you're whistling or playing a flute but without making sound) for six seconds. Repeat this breathing pattern for five minutes. During this time, you should scan your body and mind for irregularities. Notice any emotional or physical pains that present themselves. Never judge them. Just realize that they are there and coexist with them.

Once you have finished your cyclic breathing it is time to go deeper. Keeping our eyes closed, feel the heaviness of your arms, and release that heaviness to the ground. If your shoulders are lifted, let them go as well. If you are sitting back or lying flat, release all of your muscles to the ground. Feel the pull of gravity on your body and limbs and allow it to be. Next, let go of your facial expression. Feel the eyebrows bunched in the center and let them go. Feel the nose and cheeks lifting towards that same bridge and let them drop. Release the muscles in your temples. Finally, I want you to let go of your eyes. When done properly, they may begin to roll and wander about. When you feel your thoughts grabbing them back or resuming control of your facial muscles, as thoughts often do, just let it all go again. With some practice, this facial relaxation becomes second nature and also helps when you can't fall asleep.

Now that you are fully relaxed it is time to relax your mind. To do this we are going to take a break from thought, as we have come to understand it. We may wonder what thoughts might have looked like before language evolved. We may even wonder how animals think. The words we usually form our thoughts with will, maybe for the first time, not be present while we are conscious. To achieve singularity of attention, many meditations use a mantra, the most famous to the non-practitioner being *OM*. If you learn a concentration-based meditation such as Transcendental Meditation, you are given a mantra by your teacher. Some meditation disciplines let you choose your own and other types of meditation use breathing as their focal point. Feel free to use whatever works for you. Personally, I find all of them to be distracting and so I had little choice but to create my own.

Instead of imagining a sound like *OM* or a word or phrase, my hope was to clear my mind of these and other distractions, that I might allow it to float to wherever it may go and to give it a break, other than sleep, from its ever-constant calculating. The mind spends all of its time figuring out and wondering. The meditation I use, Tacita Cogitation Meditation (TCM), sets out to give that mind a break and lead it to clarity through wordless thought. Ideas will begin to form and take shape in your mind. You will be fully conscious (until you are finished, or perhaps fall asleep) but most of us will be experiencing wordless thoughts for the first time since before we learned the meaning of our first word.

I imagine a sound or, maybe more fitting, a noise in my mind. The noise sounds like a combination of the drone from a didgeridoo and the unintelligible conversation of a large crowd. Once we start the sound, it continues without our needing to put any thought into it. We simply kickstart the sounds of the crowd by imagining it and it perpetuates from there. The fluctuations this sound randomly presents allow for nothing to really focus on, and so it fades into the background of our headspace. We don't control it. We don't focus on it. It's like background music, running forever until we barely notice it is there. If word driven thoughts begin to disrupt our session and begin to take hold, we simply find that crowd of voices, that didgeridoo drone, and let the words fall into the background of the crowd's conversations. This is where things get interesting.

At some point between cyclic breathing and now, usually after letting go of my facial expressions and the muscles that hold onto my eyes, I begin to experience a strange sensation. It usually starts at the inward dip in the nasal bone where it meets the frontal bone or, pardon the expression, right between the eyes. From there the feeling spreads outward, although it has been known to form independently where the Maxilla bones meet the Zygomatic (the top of the cheeks near the center of the eye), until the feeling takes over my entire skull. I can only describe it as the feeling of my skin slowly loosening and lifting away as my consciousness separates from my physical self.

The veil that lies over the mind's eye becomes more translucent as the meditation progresses. Look hard at the darkness and you will see. At first, we may notice colors or shapes with light and dark areas that seem to blend well with each other. The entire area, at least for a moment, has equal amounts of fluctuating dark and light, almost like a smoother and sometimes colorful version of the static on an old television that was receiving no signal. Eventually the darkness and light begin to separate and what used to be just patterns start to take shape. Solid lines start to emerge, and objects may appear. Try not to think about them, just let them be. Standard concentration is the enemy of this state and will cause you to resurface if you let it. Eventually these objects become realistic, and you begin to dream. You're not asleep. You are simply experiencing your thoughts without the three factors you have become accustomed to.

Most of us think in dialog that is set to the primary language and, sometimes secondary languages that we understand. We also tend to direct that dialog toward the outcome we want rather than listening to what it is trying to say. Inner arguments are a common way of working out a problem and finding the best course of action, whether we prefer to listen to the angel or devil on our shoulder in the end is almost irrelevant. Both are us. Without the first factor of language, we are unable to use the second factor of directing or steering those thoughts toward a desired outcome. The third factor we are unable to experience, because without the others it has no use, is rationalization. Without words we cannot argue our point or rationalize our choices. This leads us to thoughts that are pure. Silent thoughts.

Through Tacita Cogitation Meditation, or silent thought meditation, we are allowing ourselves to experience our mind without any type of judgement, neither inward nor outward, tangible, or perceived. Here we no longer feel the need to make decisions. We simply exist, and that is enough for us. In this place, we are whole. The mind is quiet and relaxed, as it is when we sleep. We try to keep ourselves in this blissful state for at least 15 minutes, the whole process taking about 20 from start to finish. We can remain here longer if we feel we need extra time, but 20 minutes usually works its magic. When we allow ourselves 20 minutes twice a day for meditation, the results are a quieter mind that can be calmed when needed, less craving for harmful substances, and less of the traits we are hoping to rid ourselves of.

When it comes time to end our meditation, one can simply allow themselves to awaken, although we may find it less harsh to ease back into consciousness than to jump up and run. We hear the sounds of the room, or of nature, and smell the scents in the air. We may move our fingers and arms, touch the ground, or bring our mind back to any of the senses before opening our eyes to the physical world. This is similar to when we wake from a dream. It is more acceptable to us to slowly come out of a dream than to be startled awake, and so transition yourself as you see fit.

CRT and PRT can be used alone, together, or alternating, though I recommend using one at a time until you are used to the effects of each. Either can be used with MRT at any time. While CRT, PRT, and MRT are great for immediate relief of many conditions, the results are still temporary at this stage. Other California Sober methods are needed to reinforce this new way of thinking in order to open your mind to a new way of looking at your problems. Simply switching out your SOC for one of these Remediation Therapies is a short-term solution to a long-term problem. The next steps are essential to achieving the Golden State of Mind.

Phase 2 – Meetings and talk therapy.

Once you have found temporary relief through one or more of the remediation therapies, it is time to find someone to talk to. Many who switch to California Sober from *traditional* forms of recovery do so because they have either had limited success with abstinence from any and all mind-altering substances, or due to the fact that they have tried one or more of the California Sober methods and found them to be of more use than asceticism. These crossover CSs usually come to me with their own version of the same story. They were in one of the Anonymous programs, following the steps and remaining free of their SOC, when they openly shared about using cannabis for pain and anxiety, or using classic psychedelics for help in having the spiritual awakening that the steps require. When they shared this information openly and honestly, they were told by their sponsor that they needed to go to a rehabilitation facility and that that sponsor would no longer help them until they were back on a path to abstinence.

For those in Narcotics Anonymous I can almost see their

misguided logic, due to the false ideas circulated by the government of the late 1960s. For those in A.A. it simply goes against the beliefs of their founder and the cause of his sobriety. In turn, N.A. is built upon Bill W.'s foundation, which makes this notion hypocritical for them as well. Both systems expect the practitioner to have Bill's spiritual awakening, which he had due to the use of psychedelics and that he reinforced later in life through the use of LSD, and yet they shun anyone who follows in W.'s footsteps, but I digress.

What those who come to California Sober from the Anonymous groups long for is the comradery and support they get from the meetings those groups hold regularly. When they find out that California Sober meetings are similar to the meetings they attended in their former group, and often run by these crossover members, their reaction is always the same. *Where can I find one?* Meetings are popping up in every major city (and even in other countries). If you can't find one just yet, and you know of one person (other than yourself) who is interested, you can start your own California Sober meeting by using the format presented later in this book. If you already attend some form of one on one or group therapy, that will give you the foundation you need to follow the program until you find a meeting near you.

Phase 3 – Experience Therapy

Psychedelic Experience Therapy (PET)

The most effective method of relieving addiction, depression (including Major Depressive Disorder), anxiety, PTSD, OCD, and other conditions of the mind, is Psychedelic Experience Therapy or PET. No other treatment to date outperforms PET when it comes to Alcohol and Substance Use Disorders, according to almost a century of research, and it works on other conditions of the mind where the usual medications for those conditions fall short. PET therapy (when done the California Sober way) is as close to a cure as is known to the medical community thus far.

PET works by generating new neural pathways that circumvent old patterns of thought and behavior, thus rewiring the brain to create your most desired version of yourself. The best part is that it only changes the part of you that you wish to change. You will not simply become someone else; you will become your best self. This is due to the fact that the thoughts and feelings that guide the neural pathways are yours, from deep within. You know what it is you want to change; PET simply facilitates that change as opposed to making the same mistakes and feeling the same regrets over and over.

During PET, you will embark on a journey through your subconscious that is pure and true, uninhibited by what you have been told over and over about yourself, and without the barriers you have built in your mind as a result of life's hardships. You may discover enhanced self-compassion, reducing or erasing the judgement that you so often put on yourself. You will be able to clearly see the true path that you must take to your recovery, so clearly that you'll wonder why such a simple idea eluded you for so long. This is due to what is known as Ego Death.

While it may sound like the name of some extreme metal band, Ego Death is the temporary death of your Ego, or subjective self-identity. Don't worry. It doesn't really die. It just goes away long enough for you to realize it's flaws and discover a new way of being your truest self, the person you can be without the patterns of thought and behavior that are holding you back, allowing your subconscious to guide you to what you have always known deep down. You'll see yourself for who you are and discover who you want to become. When the ego returns, it returns with all of the new information that you realized during your psychedelic journey.

As the brain *rewires* itself, anxiety, depression, and other conditions of the mind can become a thing of the past, as does your desire to use harmful and addictive substances that have become a way of life, whether due to self-medicating or just an experimental phase that took on a life of its own. As you look at the circle of behavior that you were sure you would be stuck in forever, you will see a distinct exit that has always existed. You will quickly realize that you were never really stuck at all. The off-ramp was simply hidden from view. As if with new eyes and a freshly rebooted mind, the path to recovery from whatever it is that ails you will appear so blindingly bright that it cannot be missed.

What PET does for people has been said to be like several years of therapy in a single session. The results last for up to a year from a single dose, with the highest rates of success being in the first month. Many find that only one session is needed, while some individuals benefit most from quarterly, or sometimes monthly, PET sessions. Since the highest success rates are in the first month, monthly treatments can be beneficial until the desired results are achieved. After that, you can decide to use the treatment as little or as often as you feel it is necessary for your recovery.

In my 35 plus years of using classic psychedelics and guiding others on psychedelic journeys, I have witnessed transformations of the mind and spirit that have been life changing for both myself and other participants. When I began using them in the California Sober way, I no longer struggled to break my addictions, I simply had none. The California Sober plan has allowed me to watch that transformation occur in friends, loved ones, and everyone that has taken the advice laid out herein. There is almost no limit to the benefits that one can achieve with PET, and everyone that I have witnessed on the program has succeeded. The studies show the proven results on paper. I, and countless others, have witnessed them firsthand.

The first step Is to realize your dosage, as explained in Chapter 4. The first psychedelic experience is different for each individual, which is why a threshold dose is recommended before undergoing the full experience. While some can go all in during their first session as if they had done it before, others may need to familiarize themselves with the process. The threshold dose allows the individual to get their feet wet, if you will, so that a more pronounced experience is less foreign to them. The threshold dose allows you to get a glimpse into the psychedelic world before you undergo the full experience. After that, it's up to you to decide if you are ready for the full experience.

For those with experience with classic psychedelics, the full experience can be your starting point. The only difference between recreational use and therapeutic use is intent. You must go into PET with the intent of undergoing a change. It is necessary to focus your intent on changing the part of you that you no longer feel comfortable carrying around, prior to taking your psychedelic. From there, the psychedelic will take you where you need to go. Never fight it. Trust the psychedelic to take you on the journey you most need in order to recover. Relax and go with the flow. It's your mind. There is nothing to fear, other than fear itself.

In a safe space, under the supervision of a California Sober Mentor, trained psychedelic therapist or, if you have a great deal of psychedelic experience, a trusted and psychedelically aware friend, or friends, it is time to undergo your California Sober Psychedelic Experience Therapy (PET) when you feel you are ready to start the process of long-term change. This works for addiction, be it to alcohol or another harmful substance, anxiety, depression, OCD, PTSD, major depression, and other conditions of the mind.

Studies show that dosages of classic psychedelics, unlike the dosages of many medications, are not subject to body weight. This means that the threshold dose (or even the full experience dose) is about the same for everyone. This makes it easy to find your threshold dose and your full experience dose. What can differ is one's comfort zone. This is why it is important to always start with a threshold dose, rather than going all in on a full experience, if you have no prior experience with psychedelics.

The Importance of intent

Intent is the only way that any of this program works. I can't stress this fact enough and so I will repeat it regularly. Every aspect of the California Sober method of recovery starts with, and can only continue to work through, the focused intent to relieve the burden of whatever it is that ails you. One will not likely find relief from addiction by simply ingesting cannabis, classic psychedelics, or any other magical substance. I say not likely because these substances have the power to open your eyes to things that you may have overlooked in the past. You may, deep down inside, already have the intention to stop using your SOC or to do the work necessary to relieve another condition of the mind. Psychedelic therapy may bring that intention into your consciousness. That said, focused intent is the key to all of the California Sober methods so let's talk about what it is and how it works.

Enlightenment is the true goal of these methods. To become enlightened, one must expand one's mind beyond their current situation in order to manifest a new reality. It has been said that small minds talk about people, average minds discuss events, and that great minds intellectualize ideas. Small minds prefer to deal in the world of gossip, focusing on the deeds of others like a neighbor or celebrity, while average minds tend to involve themselves in current events and whatever is in the news. Great minds tend to look for solutions and involve themselves in the greater good. To become enlightened, one must look beyond the day to day and find their way to bringing their ideas into reality.

There is a concept that claims that the Universe is on your side and that your thoughts and intentions can alter your reality. The idea is that the Universe responds to your wants, needs, and desires if you focus your intent on positive outcomes and show gratitude on a daily basis. If you set clear intentions and focus on positivity, the Universe aligns with your intentions to fulfill your dreams. If you work towards positive ambitions, the Universe will deliver you the rewards. All you need to do is express gratitude and focus on these goals daily in order to transform the world around you. Still, there's always a catch or two.

First and foremost, you have to truly believe that it works in order to see results. You can't just say some magic words, rub a lamp, and get 3 wishes. This Universal power is not in the business of convincing you that it is real and so testing it, without undeniably believing that this transformation of reality will happen, is a lesson in futility. It's like when those of a secular nature say *if God is real than why doesn't he just show himself* when, in fact, a truly religious person believes that God shows himself in every aspect of every moment of our existence. It is belief itself that transforms that person's reality. This may either cause the religious to see God in things that are natural or open the eyes of the religious to the power of their God. The answer to that is subjective. If it truly works for the individual, the reality of how is irrelevant.

The second catch is the understanding that the Universe

knows your true path and will attempt to dissuade you from one that it knows will end in disastrous results. This is a nuance that makes many of us disbelievers. *If I focus my intent and positivity, why do I still not get what I want?* To some, it seems like an excuse for the Universe not delivering on its promise. It causes us to question whether or not this concept is a scam. The truth is that, whether or not this concept truly works, far too often our desires are not something that are good for us. Imagine an addict trying to conjure money for drugs, or someone trying to obtain great wealth without doing what needs to be done for that to happen. Far too often, our desires are not aligned with what we need to accomplish. Our intent needs to be both positive and in our best interests.

The third caveat is *be careful what you wish for, because it might come true.* I find this to be the truest of all statements. While we may have true intentions that we believe align with our best interests, we can be wrong. If we constantly focus on something (or someone) that isn't in our best interest, we beg and plead our case with all of our heart and the truest of intentions, eventually the Universe may give us what we ask for. As an example, let's say it's a person we think we wish to spend the rest of our lives with, even though they show little interest in our vision of the future. Then one day, as if by magic, that person seems to see us in a new light. They give us the attention that we desire and so we enter a relationship with them. Our dreams have come true.

At first, things are better than we could have ever imagined. Life is beautiful and all is well with the Universe. Three months in and you're having your first fight. The honeymoon period is over. As much as you try, because you are hopelessly in love, things get worse from there until you are living in a hell of your own creation. One of you is done while the other is not. Either way, the nightmare has just begun. You either have to live with the truth that the one you love doesn't reciprocate, or that the person you begged the universe to deliver is driving you mad. Either feeling is torture if you have any humanity.

Not knowing what you truly want is a terrible time to focus intent, be it on a job that you may later despise, a relationship that is not a match for you, or anything that you desired in the throes of passion, loneliness, or other desperation. Before you focus your intent, you need to think through all of the potential outcomes to find what you really want in the long term, versus what you want right now. Be careful what you wish for because odds are, if you put your focus and intent into it, it will come true. I've never focused my energy toward obtaining anything that I did not eventually end up getting. I haven't always enjoyed the outcome and, although I don't believe in regret, some of my granted wishes may have been better left as a fantasy.

When intent is focused on something as pure as changing our lives for the better, and when it is focused in such a way as to not cause any harm to others, that wish is almost surely granted. If we believe that we can overcome our addiction or mental condition, we can. Sometimes we are just stuck in the rut that our problem has dug beneath our feet. Psychedelics can show us a path to find our way out of that rut and get back on level ground. The California Sober method of recovery helps us to focus that pure intent on getting the life that we need, that we deserve, as long as we have true intentions of making that change. We can't delete who we were and start over, we can only become who we were meant to be.

Pull Yourselves Together.

When using the CRT, PRT, and PET treatments, one is not trying to get rid of any version of themselves. No matter who you have been in the past, and as much as you may detest that version of yourself, there is always something that that self has taught you, a spark of wisdom that comes from each struggle. Regret is a wasted point of view. There is no going back and whatever happened in the past has brought you to this place and time. Without those experiences you wouldn't be the person you are going to be tomorrow. The true goal is to visit and assess each self that has ever existed, incorporating the best parts of each of those realities into the current version of oneself, while also learning from the lessons that the worst parts of each of our former selves has taught us.

My favorite self is my child self. The pure thoughts he had were what I try to live by each day, but he couldn't have survived this world without the versions that came later. While I try to embrace the way my child mind saw the world, holding onto as much as I can from his point of view, I realize that my childish view of the world we live in is only a fantasy unless the majority of the planet can find their way to true peace. My teenage self learned how to navigate the underworld and my adult self learned to make his way through societal demands. By incorporating all three, I can be the peace loving, empathetic, lover of all of the creatures of the Universe while holding on to the cynical me in order to remind myself of the dangers of the world, keeping anger for when I'm backed into a corner, and wrath only for when it is necessary to find my way out of that place.

When we take all of the variants of ourselves into account, we can realize the best and most peaceful scenario for all situations. Without a grain of cynicism, we are but fools being played by the con artists and narcissists of the world. Without hope we are doomed to failure. Without anger we are easily used but without love we are hopelessly alone. Some see the glass as half empty, others as half full. I choose to see the glass as a vessel that can be filled and emptied at will, ultimately depending on your view of the circumstance. You must open your eyes and see the lies in order for the truth to reveal itself and reign supreme.

Phase 4 – Work on yourself

Now that we have found a way to refrain from our SOCs through California Sober Remediation Therapies, meetings, and Psychedelic Experience Therapy our path has become somewhat defined. There are patches where we can still become lost in the weeds if we are not careful. Since intention is the key driving factor for all of the above-mentioned phases, intention is what we need to harness in order to actualize our will. The California Sober path goals are a great starting point, leading to the 13 trails of California Sober that one can follow to reach the Golden State of Mind. Keeping our paths clear is the best way to never find ourselves lost again.

The California Sober Goals – A Guide to the New You

Goal 1 – Change your mind.

Through California Sober Remediation Therapy (CSRT) we strive to outsmart our addiction or condition of the mind by meditating and/or ingesting one or more natural and non-addictive CSRT treatments. By doing this, we change our mind's original goal of seeking out our SOC to more productive and less harmful goals. We allow our CSRT to guide us to creativity and wellbeing as it removes our desire to use harmful substances and takes away our other ailments for the immediate future. In doing this, we find temporary sanity and we are safe, if only for the moment.

Goal 2 - Rewire your brain.

We use Psychedelic Experience Therapy (PET) to examine our issues and find the clearest path to our recovery, opening our minds to future possibilities. Through PET, we better understand who it is we are striving to be and see a clear path to the best version of ourselves, the version that we see, so that we may project to ourselves and to others the self that we know and love. We do this not to appease others, but because we truly want to be our best selves, and so we use PET to light our path to becoming and remaining California Sober.

Goal 3 – Destroy Your Programming

We have all been programmed since we were born. Ideas presented to children tend to stick without any question of their truth. By the time we begin to question anything we are teenagers, programmed with a wealth of lies and rumors that we simply accept as fact. For some it's blind faith, for others it can be political. Far too often, children are programmed to become hateful adults, never for a second doubting what they have been told about the group they despise without ever getting to know them. It is necessary to question everything you've ever known on the deepest level. It was Charles Dicken's who said *Take nothing for its looks; take everything on evidence. There is no better rule.* If someone tells me that the table is solid, I question first whether it is a table and then their perception of the table. *I don't believe in violence; I don't even believe in peace. I've opened the door, now my mind's been released.*[46] We must destroy our programming in order to

---

[46] Under the Sun – Terrence Buttler 1972

open our minds.

Goal 4 – Center the mind.

Through daily breathing exercises and meditation, we attain focus and direction, calming our mind and spirit so that we may continue on our path with ease. This daily ritual assists in the rewiring process and strengthens our will so that we may achieve our long-term goal of maintaining California Sobriety and mental wellbeing. As we meditate, we achieve inner peace as well as outward empathy for those struggling with their own issues. We make a conscious attempt to help those around us, as doing so makes us better versions of ourselves.

Goal 5. - Strengthen the Self

We take pride in our physical wellbeing through movement because stretching and exercise elevate mood by releasing natural endorphins, counteracting sedentary lifestyles that lead to feelings of depression. We know that a strong body helps create a strong mind, and that stretching and exercise also help us to stay focused on our goal of remaining California Sober. We strive to do just a little more each day in order to strengthen our mind and body so that we may handle whatever life throws at us.

Goal 6 – We are what we ingest, so make it worth it.

As with our CSRT and PET, we strive to put only natural substances into our bodies. We do this because eating natural foods provides the mind and body with the nutrients it needs to strengthen our recovery and attain peace of mind. We do our best to avoid processed foods that leave toxins in our bodies, as they cause low moods that may trigger our symptoms. While no one is perfect, and sometimes life causes us to eat what's fast and easy, we realize that eating mostly natural foods helps us to limit these issues. We know that a healthy body and mind are necessary for us to focus on our long-term goal of remaining California Sober.

Goal 7 – This Instant Karma's gonna get you.

We strive to be the best version of ourselves by following the Golden Rule and treating others as we wish to be treated. We do this not only through our actions, but through our intent. Positive actions only work through positive intentions and, while faking it until we make it may be a good starting point from which our truest intentions begin to be forged, only through desire to be our best selves will we find true peace. We help others as we wish to be helped ourselves and always try to do what we feel is the right thing to do in each situation. By paying it forward with pure intentions we know that we will find the peace we need to remain California Sober.

Goal 8 - Spread the wealth (of knowledge).

While we have found our way to the Golden State of Mind through our California Sobriety, we realize that others are not so lucky and are in dire need of our help. Therefore, we make a point of reaching out to those struggling with their own issues in an attempt to show them the way. We don't preach, as each person's journey is their own, but we tell anyone who will listen the ways in which California Sober has helped us to find true freedom and peace of mind. We do this because we have been where they are. We empathize with them and wish to help them to end their struggle. Through remaining

California Sober and helping others to find the same peace, we can finally reach the Golden State of Mind.

Goal 9 - Believe in yourself, 'cause no one else is true.

It is simple, and often compelling, to follow others that we think may have all of the answers. This can lead to following those who don't share our vision or those that don't have our best interests at heart. As much as we want these solutions to be real, many who attempt to *guide* us have ulterior motives that only serve to sway us from what we know is the true path. California Sober methods help guide us to find our truth, a truth that those who wish to harm us will try to dissuade us from. By believing in yourself, you will find what truly works for you. *Don't let those empty people try and interfere with your mind. Just live your life and leave them all behind.*[47]

The Golden State of Mind

By working to meet our daily goals, and through CSRT and PET, we strive to achieve the Golden State of Mind. The Golden State of Mind is a feeling of peace and happiness that is with us when we wake each day. As long as we follow our true path, it remains with us. That's not to say that life will not have struggles, just that we will face each trial with an open mind and a confidence that comes from knowing that we will prevail. On our California Sober path, we find that we can see which obstacles are insignificant while finding new ways to deal with the ones that remain in our way. We can accept where we are in our journey, changing direction whenever something in our lives no longer promotes our mental wellbeing. We are the masters of our own reality.

---

[47] Under the sun – Terrence Butler – Vol.4 1972

This realization is the Golden State of Mind

Waiting for the Other Shoe to Drop

One of the biggest problems with being newly in control of your life is that good things start happening to you. It is a strange and, believe it or not, often unwelcome feeling for those who have been living with addiction for a long period of time. Those of us who are newly experiencing freedom from our addiction or other issues are so used to bad things being just around the corner that it can be unnerving when too much time passes between bouts of destruction. It's normal to feel that way when you have lived a life that has consisted of one disaster after another.

Time after time, whenever our lives found a way to reconcile themselves, whenever we got our acts together for a brief moment, another fuck up came to pass. In the course of an addict's life, only so much time can pass before something horrible happens again. It always seems as if whenever things start to go really well, a world of shit is waiting for us, and not far down the road. We finally paid the registration on the car and the alternator went, or we finally earned back the trust of a loved one only for them to discover something we had done in the past, causing them to give up on us once more. I've had many abusers of substance tell me that they have the addict's curse. *When things are going too good for too long, watch out. Something bad is about to happen.* The better things have been, and the longer they've been that way, the worse the problem is going to be.

While that feeling of impending doom is something that is hard to shake, there comes a time when you have to let it go. It's almost comforting, for those of us who have lived through addiction and conditions of the mind, to prepare for the worst whenever things start to go our way. It's a survival instinct brought on by years of allowing our lives to be a madhouse of recklessness and destructive behavior. While bad things can always happen, when we practice one or more of the California Sober methods, our new lives tend to limit the amount of turmoil that we have to deal with. Life doesn't have to be a roller coaster if we don't want it to be.

Through the California Sober method of recovery your life will begin to take new shape. Problems that were usually caused by your addiction will no longer come to pass, and the issues your addiction has already caused will be easier to remedy. Although they may be skeptical at first, loved ones will begin to see you in a new light. You'll be more present in the moment, increasing the level at which people in your life trust and respect you. People will be surprised at the best version of you, one that they can now clearly see. Still, those that never wanted you to succeed will never believe that you have.

When I was using my SOC, those that wanted me to keep them company in their addiction told me that there was no way that I could stop using. When I turned my life around with the California Sober method, those who truly loved me were astonished and proud of who I had become. Others who had looked at me with disappointment and disgust became envious of my new life, going so far as to accuse me of pulling off some kind of con and somehow faking my prosperity. Some said I was just on a lucky streak, while others thought I was simply lying about my lack of substance abuse and somehow scamming my good fortune.

To those who embraced the new me, I gave respect and held them close. To those who chose the dark path of waiting for my California Sober ways to fail, I simply put them aside to be revisited when they could come to terms with their own issues with my newfound lifestyle. Not everyone can understand how one overcomes something that not many survive. For those people, I will allow them their time to heal.

For the ones that never had my best interest at heart, I put them out of my mind completely. If they ever genuinely come around, I'll welcome them with open arms. If they never do, I won't waste my time trying to prove myself. My peace is all that I can offer, to myself and to others.

When you reach the Golden State of Mind you realize that you can only exist in a world of positivity. Those who present only negativity are an anchor that will drag you down into a sea of madness. By surrounding yourself with people who have a positive view of your path, you reinforce your way to California Sobriety and have the ability to bring others the same peace. Those in your support will quickly reveal themselves, and more will come when they realize your truth is a reality. Before long, everyone who has your best interest at heart will find their way to embracing this best version of you. The California Sober you.

Don't Break the Oath

We California Sobers realize that through meeting with other like-minded individuals in a safe setting to discuss our issues, recount our successes, and explain where we come from, we can reenforce our beliefs and achieve our common goal of remaining abstinent from the substance(s) that have destroyed some part of us. We acknowledge that talking with others who share in our California Sobriety, and bringing this message to others who wish to attain the same peace of mind, will help to enlighten us, and guide us on our journey.

We acknowledge that each journey is its own, and that it is as unique as the individual following the path. There is no one-size-fits-all path, and each individual must find what works best for them, as long as it leads to them refraining from their Substance of Choice. We don't judge others for doing what works for them, even if it doesn't work for us. We offer, to anyone who will listen, what it is about California Sober that works for us, ourselves, that we may help them to find their true path to recovery, and to peace of mind.

Chapter 6 - The 13 Trails of the California Sober Method of
Recovery

Recovery is about healing both the body and the mind. We
need to make both strong so that we may endure all of life's
challenges. In the same way that we make our physical selves
strong through exercise, so must we exercise our mind.
Doing the same exercise routine every day forever can result
in a stall in progress, due to the body getting used to the
program. At that point, one must change the exercise routine
frequently in order to maximize their gains. The body
requires a shock to the system, something different, in order
to grow. The same is true for the mind.

In order to help the mind expand and grow, one must exercise
it in different ways by learning new concepts and creating
new thought patterns. Many people hit a point in life where
they subscribe to a certain set of beliefs that they will never
question or stray from. They refuse to open their minds to
the possibility that their ideas may be wrong, outdated, or just
need an update. This causes the mind to become stagnant
and limits that individual's growth. Through CRT, PRT, and
PET, we discover new parts of ourselves, new ideas, and a new
outlook towards the ideas we currently hold true. In addition
to the new neural pathways that these therapies create, new

thought patterns help expand the mind and consciousness, keeping that mind young, healthy, and strong.

The 13 paths of California Sober are designed to exercise the body, the mind, and our consciousness, elevating us to a higher level of thinking. These paths keep the mind from becoming stagnant, lazy, or otherwise closed, as well as keeping the physical-self strong, and ready for whatever this world throws our way. By following these paths, we hope to become the best version of ourselves, the truest self that we wish to present to the world, the us that we believe in and are proud of. Changing our behavior is as simple as opening our minds to the reality that we can. Once there, the possibilities are endless.

Imagine a grand garden surrounded by an endless forest. There are 13 trailheads that all ultimately lead to the same place, a place where you exist in your most perfect state, yet each takes you through different areas of that realm. You can enter through any of the trails, yet all must be cleared for you to be able to wander about at your own discretion. In order to be free to wander through all of these blissful micro-environments, thus creating your perfect world, you need to remove any obstacles in your path that aren't easily circumvented. Once all of the trails have been cleared, you will have free reign over your ultimate nirvana.

Time can cause these trails to become overgrown, and obstacles can fall in the way, making these trails harder and harder to follow. Walking these paths regularly makes them easy to maintain, while staying away from any of them for too long will allow them to return to an almost impassable state. One by one you must revisit each trail, clearing them of debris from time to time. If you do so often enough, your footsteps alone ensure that nothing grows in the way. If an obstacle falls across the path, it can be easily removed, stepped over, or walked around. That is, as long as the trail has been maintained and new obstacles aren't piling up, as they are dealt with as soon as they appear.

The longer you go without walking these paths, the harder it becomes to move freely from place to place in your paradise. For this reason, you must consciously incorporate the maintenance of these paths into your everyday existence, making it an easy, almost thought-free, part of your daily ritual. As long as you re-visit these trails on a regular basis, it is easy to take yourself anywhere you want to go. Using the tools that California Sober gives us, we make sure these paths are in perfect working order so that we may walk them at will, whenever it is that we choose to.

The Paths

1 - Mindfulness of the present - don't stray too far

As we succumb to the monotony of the day to day, distractions can help us to break the cycle of repetitive behaviors. We turn to our electronic devices more than ever to overcome the boredom of repetitive tasks. Television, social media, online games and apps, and all of the various forms of communication, such as texts and email, all help us to relieve boredom and take a break from the tasks of the day. These distractions can be a blessing when sitting in a waiting room (I remember what it was like before them, thumbing through magazines I wouldn't otherwise read if I was paid to), on line at a bank or supermarket, or while waiting for someone. The problem is that we become so used to these distractions that we forget to put them down and they begin to take us away from what really matters, being *in the moment*.

It is important to be *in the moment* as much as possible, but what does it mean to truly be *in the moment*? Let's explore. On an average weekday, our alarms go off and we wake up.

We rush through the routine of self-maintenance tasks like eating breakfast, showering, brushing our teeth, getting dressed, and getting out the door to school, work, or whatever our daily lives hold for us. We then carry out our normal processes of the day in a check it off the list, matter of fact kind of way, until we reach the goal of getting back to our comfort zone, home. Finally, we can do the things we actually like to do for the remaining few hours (if any) that exist between finishing the tasks we set out to accomplish and the end of our wakeful daily experience. Rinse, sleep, repeat.

It's easy to let a thought whisk us away to a paradise of our own invention. Daydreams are the salvation to which we can wander at any given moment, escaping the mundane drudgery of our work or studies, but when our minds enact this failsafe in the opposite of situations the trouble begins. We lose ourselves in the worries of self-prophesized hardships and pending disappointments instead of experiencing what is actually going on right in front of us. When we are at a romantic dinner, or our kids are having one of those once in a lifetime precious moments, we can become so lost in the mental organization of future events that have yet to unfold that we often miss what's happening in front of us, to us, in the now. That is not being in the moment. When your lover confides their most intimate of secrets, or your daughter reveals her first love, and you awaken to *Are you even listening to me?* It can be more than embarrassing; it can leave a mark.

The same distraction occurs, and maybe even more so, with the use of our handheld devices and social media. It has gotten to the point that two people can be in the same room, on the same couch, watching the same movie together, and neither shares the experience with the other. Parties are often degraded to groups of zombies, lost in their digital lives, texting friends from across the room rather than sharing an intimate conversation. Even joking about others would be more of a bonding experience when whispered in the ear of someone you connect with, sharing a laugh, than the cold and easily forgotten text version of the same, followed by a lifeless lol.

We can walk a busy street in an exciting city, never bothering to notice that life is exploding with color in our peripheral vision while we focus sharply on the screen at the end of our arms. Then, we get home and hear the stories of an amazing performance in a park, or a robbery at a convenience store, only to realize that we walked right past both events as they transpired, never knowing that a single thing had occurred mere meters from our path. At the same time, we walked right past a friend we hadn't seen in ages, neither of us ever noticing that the other existed. It's amazing that people even find other people anymore. I suppose that they do only due to the fact that there's an app for that too.

With all of life's distractions, it is all too easy to get lost in what is going on in the external life you have created as a means of supporting the life inside your personal bubble. Work becomes your life, while the life you have been working for takes a back seat. Sentimental memory-creating moments are pushed aside to make room for *important* meetings and overtime. *There'll be time for that later*, you assure yourself. Then one day you find ten years have got behind you. What you missed is irreplaceable. What you've done, forgettable.

To be truly present in the moment is to let go of all of the thoughts that don't pertain to what is going on right here, and right now. There is a time and a place for our daydreams, our devices, our forgettable pastimes. When we are engaged in life, this is not that time. Now more than ever, a conscious effort has to be put into separating the wonder of the information technology that has the potential to catapult us to greatness from the day-to-day experiences of our universe, and all of its remarkable species that are here for us to marvel at with such wonder. We need to experience our lives, not just survive them while distracting ourselves from the sad cycle of repetition that they can become when we no longer seek new adventures.

The key to being mindful of the present is to push away all of the distractions that we allow ourselves in order to make the boring tolerable. While this can sound much easier than it is, it is also much easier than it sounds. Being used to these distractions, it takes real effort to change our behavior but, once you've made the conscious decision to do so, it's as simple as enjoying life. When you feel your thought's taking you away from what's going on in the here and now, instead of wandering into a daydream or reaching for your phone, focus on the five senses. They are our true perception of the moment. Let me give you an example.

I am currently watching a tortoise eat a red pepper in my backyard. The sun is warming the skin of my arms, face, and chest. A subtle breeze keeps me from feeling too hot as I watch a butterfly float and flutter across my sightline. The breeze shakes the flowers gently in the garden. The scent of a nearby barbeque makes me realize that it is lunchtime. As my thoughts begin to wander to what I want for lunch, I bring them back to what's going on around me. I hear an airplane in the distance, while the sound of cars on the busy street in front of my house creates a rhythm like that of waves crashing on the beach.

A cloud blocks the sun, and my skin feels cold as another plane bisects the sky above my head. A ghetto bird, those fun police and news helicopters, circles my neighborhood as a crow caws at another that is flying over on my right side. The reality is better than full HD 5.1 surround sound. As the tortoise finishes her pepper, the wind blows the scent of lavender from my garden towards my nostrils, cooling my skin and tickling the hairs on my arm in the same process. I can almost taste the California winter air. I am present in this moment, even as I write these words. I am allowing myself to experience this moment and revel in its glory. I have not a care in the world, and if one appears I simply concentrate on my five senses and allow that care to fade into the background.

My present thoughts about these senses, the words you read here, are welcomed as they are part of the moment I am experiencing. The feeling of the keys as my fingers hammer down upon them is also a welcomed aspect. What is not allowed are any thoughts and ideas that have nothing to do with this moment. The sound of my dog's tag on her collar is soothing. Thoughts about filing my taxes and having to clean the garage are uninvited guests that will be treated as such and ushered to the door. If one of my daughters were to come out and start dancing around the yard, as they often do, I might stop writing to immerse myself in that experience, or I may let it play out in the background of my moment, which I am having with you. I decide what I want to focus on in the present. As long as I am present, that is all that matters for now. How I prioritize that is decided by who I am and who I want to be.

As we practice mindful presence more, we become able to incorporate it into our everyday existence and learn to prioritize what it is, in the moment, that we should be mindful of. On a walk to get some lunch in the afternoon, we may be tempted to multi-task, making the walk more productive. We can catch up on emails and return phone calls in an attempt to allow ourselves more time to be in the moment later on, at the end of our day, but far too often this is a lie we tell ourselves and we end up using the time we freed up to further catch up on things that aren't in our moment.

It's up to you to decide when to be in the moment, and which moments are most important to be present in. That walk that you used to multitask may have better served your quality of existence if you saw the street performer on the corner across the road, or stopped at that bridge and listened to the birds singing their songs while watching the water dance over the rocks and disappear under the bridge. You may have gotten more out of seeing children at play, or a dog chasing a frisbee in the park, than you did deleting the spam email that said you'd inherited 10 million from a Saudi Arabian prince. Only you can make these calls.

The moments you will surely regret missing are ones involving your loved ones, be they blood relation or otherwise. Don't miss out on the moments that make life worth living. Try to listen when someone you hold dear has something to say. It may be just a dumb thought or a life changing epiphany, but either can hold a wealth of importance that you may have missed otherwise. Try to find a second to feel the sun on your face, and to take in the beauty of all that is natural in the world. Really taste that meal, instead of shoveling it down in an attempt to fill the void in your belly in order to get back to what you were doing. See what is going on around you instead of treating your commute like a hallway you can't wait to get to the other end of. Smell the flowers, or a campfire, or barbeque, or the Chinese food place down the street.

The trick is to allow your autopilot to take over and drift off to LaLa land when you are doing mundane tasks that you don't enjoy, being present in the moment at the times that are important, those that will bring memories that you cherish forever, or when there is beauty to be discovered and relished. Ultimately, it's up to you to decide which is which. I suppose the key to life would be to reduce the number of tasks in our lives that we consider unpleasant, saving daydreams and looks out the window for when we have to do the dishes or mow the lawn, and increase the time spent doing things that make us smile, laugh, and love. One might also suggest that we can train the brain to enjoy any task by teleporting our minds to the times we enjoy if we truly put our minds to it.

Be mindful, and be in the moment that makes you happiest, wherever life puts your physical being at the present moment, but don't forget to wake up when it's time to share intellect, emotion, and general goofiness with the ones that you love, and to take in the natural wonder of the universe we share with the other life forms. Take time to experience your connection to that energy and focus it on the things that make you smile. Connect with your senses as more than just tools to navigate the day, but as sources of pleasure to let you experience that day, rather than missing it by just barreling through.

2- Self Love

You are the most important person in your universe. Without you, your world would cease to exist. In order to make that universe prosper, you have to first realize that there is no one that is more in need of your love than yourself (unless you have kids, in which case you are a close second). If you don't meet your own needs, both physical and those necessary for happiness and peace of mind, you can't expect anyone else to, and relying on anyone to meet those needs for you is a recipe for self-destruction. Place that burden on another and you become an anchor that weighs them down while simultaneously making yourself fully dependent on that person or people. The only way to find true happiness is to relinquish the need for anyone else to make you happy.

You have to put yourself above all others in order to coexist. While this may all seem selfish and narcissistic, the opposite is true. I'm not telling you to put your wants and desires before someone else's happiness. I'm telling you that your needs should be met by you, rather than relying on others to fill in the gaps where you fall short. Until you can be truly happy with yourself and not *need* anyone, you will forever be unhappy. In addition, you will blame others for that unhappiness, never fully taking credit for your own misery. The truth is, there is only so much someone can do to keep your spirits lifted. Before long, anyone that you rely on for this purpose will become bored, resentful, or simply overwhelmed by the task. This is often how relationships, be they platonic or otherwise, end.

CRT, PRT, MRT, and PET can all help on your journey to finding the you that you love although, ultimately, you have to maintain that relationship. No one can truly love you until you love yourself. This starts with positive thinking about yourself, but that's not the end of it. You have to treat yourself well. Take care of your physical being through daily maintenance such as stretching and exercise. Take care of your world by taking pride in and caring for the things that bring you happiness, be that your relationships, your home and belongings, your career, or any other source of joy. Still, you have to take care of the one thing that can make or break your wellbeing, your mind.

Through breathing exercises, meditation, and positive thoughts, you can bring any mind to a state of bliss. Even if you have to force them at first, positive thoughts are the key to self-care. Try to see the positive in any situation that makes you want to feel negative. Find a gem of goodness in a bad situation. I've found that whenever I've tried to force my will upon the world in order to hold onto something I thought I needed, I eventually lost it. After a mourning period, something new and better always presented itself. Like the old adage, when one door closes another opens. Usually, if you're living a California Sober life, the new door opens to something better than what was lost.

When a job I loved ended, a better job came after. When a love was lost, a truer love came around a little while later. In retrospect, the one that was lost was not worth holding on to.

As long as you keep a positive attitude and a true love of yourself, what comes after is always better than what comes before. Sometimes there are occasional situations in between that don't live up to what were before, tricking you into thinking that things are in a downward spiral. With enough time, the future can always outperform the past. Patience and positivity are all you need. This is why you must not rely solely on anything (other than yourself) for your happiness.

The world is fluid and change is the only constant. Characters will enter and leave your life on a regular basis. Some will stay longer than others and, with any luck, you'll find a few to transverse decades with. The better you take care of yourself, the more positive you allow yourself to be about yourself, the more like-minded people you will attract. Solitude should not be something you fear, it should be something you need from time to time in order to reflect on who you are and who it is you want to be. The one person that you will definitely spend time with from the day you are born until your last waking breath is you. Be good to that person and everything else is simply a bonus.

3- Self Responsibility

Taking responsibility for our own actions is something that often gets pushed aside when we are addicted to alcohol and other harmful substances. We tend to make excuses for our behavior even when, deep down, we know we are falling short on our commitments and doing things that we probably shouldn't be doing. We relinquish our responsibility to whatever person, circumstance, or universal power that we choose to think has gotten in the way of our otherwise perfect track record for not screwing things up (ha-ha). We blame our bosses, teachers, loved ones, even our God, luck, or the Universe.

We excuse these digressions with thoughts and proclamations like *it's not my fault* and *I couldn't help it* when in fact we honestly know we can do better. We blame our shortcomings on situational factors when these faults are truly caused by our own misbehavior and lack of presence. *My landlord is a dick* when we haven't paid our rent on time and have been served with a notice or *I didn't hear my alarm go off this morning* when we are once again late for work after partying well into the night are common cop-outs. I've even heard *God hates me* from a man whose health was continually failing due to his abuse of alcohol, pharmaceuticals, and cigarettes. The worst excuse you can make is *I'm a fuck up*. You're literally blaming yourself without taking responsibility, as if being a fuck up is genetic, or some cosmic force at work against you.

The problem with blaming anything and everything for our own deficiencies is that, by doing so, you rob yourself of the chance to fix the root cause. You can't make an alarm wake you from a substance induced coma, you can't force *God* to be nice to you, and you can't make your landlord want their money any less. By relinquishing your responsibilities, you give them a power greater than yourself, thus greater than anything you have the ability to respond to. You transform yourself into the perpetual victim, a weak and insignificant annoyance that life is constantly pushing around and bullying until your eventual demise. You create a life without hope.

Taking responsibility for your own actions is the first step in empowering yourself to make the changes necessary to better your situation, to better your life. Instead of claiming that you are powerless over the circumstances that have brought you to this point, you are proclaiming that you, and you alone, have the power to take back your life and become the best version of yourself. By admitting that your problems are caused by your own actions, you create a world in which you have the ability to change those actions and fix the problems that you have caused, thus making a nearly perfect future possible.

Once you have admitted that, by some action, reaction, or misdeed, you have caused the problems that you now face, you can begin to take steps to alter your behavior in order to limit the actions that cause said issues. You also show people that you know who the culprit is and are willing to accept responsibility and make an attempt to do better in the future. Once those you have wronged see that you are willing to accept the consequences of your actions, they are often more likely to forgive, and maybe even help you remove the obstacles in your path.

These pardons don't come too often, so empty apologies will not release you from these debts (and will likely make them worse). Taking responsibility means doing what needs to be done to rectify the situation not just through words, but by altering your behavior in the present and future. Truly owning your transgressions means believing that you will do your best to never let these things happen again. It's honestly owning your mistakes, not just claiming to in order to gain a second chance to fuck up again. Trust is not easily regained but, if you put in the work, those who love you will see the change for what it is.

Once you genuinely own up to all of your transgressions and make a faithful attempt to rectify the situations you have caused, you will already be a better version of yourself, one that you can be proud of even as you falter, as we all sometimes do. With time, taking responsibility will help you to make less of these types of mistakes, and you will find yourself in better circumstances as a result. Remember, only you have the power to change your life. California Sober can give you the tools and the natural remedies to facilitate this transformation, but only if the desire for true change is within you.

4- Let go (the power of positive thinking and discarding toxic people)

When we are in a good mood, when something positive

happens or things are just generally going well, we are elated. We associate these positive feelings with being up, elevated, or high on life. That's because the body rewards us for positive experiences with endorphins, among them endomorphin, a chemical made by our bodies that is similar to Morphine. Endorphin is a portmanteau (two words squished together) of endogenous (from within) and Morphine (a substance that activates the pleasure centers of the brain) that literally means as it says, the morphine within.

When things are not going so well, or when things in our life are downright shitty, we say we are down. This feeling can be caused by outside influences, chemical depression, or coming off of a high from ingested substances. It can also be caused by our bodies making less endorphins due to problems we are facing or some other real-world factor, or through a process where our bodies make an enzyme called monoamine oxidase A (or MOA-A) that breaks down key neurotransmitters, resulting in low endorphins, a chemical depression.

Our moods are regulated by chemistry. Many of us self-medicate in order to alter the chemistry of the brain, tricking it into being elated when outside circumstances don't promote those feelings or fixing a chemical problem within. We can also regulate these brain chemicals quite a bit by controlling the external inputs that our brain receives. In other words, we can boost our levels of happiness by reducing the things that make us unhappy in our lives. This may seem obvious, but many people live their lives with these negative inputs and still wonder why they are unhappy. There is a natural remedy, if you are willing to make the hard changes needed to boost your endorphins and lower the negative inputs in your life.

Think of your mind as a hot air balloon. Adding heat will bring it higher into elation, reducing heat will make it go down, but you have to keep the heat on to keep it fully inflated. To keep your balloon afloat without climbing too high, there are sandbags attached to the sides to weigh it down. The heat that warms the air and gives the balloon its lift can be anything that makes you feel good. Positive people, good news, a great movie, sex, the sun on your face, you get the point, take you up. The warmth you get from these things heats the air in the balloon causing it to rise to great heights. The more heat you can get, the better. Your first priority is heating the air in the balloon enough to, at the very least, keep it inflated and, hopefully, give it some lift.

Sandbags are different. Unlike heat, which is (for our purposes) a form of positive energy that creates a lightened feeling, the sandbags have weight. Different types of sandbags have various weights, some heavier than others. Sandbags can be emotions, people, situations, even items that cause an emotional response. Some sandbags appear to give off heat, at times. These sandbags, the heat giving ones, are your favorites. You want to keep them. Even though they weigh you down, they sometimes provide the extra lift you need, balancing themselves out and making themselves neutral, for the most part, and even positive at times. The heat generating sandbags are usually people in your life but can be items that provide an emotional response and even situations that you find yourself in on a regular basis.

Your job is always to keep your balloon inflated and floating on a level plane. Positive people, positive experiences, even positive places can all provide the warmth necessary to lift you to great heights. Warmth can come from something as simple as that smiley face that the waitress drew on your check, or that song that always makes your cheeks rise when it comes on. Warmth can radiate from a child at play, or from a family member that is always there to help you along in life. Think grandma baking cookies with a smile, that friend who pops into your world to share their good day or see about yours, or when your kid makes you a card that says I love you for no reason other than they felt it in their heart.

Surrounding yourself with these positive experiences and people will give you a steady and relatively warm heat source that will provide an even lift throughout the day. If you don't have many (or any) of these people in your daily routine, you may want to find some (just because they make it easier), but, if you prefer to go it alone, these can be the strangers that you see every day that are kind, your pet, music, the world you've created in your apartment, and environmental factors that you have arranged to make your world just the way you like it. That last one is my favorite because you have total control of it and no one else's bullshit can get in the way of it. It's your world. Create the space you want to exist in. As long as you have enough steady warm flowing heat sources, your balloon will stay inflated and give you some lift throughout the day.

Other heat sources are blistering. They provide quick, intense bursts of energy that are short-lived. They'll make you jump to dizzying heights for a moment, yet when they burn out, they seem to suck the majority of heat from your balloon as they go, causing you to lose a bit of altitude. Afterwards, you find yourself low until you can get enough warmth to even things out. This type of heat can radiate from new love, a roller coaster, a motorcycle ride, skydiving, or scoring great tickets for your favorite event. Passion drives this heat and it's hard to learn how to regulate it but, if you do, it can be an amazing source of lift when you need a boost. Just be careful. The hotter it burns the further you'll drop when it's no longer available.

You also have to evaluate the sandbags in your life often to see if they are dragging you down or keeping you at an even altitude. It can be hard to determine, as some sandbags appear warm and light while concealing their crystal density. They may appear to be as light as a feather and feel warm to the touch, when in fact they have a core that is heavy and cold. As much as you love these sandbags, there will come a time when you have to choose between cutting them loose or having your balloon crash down upon you. These are personal decisions that cannot be made by other people. Still, you should always be welcome to suggestions when they are given and keep your mind open, even when your heart stands in the way.

Toxic people, places, and sometimes items, can be the ones that mean a lot to you. Cutting them loose does not mean that you don't love them. It only means that you can't rise with them weighing you down. Abusive family members and lovers, places in which you can't shake the memory of horrible experiences, and even items that remind you of a bad time in life, can weigh you down. Sometimes you have no choice but to cut them loose so you can soar above. There should be no guilt in this as they, especially when it comes to loved ones, have the power to change while choosing not to. You can always revisit them later in life to see if they no longer weigh you down but, for now, you may have to let them go.

Remember this. No person's happiness, other than your own, is your responsibility. As good humans, we want to make the ones we love happy. We want to lift their spirits and be the hot air in their balloon. A problem arises when, as hard as we try, we cannot keep them afloat. At times we seem to lift them up while other times, while being our most genuine selves, we cannot. We aren't doing anything different and yet their moods rise and fall. As much as we want to try harder, there comes a time when we must realize that the attempt to lift them up is weighing us down and, what's worse, they don't seem to care either way. They make attempts at verbal apologies only to drag us down with them as soon as we forgive and forget. As much as we love them, their parasitic nature drags us to unbelievable lows.

There was a time in my life where I had to release all of my sandbags just to keep my balloon off the ground. There was no time to figure out which ones were dragging me down the most, and so I just cut them all and floated toward the setting sun. They included my hometown of Spring Valley, New York, and the entire county and state. They also included my entire family and every friend I had made along life's long journey to where I was stuck. By cutting them all loose, I was able to rise to great heights and become the person I am today. Had I not, I would likely still be stuck in the hole I was in. Since then, I have revisited each and every one, allowing some back on board my balloon, leaving others where they fell, and arranging the possibility to revisit some important ones at a later date.

This process is constant and fluid. I pick up brand-new sources of heat, a few new sandbags, and maybe even pick up some old versions of each as I rise and fall through the atmosphere of my existence. A rare few are forever gone and the new ones I have found can never replace them. Still, the new can help fill part of the void left by the old, and some allow me to rise higher and higher every day. I check my heat and sandbags on a regular basis to ensure I'm not being held down, and also to make sure that nothing is getting me too far up that I can't see the ground. I like to stay even, balanced, and steady, as you will learn to with time, as you drift along on your journey.

5- Pleasure - and Smile therapy

Pleasure is something that we all must indulge in in order to have a balanced life. This may sound obvious, but some people don't allow themselves enough daily pleasure to balance out the negative impacts of life. Taking the time to feel pleasure is something that should be consciously included in your daily routine, whether it be a favorite television show, music (which I believe is essential to a happy existence), friends, family, gatherings, a day out, etcetera. Sex is an obvious source of pleasure, be it with yourself or others. Anything that brings you joy and happiness, promoting a boost of endorphins, should be considered part of your daily routine.

Make sure to include music in your life. For many of us, this is such a necessity that the music never stops playing, especially when we are young. As we grow older and life's chores get in the way, we sometimes forget to take the steps to allow notes to fill the air. We become so distracted by the routine of life, the work-clean-sleep-repeat, that we have to remind ourselves that the music we love improves our existence, so much so that the simple act of turning on our favorite song can transform something as monotonous as doing the dishes into an evening ritual that we can even look forward to. Turn it on in the background of everything you do and enjoy the soundtrack of your everyday existence.

Be wary of things you use for pleasure that make you feel down afterward. What goes up must come down, but most of life's natural pleasures don't make you fall below your normal baseline afterward. Things that boost you up only to have you crash should be used sparingly. These can include sex (usually with people who don't treat you well or that you have little or no connection with), substances (which we are California Sober to avoid anyway), and anything else that makes you feel bad after they make you feel good. When you're down, don't reach for these things. They will only make you feel worse in the end. Instead, try some tricks that pick you up without letting you down.

At some point in all of our lives someone has said to us *smile, things will get better.* If you're anything like me you probably thought to yourself, or maybe even said out loud, *shut up, you don't know what the hell you're talking about.* They truly may not have had a clue what you were going through at the moment, but they were giving you good advice. You see, smiling is a two-way street. We all know that when someone or something makes us happy, we smile, but did you know the reverse is true as well? Yes, the simple act of smiling can actually reinforce positive feelings and can even create them.

When the muscles in our faces pull the corners of our mouths into an upward position, cheeks lifting until they ball up under our eyes, our bodies release hormones including dopamine and serotonin. Dopamine (natures dope) increases feelings of happiness and serotonin reduces stress and causes a generally good mood. While happiness causes us to smile, smiling also causes happiness. It's a life hack that allows you to feel the way you look, and it works by tricking your brain into thinking something good is happening.

Our bodies are made up of complicated machinery that has evolved over millions of years. Throughout this evolution, chemicals and muscles have interacted, back and forth, to produce the best results possible for optimal performance. One has triggered the other for so long that the muscles and their respective chemical reactions have become codependent. Either can be the cause or the effect and, therefore, work interchangeably. As elevated levels of endorphins cause us to smile, smiling causes elevated levels of endorphins in a chain reaction that can help us overcome a bad mood.

Studies show that the act of smiling can lift your mood, lower stress, and heart rate, boost your immune system, lower your blood pressure, and even prolong your life.[48] Before I ever researched the subject, I noticed that forcing a smile when I was sad, mad, or just having a bad day, I would start to feel better. The longer I held the smile, the more it seemed to

---

[48] Tara Kraft and Sarah Pressman - Grin and Bear It: The influence of Manipulated Positive Facial Expression on the Stress Response - University of Kansas published in Psychological Science Vol. 23 Issue 11 - September 24, 2012

work. At first, I thought it was all in my head until I eventually told my wife to try it. Ever the cynic, she made fun of me at first, she eventually came to me to report her success with it. I even had my, at the time, 5-year-old daughter give it a shot when she was crying. It worked and she couldn't help but laugh.

Since my accidental discovery of what I refer to as *smile therapy*, it has become a handy tool for fixing everything from ouchies when the little one falls down, to potential meltdowns when aggravation reaches a boiling point. It prevents unnecessary arguments and lifts spirits when you need to get your mind past the small stuff and on to better things, and it's fun to try when you need it the most. As silly as it may sound, *smile therapy* is a scientifically proven way to trick yourself into being happy when you are not quite there, and to improve your overall health while you're at it. When life hits you with an unexpected bummer, laugh it off. It'll make you feel better. I promise.

6- Karma and the golden rule

Religion is a sticky subject and one best left to the hearts and mind of those who truly believe in whichever one they choose to, or choose not to, follow. Let the theologians argue their points to their collective hearts content and indoctrinate their offspring accordingly. As for me, I like to reflect on the lessons of them all, take what I need, and leave the rest. While all religions have their wisdom, each also has its shortcomings, if only that the blind faith that religion requires doesn't allow for much free thought. Each causes its followers to *know*, without any doubt in their mind, that they are right while everybody else is surely damned.

This fault is the cause of some of the greatest atrocities of man, including the erasure of entire belief systems that would have brought a wealth of great knowledge to our current society. Some of those lessons have been rediscovered and are presented to you herein. The California Sober method of recovery uses ancient substances that were used ritualistically, and even worshipped, for millennia prior to their damnification as the current world's religions swept across Europe and, eventually, to the Americas. Each religion destroyed the next in the name of spreading the *truth* of their own, thus saving savages (such as us) from their ungodly beliefs.

Still, all the worlds remaining religions share one very basic and yet often complicated truth, a concept that is so simplistic and necessary to mankind that it is one of the very first lessons we instill in our children. It is then reenforced by teachers, clergy, and peers, so often that we forget where we first heard it and, if we are lucky, carry it with us forever and pass on to our offspring. The older we get, the harder it is to stick to, making excuses to why it doesn't apply to certain situations. The younger we are, the easier it is to understand in its purest form. It's known by many names, but my preference is to call it by its most fitting moniker, the Golden Rule.

Christianity, Hinduism, Islam, Buddhism, Taoism, Confucianism, Jainism, Baha'i Faith, and Wicca all have a similar sentiment. Judaism goes so far as to say that all of their teachings are simply interpretations of this same rule. Even Satanism has a bastardized version that loosely translates to *practice the Golden Rule on those who practice it themselves* or *Do onto others as they do unto you.* That particular nuance allows its believers to excuse themselves for acts of vengeance, which many participants in the former religions do anyway, and can more purely be interpreted as *follow the Golden Rule unless doing so allows you to be victimized*, but that's a whole other discussion.

As mentioned previously, the Golden Rule is as simple (and often complicated) as you allow it to be. *Do unto others as you would have them do to you.* If every religion that exists today, and all that were wiped from history, says the same thing, it may be of some value, right? We ask our kids questions like *how would you feel if someone did that to you?* or some version of the same, while we run around doing things that we would never want done to us. Through all of this hypocrisy, we often feel victimized and ask life *why is this happening to me? What did I do to deserve this?* While asking this, we rarely stop to reflect on our misdeeds of the day, we just want what we think is owed to *us*.

Karma is a concept that takes the Golden rule to a new level in an attempt to explain the answer to the question *why me?* It's answer, simply put, is *because you fucking deserve it.* While we find the maxim of reciprocity's origins in the 4000-year-old Egyptian story of the Eloquent Peasant, which reads *Now this is the command: Do to the doer to make him do*, and later the Sanskrit philosophy *Truly, one becomes good through good deeds, and evil through evil deeds*, it is reiterated in Hinduism, Buddhism, Jainism, and all the other isms and more. One may choose to believe in the Golden Rule or not, but its widespread respect has brought it into the hearts and minds of most, whether or not they practice what they preach.

That's not to say that karma is a definitive reason for every bad thing that's ever happened to you. That would be absurd (as long as we are assuming that this is our first time living). There's plenty that life throws at us before we ever make a single moral choice. Some of us can live a life of kindness and self-deprecation while having a world of shit thrown in our laps for seemingly no reason at all. Still, there is great good that can come from the practice of this belief, and what could be wrong with practicing moral accountability other than the selfish need to blame others for our misfortune?

Karma adds to the Golden Rule's *do unto others* with the

consequence of *or get what you deserve.* It's a concept taught by the world's religions, music, and even television sitcoms. My daughter inherited her view of Karma from the T.V. show *My Name is Earl,* which was later reinforced by the band Sublime when they sang *It all comes back to you, you're bound to get what you deserve. Try and test that, you're bound to get served,*[49] and in John Lennon's *Instant Karma.* If you haven't yet grasped it, let me reiterate.

The simple explanation is this, *what comes around, goes around.* If an individual runs around in life being a selfish dick, a bully, a person who continually puts their needs above others and is out for their own, severe consequences usually arise, leaving that individual crying to whoever might still listen, *why does this always happen to me*? If a person is courteous to other's needs and is always doing things to make the world a better place, good things happen to them in reciprocity.   Again, there are countless exceptions to the rule. Still, Karma seems to often reign true.

That said, even if it weren't a hard fast rule of law, even if it only proved true because people recognize and respect those who treat others well, why would you not spend your life trying to live by it in the hopes that it's benefits would be bestowed upon you? There is no one that could have a worse life by treating others with the same respect they feel they deserve. There is no one who will suffer because they were kind to someone they didn't know, as opposed to being an asshole for no good reason. Why then do we go through life sacrificing other's wellbeing in the name of our own happiness? The answer is simple. Selfishness.

I had a hard childhood; one I would never wish for another. I spent those early years trying to practice the Golden Rule, even in the face of abuse and misfortune. Then I spun my life

---

[49] What I got – Bradley James Nowell / Eric John Wilson / Floyd I Gaugh IV / Lindon Roberts - 1996

180 degrees and spent my 20s trying my best to overcome and ignore that rule when it came to anyone but my chosen family. When I turned around again and gave the rule another chance in adulthood, I found that my work paid off in many ways. My life turned around and, on the other side of things, I was a better person because of it. Whether or not it was because I followed the Rule is irrelevant. It made me feel better about myself and appreciate all of the good things that were happening to me, giving back more each day, until I could no longer question (or didn't care to) whether or not it was this Rule that was causing my good fortune. Why care if it worked universally, as long as it was working for me?

It doesn't matter if there is some Universal power that governs how we behave. It doesn't matter if what comes around truly goes around, or vice versa. What matters is that it doesn't hurt to treat people the way you want to be treated (with the exception of some extreme assholes that may deserve to be dealt with), and it makes you feel like a better version of yourself when you do. So again, I ask you, why not try it for a few years and see what happens? At the end of it you can go back to being the same miserable prick you want to be but give it some real time and see how it works for you. It really can't hurt.

7- Take care of your world (from your personal bubble to the planet to the universe)

Taking care of *your* world means different things at different levels. In the beginning it starts out small, slowly snowballing into whatever you let it become. The more you follow the concept, the easier it is to follow. That's because the mind works like a muscle. The more you use it, the stronger it is. The lazier you are with it, the less it can do until, ultimately, it becomes mush. Concepts are like weights for the mind. They can expand your consciousness if you let them, while leaving the closed minded with nothing. The more you work on a concept, the easier it is to work an even bigger version. In this case, the concept is your world.

When you first embark on this journey, the job is simply to take care of yourself. That's your entire world. Your body, your mind, and the 25 square feet in which you exist. That's all. And while that is remarkably simple for some, it's overwhelmingly complicated for others, and so this is where we start. Practice decent hygiene, exercise, and eat the healthiest things you can. Stay away from your SOC through remediation therapies and meditation while working these concepts to your best ability. That's the goal. Take care of *you* so that your world may exist. As easy as this task may seem, don't take it lightly. Be diligent in the most minute aspects so that you may endure whatever is to come.

Even these simple practices are graded on a sliding scale, so try not to feel overwhelmed. For one person, an 8-mile hike or an hour at the gym is exercise. For another, it's a good stretching session and a walk around the block. While eating healthy can be a kale salad for someone who generally eats well, it might be a glass of OJ or water instead of soda for a person on the other end of that spectrum. Some may floss 3 times a day, others may skip a shower on Sunday because they aren't in the mood. The key is to improve upon what you did yesterday, even if it's only a little. Slow gradual improvements add up to major change in a relatively short period of time. Small changes evolve into huge gains, and so we need only accomplish a little more today than yesterday.

Once you're good at taking care of you, and getting a little better every day, it's time to take care of your things. Your personal belongings should be organized and easy to find. Things should have a home and live in it. When you use something, put it back. Still, one's idea of a mess is another's idea of cleanliness. The object here is just to make sure that your stuff is where and how you want it. Someone else's idea of order doesn't have to match yours. It's your world. Take pride in it and make it comfortable for you. If you let things pile up until there's an overwhelming mess, you'll be less likely to get to it anytime soon. The depression of living in disorder will lead to less motivation, causing more disorder, causing more depression, and so on until you break the cycle. If you put things away as you're done with them, no mess will ever accumulate. Still, if you're truly content with your mess, that will do for now as long as you improve a little each day.

Once you're taking care of yourself and your stuff, your world has room to expand. If you're walking in your neighborhood and a plastic bag floats by and hits your foot, instead of kicking it off, reach down and pick it up, walk to the nearest trash can, and throw it away. You'll be surprised how good it feels to do something for your new and growing world. When you're out in nature, take out more trash than you brought in. This is your world. You have to live in it. It's easy to just look at a garbage strewn park or beach and think *what dirty assholes we humans are,* but if you don't try to change things, it's as much your fault as anyone else's. Take pride in your world. It's yours. You're here and you have to live with it so make it better.

Recycle, use renewable energy, pick up that bag that keeps hitting you in the foot. Do whatever you can. The better you feel about your part in the world, the better you will feel in general. If it's too much for you, do a little less. Just be a little better every day. Remember first and foremost to take care of yourself, then your area, and then your world. Prioritize from the center of your bubble outward. Eventually you might be taking care of the universe, but that's something you can concern yourself with later. For now, you can simply take care of your world, no matter how big or how small you want that world to be.

8 - Promote positivity (even if you're a cynic – get off of my cloud)

Energy is contagious. This is truer for some than it is for others but, in any case, it's a simple reality. If you surround yourself with negative people, you will be a negative person (or at least live a tortured existence). If you surround yourself with positive people, you will have a more positive outlook. I can say this with certainty because I am a realist. I'm not comfortable around people who are overly happy and bubbly because I feel they are missing something, that they are not aware enough to see the truth. It's like they're missing the point. The world is not perfect. Society is not perfect. Something has to affect you, living in this world.

I'm just as out of place among truly negative people, people that complain all of the time and are ready to fight at the slightest injustice. These include the intitled people that yell at food service workers or front desk agents at the post office for not being fast enough, because there aren't enough tellers, or because of something else beyond that employee's control. On the other end of that same coin are the people who constantly bitch that they are the victim of circumstance after circumstance, never actually taking an ounce of responsibility for their situation. The truth is this, all negative people are trying to look tough during sadness. They hide their tears by yelling and complaining but they are still just crying.

Most of us can find our way to the middle. We aren't always happy because that would be absurd. Life has its problems and even the most positive people get negative at times. We aren't always mad because that would just suck. Still, we bitch about injustices and get angry when faced with opposition. We get as excited as children when something awesome comes into play. We whine a little about our issues, until we find a way out the other side, and we hope that we can laugh when the irony of it all reveals itself. We have good days and bad days, ups and downs, and we always find a way back to the middle.

There's nothing wrong with being in any of these categories, as long as we don't impose our negativity on others. All of us are trying to live our happiest life. Each person you see has struggles that you don't know about whether they look the part or not. That person you were rude to may have just lost their job, their home, or a loved one. Many people are good at hiding their misery and you might add just enough to someone's heart ache that it pushes them over the edge. You don't know what is going on in their lives, so don't go spreading your negativity just because you're in a shitty mood. You don't have to pretend you're on cloud nine, just don't be a dick to people for no reason.

Some of us are happy being negative while others can't get enough of being the light in the room. The rest of us veer back and forth between. The problem is that if we put too many negative people in our lives it drags us down. The key to a healthy attitude is confidence that it will all work out. Whether we choose to be cynical or to be ever the optimist is fine, as long as we are true to the belief that we can overcome any obstacle. The more we choose to see the light at the end of the tunnel, the closer we get to that light, and that brings us closer to the end goal, finding our own version of happiness.

9- Self Respect

Self-respect is a concept that many people don't fully grasp. By respecting ourselves we gain the respect of others, but what does it mean to respect ourselves? One might say that self-respect is taking care of yourself and maintaining appearances. Another might say that self-respect is not letting others walk all over you. One might even think that self-respect comes from standing up to those that would disrespect you. While all of these are aspects of respecting oneself, self-respect is something that needs to be practiced regardless of any outside influence.

When you truly respect yourself, you see the world and others as they truly are. When you believe in your heart that you are worthy of respect, and in turn give yourself the respect that you deserve, it becomes clear that anyone who doesn't give you the same is not worthy of your time. Once this level is achieved, disregarding those who would show you less is instinctive. This doesn't mean that you should treat anyone with less respect than you would expect, only that through this process you will see who is no longer beneficial to your life. Treat everyone with the utmost respect and disregard those who don't show you the same.

Self-respect also means that you shouldn't do things to yourself that would cause you harm. This can include using your SOC, staying in toxic relationships, or compromising your beliefs in order to appease another. Doing things that make you feel like less of yourself is personal disrespect. Be true to yourself physically, mentally, and spiritually and you will see the path clearly. Follow another against your own gut and you will quickly become lost. The longer you allow yourself to stray from the path, the longer it can take to find your way home. Simply put, to thine own self be true.

10- Outward Respect (for all life)

Having respect for yourself is useless without having respect for others and for the world around you. One needs to respect the gift of life, not only for oneself but for all of life. If you think you have it hard, think about the creatures and plants that can't speak up for themselves. Before you step on that bug, imagine something giant crushing you because it didn't like the way you looked or because it thought you were scary or dirty. Put yourself in the place of the plant that is dying from lack of water, or the cashier you yelled at for ringing you up wrong who's making minimum wage to feed their children or take care of their aging parents. It all comes back to the Golden Rule. Self-respect without outward respect is simply narcissism, and too much of that will stall all progress on your path.

Take a moment to put yourself in the place of everything you see. None of us asked to be on this planet (as far as we know), and yet here we are. We all endure the same basic struggle, to survive in peace and health for as long as we can, and hopefully to find some joy in it. The mayfly spends two years under water as a larva. Once it emerges, it has but 24 hours to roam, to eat, to live. When you cut the life of an insect short, you're denying it the few precious moments it gets to experience what we call life. Plants make sounds that we can't hear. When they are cut or in need of water, the sounds get louder and faster.[50] Imagine it as a cry for help. We are all born to die. Hastening that experience for another life form is a cruelty.

Once this concept is broadened to include humans and their pets, we seem to understand it without question. Still, when it comes to what we consider to be lesser forms of life or, in the case of plants and fungi, inconsequential life forms, we tend to lose all empathy and treat the species as if its existence is at our pleasure and only exists to serve us. It takes quite a bit of thought and enlightenment to realize that every life form has similar struggles, or worse, than our own.

---

[50] Cochard H, Badel E, Herbette S, Delzon S, Choat B, Jansen S. Methods for measuring plant vulnerability to cavitation: a critical review. J Exp Bot. 2013 Nov;64(15):4779-91. doi: 10.1093/jxb/ert193. Epub 2013 Jul 25. PMID: 23888067.

It takes an even higher consciousness to muster empathy for their struggle and truly care enough, on an intimate level, to make that struggle less (or at least not add to it). Listen, I get it. If you don't cut the lawn the city can fine you. If you let rats live in your walls they can give you disease, and a cockroach infestation is just plain nasty. On top of that we all have to eat, for fuck's sake. To survive this planet, you can't be so empathetic that you are not the master of your own domain, but there's no reason you can't handle these problems in a humane fashion. I'm not saying everyone has to be a raw vegan that doesn't eat root vegetables and has a garden full of weeds because they don't want to end any life. I'm not telling you to let tics, mosquitos, and leaches feed on you. I'm simply asking you to consider the lives that you do take, and why.

If there's a spider or a slug in my shower, I escort them outside. Bug infestations are usually caused by living a slobbish lifestyle. Keep your world clean and you'll have less to deal with. Don't stomp a bug because it looks scary. You look scary to them too. It's your fear you are overcompensating for when you kill them. In the same sense, have some empathy for the people whose paths you cross in everyday existence. When you lash out at someone for getting in your way, either literally or figuratively, you're just making their world harder. Empathy and the Golden Rule can guide you towards becoming a better human, and the feeling you get from that will make you want to be better every day. The gifts you receive from being a better human start in the mind and later manifest in the physical world. Be the best you and you are guaranteed the best possible version of your life.

11- Be Ritualistic

From your daily routine to holiday traditions (be they inherited or created yourself), rituals play an important part in making us, well, us. From family traditions that are passed down through the generations to weekly, monthly, and yearly activities that you and your friends and/or family participate in without fail, they help to make up your sense of self. Even the things you do when you wake up and before you go to sleep, including the time of day that you do them, can be a comfort that makes you feel at home, no matter where you are in the world when you do them.

When we are trying to rid our life of alcohol or other harmful substances, one of the biggest issues is trying to stop ritualistic behavior. That's because our minds love routine. An after-work drink, partying to set off the weekend, or something to help us sleep, rituals of this nature tend to become so engrained in our lives that it seems impossible to live without them. Taking them up was easy. The boost they once gave us taught our brains to crave them. The rituals we created around their use made them such a part of ourselves that it almost hurts to cut them out, regardless of the damage they are doing to every other aspect of our existence.

The science of addiction is simple. Relief from it can be as well. We know that these harmful substances replaced (or sometimes filled a void from a lack of) chemicals created by our brains. Once we have found a way, through California Sober methods, to abstain from these substances, we may still find it difficult to stay away from them during certain ritualistic moments where we used to consume them. It's much easier to create a habit than it is to break one, and so we may find it easier to replace these old patterns of behavior with new and healthier customs. The California Sober methods can help do just that.

Instead of having a drink after work, exercise or meditation can be the stress relief we need. Instead of setting off the weekend by getting high, attend a gathering of California Sobers, take a hike in nature, or just meet some friends or family for dinner. Replace whatever rituals trigger your addiction with rituals that don't include your SOC. Fill your time with positive experiences that make new memories rather than passing the time reflecting on old ones. If you're an introvert, take up a new hobby or put more time into one you already have. I have so many hobbies and go on so many daily adventures with my family that I wouldn't have time to think about my former addiction if I wanted to, except when I choose to write about it.

Rituals like these also help relieve other conditions of the mind such as anxiety and depression, PTSD, OCD, etcetera. By focusing the mind on what you like to do and keeping your schedule as busy or relaxed as you prefer, you give the mind less time to have negative thoughts and patterns. Put on some music, light some candles, watch a movie. Whatever makes you happy and takes your mind off the things that are detrimental to that happiness should be ritualized and renewed as needed. Rituals are by no means a cure, but they are one of the paths you can follow on route to that place.

12- Change it up

Being ritualistic in your daily activities doesn't mean you allow your days to become stale. Life can be monotonous. The same old same old can make us lose our sense of self, of who we are. When life becomes a series of repeated tasks with no end in sight, work, chores, TV, sleep, repeat, it's easy to become depressed. We start to think, *is this all that life is? If so, then what's the point?* We forget, especially as we get older, to believe in our hopes for the future, and our goals that seem so distant that they start to feel like a pipe dream or, worse, a waste of time. That's when many of us reach for some harmful substance, be it alcohol, opiates, cocaine, meth, or whatever we use to escape the day to day.

The mind likes routine, at least for a while. Routine and daily rituals are soothing to our sense of normalcy. Then, when that groove we are in is so deep we can't see anything outside of it, that same mind detests the repetition of it all. It's great to have a routine that fits in all of the daily things that we have to accomplish, otherwise some of us would never get everything done. When those chores pile up, making them feel even more like punishment than simple tasks, we can make them more fulfilling by incorporating music, company, and other simple pleasures into them. Still, what we really need is to mix it up a little.

No matter how much we feel the need to pack our schedule with the things that need to get done, we must find time every day to do something that isn't part of our daily routine, even if only for an hour. We need at least an hour to step outside of the rut we have created so that we can see the path we are on from higher ground, an hour to look at something that we don't see every day, even if we may pass that thing by in our daily travels. We all need to take the time out of our busy schedules to let the mind wander and to see a part of the world that we don't allow ourselves a break to take in otherwise.

If you're someone who sticks to a strict timeline, schedule that hour into your day. If you're someone who just wings it, pick a time of day, and wing it in a different direction. Anything to get out of your element could be enough to reset the brain and observe a different point of view. Take a different route, whether it be on your way to and from work or while running errands, and you create new neural pathways in the brain, leading to better cognitive function. Reconnect with old friends, or make a new one on your daily travels, and it's bound to brighten your day. A simple walk in nature has a restorative power similar to that of meditation. Whatever you can do to change it up will help to remind you why it is you're working so hard.

There are plenty of studies that show that a walk in nature

has physical and psychological benefits.[51] Walks in nature can relieve anxiety and depression,[52] reduce stress, lower heart rate, and improve memory. They can also restore attention (for those of us who get burnt out during certain daily tasks) and lessen symptoms of ADHD[53]. These nature walks also improve creativity and increase feelings of generosity. A 90-minute walk in nature lowers rumination,[54] the repetitive thoughts focused on negative aspects of the self and reduces neural activity in an area of the brain linked to risk for mental illness. A stroll in the garden, a hike in the woods, or a day at the beach, a simple walk in a natural setting is all we need to alleviate so many conditions of the mind that it would be silly not to give it a try.

Whether you're going to take a hike, find a new path to your destination, stop at the museum, or treat yourself to lunch at that new restaurant that you've been eyeing, do something different today. Then do something else tomorrow. You'll feel better about life in general and you might even expand your mind, literally. There's no harm in letting yourself live a little, and it may be all you need to remember why it is that you're living the life you choose. Life is too short to spend it stuck in the same basic routine, and one hour out of 24 won't

---

[51] J. Thompson Coon, K. Boddy, K. Stein, R. Whear, J. Barton, M. H. Depledge. "Does Participating in Physical Activity in Outdoor Natural Environments Have a Greater Effect on Physical and Mental Wellbeing than Physical Activity Indoors? A Systematic Review." Environmental Science & Technology, 2011; : 1102031151020046.

[52] J Clin Med. 2022 Mar; 11(6): 1731. Published online 2022 Mar 21. doi: 10.3390/jcm11061731 PMCID: PMC8953618 | PMID: 35330055

[53] Andrea Faber Taylor and Frances E. Kuo. "Children With Attention Deficits Concentrate Better After Walk in the Park." Journal of Attention Disorders. 2009 Mar;12(5):402-9. doi: 10.1177/1087054708323000. Epub 2008 Aug 25.

[54] Bratman GN, Hamilton JP, Hahn KS, Daily GC, Gross JJ. "Nature experience reduces rumination and subgenual prefrontal cortex activation." Proc Natl Acad Sci U S A. 2015 Jun 29. pii: 201510459

take much time away from what you have to get done. You may even be more productive because of it and, after all, that TV show you missed will still be there when you get to it.

13- Teach the Children Well

When my daughter comes home from school, I ask her to tell me three things that she experienced in her day. Two of them have to be academic, usually math, where I make her explain what she learned and how to do it, and reading, from which I make her recall the story in her own words. These help her to reinforce the concepts in order to remember them. For the third item I allow her to tell me about what we call playground drama in which she describes whatever social issues she is confronted with in her day. While they can all be great teaching moments, one instance stands out that we could all benefit from.

My daughter was playing with her group of friends. At seven years old, a lot of drama comes about from this exercise that can naturally teach them life's lessons. Still, we as parents must guide them through the process if we don't want animal instincts to take precedence and allow a *lord of the flies* situation to develop. My daughter started the story by saying that her dear friend to whom she feels protective over, "just tapped [some other child's] hoop fort nicely." This was my first indication that she was protecting that friend from becoming the villain of the story. My instincts were correct, I learned as the story unfolded.

She told me that she and her second grade quintette (because quintette sounds cuter than gang) were playing in a particular area of the playground. They changed positions to do something else and, when they came back to their area, some first graders had erected a fort made of hula hoops. One first grade girl stood at the center of the tower of hoops, smiling and laughing, as the rest of her crew made the fortress taller and taller by adding more hoops to the pile. When my daughter's quintette arrived back at their place of play, it was no longer available as their lair.

Seeing this, the alpha of my daughter's crew immediately approached the situation with the intent to regain the coveted land. Their territory had been invaded and she felt the instinctual need to reclaim it. This is an instinct that is seen among all primates, an action that is not dissimilar to any of our ancestors. *You girls are in our spot,* she announced. *No one was here when we started,* one of the first graders responded. With that, my daughter's friend struck down the fortress of hoops in a single blow, the first graders running to tell a teacher of the misdeed.

My daughter's protection of her friend was understood. In a similar situation, and at a similar age, I may have done the same. Loyalty is admittedly a virtue, one I would teach her in another way, but here was a chance to strike down the pack behavior that helped us evolve into the strong society that we are while not dismissing it entirely, as it is useful in other situations. It was time to teach her the Golden Rule, and the caveat needed to ensure she wouldn't be taken advantage of for having such moral standards.

The Golden Rule seems simple. *Do unto others as you would have done unto yourself.* It sounds easy, pure, and righteous, but it can have negative consequences. If everyone were to follow the rule, no other rules need apply. The problem is that the rule only works in all situations if everyone abides by it unconditionally. That is not the world we live in, and it is certainly not human nature, so I had to teach the rule as it applies to the world as we know it. That nuance in the concept is not as easy as it sounds.

I told her to imagine a line for food. Everyone is starving and the food is distributed on a first come, first served basis. No one monitors the distribution of food, but everyone is told to take a single portion and, as long as they all follow this rule, there is exactly enough for everyone. Then I told her to imagine that a few people on that line, the bigger and more confident kids, were taking double portions. They are breaking the rule, and, because of this, some kids might not be able to eat. Something has to be done in order to ensure that the weaker kids at the end of the line do not starve.

There are several political ways in which this scenario could play out. The first, and most important, would be to reason with the small group that had taken more than their share, appealing to their sense of empathy, and explaining the hardship that the kids at the end of the line would endure as a result. If that didn't work, the options become less civil. When reason doesn't work, force is what most will turn to right the wrongs of an injustice. The empathetic could barter with the bullies, but why should one have to work for the ruling class in order to receive their fair share? The only thing left to do is to stand up for your rights as an individual.

I told my daughter to always follow the golden rule but, in the face of injustice, to always stand up for herself, and for the less formidable, when all other solutions were exhausted. I told her that forming an alliance with all that were on the side of justice would create an impassable force. I explained that bullies are the few, and when the many stand up to them justice would prevail. I actually said something like *if all of the kids stand up to the few bullies, the bullies are outnumbered and will give in* but, while that concept is tried and true, it's hard to convince kids that numbers outweigh *toughness* and I wanted her to grasp the concept that the Golden Rule comes first and foremost, and that any escalation should be as little as possible until the ultimate goal of justice is achieved. As limited as my explanation may have been, she truly understood and practices the concept to this day.

But *teach the children well* means more than just passing on the Golden Rule and the nuances that may accompany it. It's the culmination of all of our years of wisdom being passed down through the generations. If you don't spell out the things you have learned, you can't expect the next generation to just look at you and know how to act. While you need to practice what you preach, you still need to preach a little. Teach the children well is to bring the teachings you have learned throughout life into the minds of the children, and not to just assume they will learn them on their own.

What I learned most from my parents was how to survive, and while those lessons were more than enough to do just that, everything else was riddled with hypocrisy that was never reinforced by actions. I'm sure they had plenty more wisdom to hand down, other than how to work, pay bills, cook, clean, and the basics of existence, but the best they could do to advise me was *work hard and pay your bills on time.* Happiness wasn't something they had or could elaborate on. That may be why I went so hard in the way of pleasures of the flesh.

Don't be afraid to tell your children, before they enter their teenage years, the hard battles you had to fight. As much as you don't want them to think less of you, the lessons you teach will show them the mistakes they are not to make. Honesty, without glorification, is the key to showing them the struggles you've been through. Sheltering them from the truth of the world only serves to leave them blind to the harsh realities that exist in the world you're supposed to be preparing them for. In a selfish attempt to hide the parts of you that failed, you rob them of knowing the true you and what you have been through, a lesson that may save them from their own self destruction.

The Sum of all Paths

We all forget to wander through these paths from time to

time. The secret to maintaining all of the wonders of your garden is not to constantly worry about the paths, but to get to each as soon as it comes to mind. Remind yourself of each path daily. Follow the paths that you feel are most important for that day, knowing that you will embark on another journey tomorrow, and the next day, and that you will keep each path maintained throughout these travels. The most important aspect of change is the desire for that change to occur. Once you have set that desire in motion, it takes but the slightest grain of will to cause it to snowball into the greatest of all achievements, peace of mind.

The more of the California Sober treatments and paths you incorporate into your everyday existence, the easier it is to remain California Sober. Keep your paths clear and your mind open and the Golden State of Mind is easily attained. Psychedelic Remediation Therapy, followed by Psychedelic Experience Therapy, allows the mind to find its own way toward the ultimate goal of achieving peace and harmony. How you get there is ultimately up to you, but the methods contained herein, if followed precisely, give the best chance at recovery known to date.

Conclusion

I don't come from a pretty place. My existence was rough. Scars, both mental and physical, riddle my body and soul. I've suffered from depression for as long as I can remember, endured an abusive childhood, life on the street, incarceration, and addiction to everything from alcohol to crack cocaine. I've been beaten, jumped, and abused in almost every way imaginable. I've overcome PTSD from that life and come out the other side with a smile and a new outlook, and I owe it all to the California Sober method of recovery. If I can find peace, anyone can. I'm not going to say it was an easy journey, only that once I found the California

Sober way, I have never been happier and free of the addictions that plagued my existence.

I'm glad that I finally get to enjoy the lessons of my misguided youth. The lessons I learned first were the first lessons that I forgot when I was at my lowest point. Once I realized that they were true, that sticking to the naturals was the way to go, I never had another hard decision when it came to addiction, alcoholism, depression, PTSD, or any other condition of the mind. Once I realized that the way out was to simply start from the beginning, I've never needed another way. Spreading the word to others who share similar obstacles has been another saving grace that has kept me focused on the true path, the California Sober path to recovery from all conditions of the mind.

A Word about Negative Experiences

Individual psychedelic outcomes vary greatly depending on the transcender's mindset and what they are looking to accomplish. The setting can cause variations but, as long as it is safe and serene without dangers or items that trigger the transcender's phobias or create potential for harm, this should not be an issue. At this point, the transcender's mindset is the only true factor that can direct them to a place of fear or despair, these being the root cause of negative experiences.   If one doesn't understand what is happening to them, they may become fearful of the journey itself, which is why it is recommended to have one or more experimental sessions using a threshold dose prior to going on a full experience.

If one has had severe trauma in their life, the session may involve momentarily facing that trauma head on. In this case, it is up to the guide to usher that transcender towards peace and tranquility. The issue is realized, and a positive resolution is searched for. Most who undertake this journey will default to a positive mood due to the effects of the psychedelics and their ability to help the transcender find their way to reconciliation. Moments of uncertainty should be met with reassurance and positivity until the transcending party flows to the next wave of perception.

To reconcile individual psychedelic outcomes undeniably, trancenders always need deliberate love & individual strength to eliminate negative trauma, otherwise behavioral limits are challenging. Kindred spirits and benevolent beings are the heroes.

Reset and Oneness

Whether the natural ways contained in the California Sober method of recovery actually make you One with the Universe or they simply feel as if that is happening may be up for debate, but does that really matter? The outcome is the same. Using the California Sober method of recovery, we are able to reset the brain and aim it towards better goals for ourselves and, after all, isn't that all that matters? If you're spiritual, maybe PET brings you closer to that Universal truth. If you are more scientific in your beliefs (although they aren't mutually exclusive), the facts are there. The California Sober method of recovery can give you both, or either, depending on what it is you subscribe to. In any case, what works cannot be denied.

California Sober treatments create new neural pathways and open your mind to the possibilities, and the possibilities are endless. You can overcome Alcohol and Substance Use Disorders, treatment resistant depression, behavioral addictions, existential depression, grief, OCD, PTSD, and feelings of being stuck (also known as burnout). There is almost no condition of the mind that these practices can't guide you through, and you will be a better person as a result. Open your mind, expand your consciousness, see a world that you never knew existed even though you have been living in it your entire life. And so, in the spirit of William Blake, and later Aldous Huxley, I leave you with this. Once the doors of perception have been cleansed, everything will appear as it truly is, infinite!

The End

Acknowledgements

Acknowledgments. What an impersonal title for the part of the book where you thank the people without whom your work may never have seen the light of day. When it takes a lifetime to amass the knowledge, at least one trip around the sun to put those thoughts into words, and another to make sense of them, there is a lot to acknowledge.

I would like to start by acknowledging that it took a lot of pain and suffering to get to the idea in the first place, that before the first keystroke many would have to fall victim to incarceration, institutionalization, hospitalization, and the ultimate price, early demise. Since the answer was given before the Demon ever peeked out from the darkness, I'll have to start at the beginning. Forgive me if I miss anyone, or if my words don't all make sense, but it has been a long, strange trip with many twists and turns, and this is the only way I can repay a debt to those who didn't have the privilege of growing old. It's time to acknowledge the truth. Without the agony of loss, without the pain and suffering, I would have never been in a position to help anyone. That leaves a list too long to acknowledge, but I'll do my best.

Without my parents I, of course, wouldn't exist. They taught me how to survive with next to nothing. For that, I'm forever grateful. Without their particular set of issues, I don't imagine I would've been on the dark path of destruction that led me to my eventual revelation. Without their particular set of skills, I may not have survived. I'm not sure that thanks are appropriate in this particular situation, but I acknowledge their contribution as this book would never have been written without them.

To my first teachers, the Guys (plus none, minus none), thank you for breaking me out of the aforementioned insanity and for showing me the way. I only wish we hadn't all forgotten the earliest of lessons that you all taught me; stick to the naturals. Matt Harshner, Matt Sicher, Stef Fetcho, Adam Baum, Louie Lehman, Eric Wachter, Mark Lamphier, and my brother Mike Simmons, when it started it was pure, albeit mischievous. Who could've known it would end the way it did?

To the second and ever-expanding incarnation of that crew, the S.V.D.C., fate must've brought us together for how else could so many like minds gather to form a family like ours? For this reason, I do not believe in regret, for to change one thing could change it all. You all taught me how to live free and without the chains of our childhood programming. While there are way too many to list, let me at least mention the ones that are no longer with us, as they paid the price we did not have to, yet. Matt Sicher, Bob Hanauer, Gary Berger, Gary Gataldo, Warren Archumbalt, Louie Lehman, Jeremy (Jake) Prozeller, Jeff Riemer, Chris White, Reefer Rob Tomassi, The Diaz brothers (Joey, Ronnie, and Michael), Prentice Polk, Jeffrey Balk, Mike McCarthy, Marc Raimondi, Mikey Dreads, Dennis Fitzpatrick, Diane Palmer, Philly(blunt) Rodrigues, Paul Chin, Jeff Janesak, Meaghan Fasano, Marsha Harshner, Joelle Savas, Lauren Kahn, Robert Kimbrough, Stacy Burkowski, Dave Berlingeri, Mike Fitzgerald, Jacky DePaolis, Renee Fullerton, Mike Westervelt, Pat Stuhmer, John Resner III, Ed Romanoff, Lynn Segan, Alice Fetcho, Mary Polk, Aunt Carol, Aunt Linda, and my mother, Pat Simmons.

I think about them daily, as almost everyone I love is dead. If I missed a name, it's only because there are so many grand characters that it is hard to gather them all in the space of one simple mind. I acknowledge their sacrifice and I only hope that one day we can all be together again. See you on the other side.

About the Author

W. E. Simmons is an ethnobotanist and researcher from Spring Valley, New York. His introduction to psychedelic substances in the mid-1980s inspired his fascination with their potential for relieving alcohol and substance use disorders. He has spent more than 30 years researching the effects of psychedelics and other mind-altering substances, specifically in the context of addiction and recovery. After moving to California in 2002, Simmons dedicated himself to developing a revolutionary method of recovery. With the help of the latest science and a network of recovering addicts, he carefully honed his work into the first truly unique guide to recovery from addiction (and many other conditions of the mind) in almost a century, one that has been successfully used by W. and countless others to finally overcome their struggles, the California Sober method of recovery. In addition to ethnobotany and the exploration of mind-altering substances, Simmons also authors works in philosophy and fiction. He is an addiction specialist, a medicinal botanist and ethnobotanist, an experienced psychonaut, and freedom fighter in the War on Drugs.

Reference Material

Meeting Guidelines (How to hold California Sober meeting)

1. Hello everyone and thanks for coming. Welcome to our meeting of the (group name) group of California Sober. My name is_____________and I am California Sober. I will be the meeting Host.

2. Let us open the meeting with a moment of silence for those who have paid the ultimate price of addiction and for those who have yet to find the California Sober way. (Briefly pause in silence)

3. California Sober is an association of individuals who have found common ground in their battle with addictive substances and other conditions of the mind. We share our experiences with each other so that we may confront and tackle our addiction and help others to recover from alcohol and substance use disorders, and other unwelcome conditions of the mind.

The only requirement for membership is a desire to stop using harmful substances and to be free from unwelcome conditions of the mind. There are no dues or fees for membership; we are self-supporting through our own contributions.

California Sober is not allied with any sect, denomination, politics, organization, or institution. We do not engage in any controversy; neither endorsing nor opposing any causes. We welcome all individuals regardless of race, religion, sexual orientation, or anything else some may view as different from themselves. We are all unique, but we find a common goal on our California Sober paths.

Our primary purpose is to remain California Sober and help others to achieve California Sobriety.

We ask that you do not endorse any product or attempt to persuade others to try specific products or offer them for sale to fellow members.

That said, we encourage talking about what we, as individuals, are doing to help us maintain our California Sobriety.

4. ______________will now read our Oath.

Our Oath

We California Sobers realize that through meeting with other like-minded individuals in a safe setting to discuss our issues, recount our successes, and explain where we come from, we can reenforce our beliefs and achieve our common goal of remaining abstinent from the substance(s) that have destroyed some part of us. We acknowledge that talking with others who share in our California Sobriety, and bringing this message to others who wish to attain the same peace of mind, will help to enlighten us, and guide us on our journey.

We acknowledge that each journey is its own, and that each is as unique as the individual following the path. There is no one-size-fits-all path, and each individual must find what works best for them, as long as it leads to them refraining from their Substance of Choice. We don't judge others for doing what works for them, even if it doesn't work for us. We offer, to anyone who will listen, what it is about California Sober that works for us, ourselves, that we may help them to find their true path to recovery, and to peace of mind.

5. Ask any new members to introduce themselves. Ask any visitors to introduce themselves and say where they are from.

6. Introduce any scheduled speaker. If the meeting has no

speaker, the host conducts the discussion.

7. Pick one or more of the 9 goals or 13 paths to discuss.

8. Talk about intent, as it is the driving factor of the program.

9. Thank the guest speaker (if any) as well as any others who read.

10. Go around the room and ask if anyone would like to share their California Sober experiences.

11. Make any announcements about group business, events, and other California Sober events. Ask for any announcements from the floor.

12. Pass the donation vessel (unless it is an online meeting). The Host can say something like: We have no dues or fees in California Sober. We are entirely self-supporting. This self-support includes our rent for this space, refreshments, and contributions to the California Sober network.

13. Close the meeting with a positive message.

This format is suggested only.

Testimonials

The following section is composed of testimonials from California Sobers (CSs) that wanted to tell of their success. Last names have been omitted for privacy.

Hey everyone, I just wanted to introduce myself. I joined the group a couple weeks ago. I have 5 years clean from meth, heroin, suboxone, and pills. I just smoke and in the past couple years have integrated some psychedelics occasionally as well. I've managed to go from homeless, hopeless, broke with a needle in my arm to having my own apartment and car and holding a job down for 5 years now even being Cali sober. Recovery is possible! I'm so glad I found this group because I don't feel like I fit in with NA or AA because I smoke but I still try to work on bettering myself every day. Anyway, that's a little about me. Thanks for letting me join the group. - Kayla M

Hi new member here 👋 happy I found this group! In August I will be 3 years California sober after shooting heroin for 10 years. Cannabis and psychedelics have saved my life 🤲 much love to all of you open-minded, strong, and beautiful creatures 💚 - Mandy K

(A peek inside my brain) Hello Everyone 👋

My last drink was a little over 3 years ago. I initially quit cold turkey, but the withdrawals were pretty brutal to deal with. I began using CBD along with an antidepressant shortly after to help with anxiety, headaches, stomach issues, and sleep patterns. I immediately felt the difference and felt so well. Both gave me hope that I may be able to kick my nasty drinking habit and stay sober. Of course, you know the more you do something the more your tolerance goes up, so CBD products were not as effective for me anymore and around that time delta 8 (THC) really became popular in my city. Delta 8 was really beneficial for me and wasn't too intense to make me paranoid or any other negative side effects. Up until about 5 months ago I used D8 to help with everyday life- now I smoke mostly THCa flower. - Kaylee J

Heck with it. I've been... Cali Sober... A bit over a year. I guess technically I use plant medicine, holistic things, spiritual path, etc. to not use my DOC (Drug of Choice), but my brain has been mean lately and thoughts are creeping in. I found that 12 step format kind of helps, and I've been working a fourth step kinda loosely... I found someone to help me through it that isn't NA or A.A., they definitely haven't been compatible, and I found more judgement than anything even though it seems that goes against the whole program? 😕 anyways... I'm here, I've not used for today, and I'm grateful... Thanks for reading. – Codi H

I am EXTREMELY grateful to be Cali sober.. it has gotten me away from extreme opiate and amphetamine use, and what was shaping up to be alcohol addiction. I use what I need to manage chronic pain condition and severe mood disorder, and I have finally become a functioning adult and a great mom again. I don't go shooting money in my veins or up my nose or down a bottle, and I enjoy life again. I don't get high, I don't get drunk, and my son has his mother and my husband has his partner back after almost 15 years of addiction struggles. I may not be 'sober' but I'm clean of the mess and toxic habits surrounding addiction that tried killing me and damn near succeeded last year. Welcome. 🖤 - Codi H

It worked for me, going on 3 years sober, - Charles M

I am an alcoholic. Full on alcoholic. I had many, many, many rock bottoms and many "day ones" trying to start over and recover. When I had finally had enough, I checked into detox and put down the bottle for good. I also suffer from mental health issues and chronic pain. About 9 months into being sober I had a terrible triple whammy of crippling pain, headaches, and panic attacks. I almost picked up a drink to "get through it" but my husband brought me a Delta 8 gummy instead and my whole world changed! I was able to avoid relapsing back into alcohol and as of today I am 13+ months alcohol free! I have no desire to drink under any circumstances anymore. I take a quarter of a gummy most days. I treat it like medicine, and it helps so much with my pain, nausea from the pain and with my anxiety. It's a game changer. Some people judge me for my usage, but I don't care. There is much more I could share about my journey, but the bottom line is that alcohol was killing me and [California Sober] help me live my life. I know there are many ways to get and stay alcohol free but for me Cali sober is the best option! - Amy C

I haven't gone to 12 step meetings in years [because] the advice I got was to not even bring up weed, psychedelics, and medication because the majority in those groups consider it the same as a relapse. I had an old timer bug out on me because I chaired a meeting after I got past 3 months just because I'm [California Sober]. That shit saved my life but most people I met in meetings tried getting me to just stop cold turkey which is horrible advice for someone that takes subs or methadone. The funny thing though is that Bill W had his "spiritual awakening" after being dosed with [Atropa Belladonna and Henbane] which are both hallucinogenic deliriants. He also was looking into using LSD to help addicts and alcoholics. Bring that up [at an A.A. meeting] and watch the room go nuts lol - Dylan B

Hi, my name is Jonathan [G], I'm from Washington state, and I've moved back down here in So- Cal to be near my son.   I've been in the struggles of Alcoholism, and drug addiction since 1977 I'm 60 now. I'm really interested in your California Sober, so I joined, I live in Redlands now. I've done the Traditional AA& NA for over 25 years... Sounds refreshing, thanks you all. - Johnathan G

I started my journey 3.5yrs ago. AA sponsor worked the steps ... as part of my 11th step I kept seeking other forms of recovery. Seen the research on psychedelic therapy and decided to seek myself. In the last year, using the [California Sober] books and research ... I started using psychedelics 1yrs ago. My growth has skyrocketed. I started a meeting at my house for likeminded people who weren't getting all they needed from traditional 12step meetings ... We're growing by leaps and bounds. It's hard when your "conservative 12 steppers" walk away ... but I'm so in sync with the universe and in flow state all I can do is share my experience strength and hope and be an example of what MY program has done for me. Attraction not promotion, right :) I'm so glad I'm not the only person out there that knows the benefits of [California Sober]. Keep shinning beautiful souls - Amy C

Hi all, my name is Jill. My sobriety date is 11.18.2013. I haven't been to a meeting in years due, in part, to judgment I feel related to me being California sober... Thanks! - Jill E

702 days no alcohol.

As Muslims believe, I believe; alcohol changes a person. It wasn't that alcohol controlled my life, alcohol controlled my thinking and emotions; the thinking and emotions then controlled my choices. I had to accept that good, bad, or indifferent alcohol changed me. I had to accept that. The biggest challenge "is not to not drink," it's the rewiring of my hard drive that I've had my entire life. The thinking about my thinking…dealing with emotions that I simply have not before. Tried different groups, AA wasn't for me although time to time I'll pop on zoom, really found benefit in [another] program but that shit is costly…so healthy lifestyle apps and fitness apps, … California Sober…better choices and sharing. And not all choices are "good"; they are better than the alternatives. It's a "take what is useful and leave the rest" daily and that is what I been doin.

I do micro dose with mushrooms, and I've been a mmjp (medical marijuana patient) since 2010; both of which have been extremely helpful for PTSD and mmjp for chronic pain management as well. I've been judged as "not being sober" because of that; I disagree. I am in a much healthier and have sobriety of the mind, something I would not have been able to say and stand by 702 days ago. - Robbie D

Hey there!! I'm Cher and I'm 101 days alcohol free today! I'm Cali Sober and feeling the best I have ever felt in my 46 years! I live in Charleston, SC and am happy to find this group and meet likeminded people. California Sober … I've been mulling over my story for some time now and not sure where to start. My addiction with alcohol started in my mid 20s and I finally got sick of blacking out, being a mean, aggressive and just plain miserable drunk. I emotionally, mentally, and physically hurt a lot of people and I've taken responsibility for those actions. I'm on this healing journey solo but with a few close friends who are my supporters and rocks. When I cut out the alcohol, everything changed in my life. The people who were benefiting from it disappeared out of my life and the people who were waiting in the wings to come back and be encouraging showed up. I'm 106 days alcohol free and 60 days single today. It hasn't been all rainbows and sunshine, but I have committed to becoming the best version of me I can be and so far… I love the new me! - Cher N

Thank you. I've been searching for a group like this since my sponsor abandoned me for using psychedelics to help my recovery. After years of struggling with relapse with my addictions I finally feel free. I'm in no way cured, but I feel more at ease and free from addiction than I have in, well, ever. Knowing there are others like me makes me feel less alone in my journey. Thank you all. – Anonymous

Hello. I'm Scotty. I have fought with alcoholism, depression, and anxiety. I am a veteran. I have had 3 cancer surgeries and I have to say through all of it I took zero pain pills... I used cannabis. It has helped me relieve my anxiety so I can deal with my medical realistically. I have my appetite. And my Sponsor backs me up 100%. I just want to join a group that gets it. In return, have fun with it. – Scott D

Anyone else felt like they have been shunned from AA. My old sponsor cut me off because I started smoking weed and now, he won't give me any advice and says that I've turned my will back - Gabriel B

Hello, my name is Ashley, and I am proud to say that I am two years and three months, California sober! When I finally decided to get sober, was at my rock bottom. I was about to lose my daughter, my family and everything and everyone that I loved. Although I have completely given up alcohol for good, I have found Marijuana has helped me tremendously with my stress and anxiety and has never caused me do anything that I regret! I would rather smoke weed than take prescription medication any day! Not only do I use marijuana to help with my stress and anxiety. I am also an occasional user of classic psychedelics. Not only did micro dosing mushrooms help me to become sober. It has helped me to become the person I am today and opened up my mind to so many different things, and become closer with nature, myself, and the world we live in and beyond! I've never been so happy and proud of myself as I am now! - Ashley S

I have one year and three months using the Cali Sober method. Nevin R

I also enjoy 12-step recovery and still participate. I struggle with how to be authentic in the meetings because I feel judged for cannabis use. Ugh. The struggle is SO real. One year and some change with no alcohol here! I do attend AA because it has been a lifesaver for me. However, I struggle on a daily basis with feeling outside the group because I use cannabis daily and this is ... very judged within AA. I was lucky and found a great sponsor who works the steps with me. These sponsors do exist! - 😩 Tracy W

Hi! I'm new to this group. I recently joined because I've been in recovery for almost 2 years, and I just recently got my medical marijuana card and everyone in recovery looks down on me for it. But it is helping with my anxiety, depression, pain, and PTSD and is helping me get off subs (suboxone) which I also recently started using bcuz I was afraid of going back out - Ashley C

I too have had trouble with this in early sobriety. I have six years Cali Sober. The guy I sponsor has a year of sobriety asked me to do the 4th step with him. Thru his year of sobriety, he did the step without knowing. He made amends. By living sober. The 12 steps are a guide. No right or wrong way. Do the right thing. Help people. Don't lie. Do things your way. As long as you live it. - Scott B

I stopped smoking Crack and drinking 8 years ago. Along with Life Full Blast came depression. Weed all.my life kept me from being depressed. It is my clarification. I have never once stumbled in my quest. Because weed is my clarification! Nature's Ritalin... I am bipolar with a few other head things thrown in. I take my meds every day of my life. Weed gives me clarification to never doubt them. Take them, smoke weed, love life! - Billye S

I'm so happy you found me, [California Sober]! I've always believed some non-addictive drugs are ok. for many people but I went to aa for years in 1980s. I have 45 years off heroin. And found aa helped but not a good fit for me - Odette B

7 yrs.+ no booze, no hard shit. Absolutely no way could've happened without [California Sober]. I've been to 4 detox, 2 rehabs and managed to stay clean 12 yrs. Then I went on a 12 yr. binge, drug of choice was MORE! I don't smoke to get obliterated, just a little to help with the symptoms of the disease, anxiety, depression, pain management, etc. and I've no need for this God given medicine till evening time. I've never felt better. The abstinence works for many, but I was a miserable son of a bitch and that's no way to live. - J.d. S

I have 16 years free from meth and cocaine after being pretty bad into addiction as a young person. I was never an alcoholic but used to drink, do X and be a party girl. I've got about 5 years... Marijuana is a daily medicine for me, and now my life is not a mess, though not always a roaring success either. But I'm grateful to be Cali sober. - Mindy S

I am micro dosing with silly sigh ben as well as daily MMJ for appetite. I can tell that the silly sigh ben is helping with overall mood. I should start a mood journal to track better. I am also a week shy of 2 months sober from alcohol after day-drinking for 3 years. Yes, this is why I did not get sober through AA. Also, because I am agnostic. - Myfanwy T

I have over 6 years of [California] sobriety. I have used this method before they had a name for it. I was in rough shape physically and mentally to the point of committing suicide. It was Feb 13. It didn't come easy, but I went to aa faithfully for the 1st year or so. I now have a great relationship where there is no alcohol. I'm in bluegrass band, bought house, Grandkids here almost every day. You might say the promises came true. - Scott B

Hi Friends!! I stopped drinking one year ago yesterday! Yay! I am def an alcoholic and my method for getting sober has been AA. I love AA for helping me with my drinking problem. However, I don't feel like I can really celebrate my year of sobriety because most people in AA don't consider me sober 🙁 As I celebrate this huge milestone, I realize how much those of us who are continuing to use cannabis need support for the positive change made in our lives! I feel like the change is minimized in my AA circles because I'm still … "using", etc. Can anyone relate? – Danny w

Over two years with no alcohol [using the California Sober methods]. I have PTSD, chronic pain from multiple injuries, a few life-threatening…. went through a 10-day detox solo and did not realize the risk even that was till after. I've been a mmjp since an auto accident in 2003 that I should not even be here to type this. It was then I realized the benefits of mmjp. Since then, I've used other natural ways for my PTSD. Humbly in a nutshell. - Robbie D

I'm interested in giving testimony to my experience getting off of heroin and meth [using the California Sober methods], and the new neural pathways magic mushrooms and LSD seem to have played a big part in my mental health. - Christopher J

Last year got super wasted at Passover and was so embarrassed when it was called out how much wine we drank. This year is so much better and different! I'm almost six months alcohol free! Ready for Easter (we celebrate both, each with one side!) 👌. - Lindsay N

If AA helps you not drink, you can celebrate there. I use herb at night, ultimately to help me sleep. My cannabinoid receptors were being flooded, I finally figured out that I don't need as much as when I used to drink and get hungover. You have no reason to feel guilty if AA and herb help you not drink. If you're not hurting anyone, and it's not a problem for you, what you do is your business and nobody else's. - Lisa W

Got sober in 87. Use cannabis. Only went 14 years, divorced, chose to drink, on the brink of homeless. Coming up on seven years [California Sober] through the use of cannabis and mushrooms. Standing on the threshold of homeless 6 1/2 almost 7 years ago [to] sitting in my house that I own, on the couch watching football today - Fred K

I'm 17 months [California] Sober from FETTY [fentanyl], straight out of treatment they try to give me psych meds, antidepressant meds, anxiety meds. I had to go to jail withdrawals from those meds so today I put nothing in my body I can withdraw from …. In retrospect, that's just the tip of the iceberg. Thank you for letting me share. Jesse N

I started [California Sobriety] with AA/NA and slowly integrated mushrooms and Marijuana... coming up on 4years ... I'm here if you need/want - Amy C

I have just over 4 years, being Cali Sober. 🖤 - Remy R

Over six years Cali sober and wouldn't be if not for this method - Fred K

3 years as of 7-27-2020 - Charles M

51yo autistic/ADHD here, with 6 years meth clean, 5 years sober, 4 years nicotine free. PTSD was the tipping point. - Robert B

I have 863 days Cali sober. Battled hard drugs and alcohol from ages 14-35. Working hard to get better every day! Bennett S

Yes! I still smoke, Drinking is what hurt me - Laura M

I would micro dose on mushrooms to realize that I wasn't that kind of person [an addict], I don't know how to explain it, but I've been [California] Sober 3 years and counting - Charles Myers

Hello all, I've been California Sober since I arrived in San Francisco in 1968. Before that anything went. So happy to see there is finally a name for natural medicine. Sticking to organics works for me and has changed my life into a well-balanced way of life. - Rose B

Hello and thank you for the add. I will be four years alcoholic free this upcoming 27th of June. I found cannabis about two years in my recovery. I absolutely love it, but I have completely mixed feelings on where I belong in the recovery world. Saying that after joining a ton of groups I realize I have to be comfortable with it myself. I keep searching for approval from others but that's not gonna work until I find it within. I'm getting there. Happy to be here. - Shannon H

Hey everyone! New to the group, and thanks for the add. I've been California Sober since 6.24.22 and looking forward to hitting my year. Here to support the cause because it's changed everything for me. Thanks again y'all. - Deborah W

Hi! I'm new to this group. I recently joined because I believe in the power of psilocybin to aid in recovery. - Ricky M

Hi all! I just wanted to introduce myself and share a photo I took. Andi alcoholic. I enjoy the fellowship of the 12 step programs. However, I'm kind of just doing my own thing. Plants over meds here. - Andi S

I'm a fellow alcoholic. Currently 413 days alcohol free. [California Sober methods] have saved my life so I'm right there with you! Welcome! - Amy C

My sobriety date was 4/20/12 and after 10 years of sobriety (off everything. Opiates were my DOC), I got a medical card. I tapped out of the program, but I still stay in touch. I love [California Sober]. - Steve W

I have 3 years Cali sober and still in the program … 🙂 Mandy K

Hi, I'm Scott, New To The Group. I'm In A 12 Step Program. I Also Have Been Diagnosed With, Borderline Personality Disorder. !!! But, The Program Insists Using MJ Is NOT SOBER !!! 🐇😕😎 – Scott M

I don't care if it means I'm not sober. My goal is to be AF —alcohol free, and it took me decades to get to this point where I have 249 AF days. I also don't use, or have issues with, other addictive drugs. I don't consider cannabis to be addictive. There's no withdrawal (hangover) the next day, I can go without it and the amount I use doesn't keep increasing. Indeed, I don't like the feeling of doing too much; whereas, with alcohol, I had a hard time drinking enough to feel satisfied. - Harry B

The recovery community doesn't consider me sober, because of pot. But I have over 17 years of not doing coc[aine], meth, and crack. My life isn't a mess. I'm not behind on bills. I'm not doing crappy things to stay high. I never want to stop smoking weed. It doesn't trigger me to want to use hard drugs. I'm grateful for my Cali sober recovery and life. - Mindy S

Being sober is abstaining from all mind altering substance, well if that's the case people need to stop taking there meds for depression, ADD, bipolar disorders etc. IMHO, as long as you are able to pay you bills, stay away from what nearly killed you and be a human not an ass hat. You are doing well. If weed works, don't try reinvent the wheel. – Debi R

Marijuana is my medication for pain, ptsd and depression! I use this instead of being out of my mind drunk. It also keeps me from using opioids and believe me with 10 herniated discs, a rod through my pelvis into my sacrum ect ect opioids and lots of booze were my go to! So I am sober af and opioid free. No regrets! - Daunine P

I didn't get away from heroin and alcohol until I told myself it was ok to use cannabis and psilocybin medicinally. I have been free from heroin ,meth and being drunk for 5 years. - Bryan B

www.ingramcontent.com/pod-product-compliance
Lightning Source LLC
Chambersburg PA
CBHW040134160726
48006CB00014B/1486